Warrior Prince

By the same author

George Malcolm Thomson

Warrior Prince
Prince Rupert of the Rhine

Secker & Warburg
London

016004

To Else

First published in England 1976 by
Martin Secker & Warburg Limited
14 Carlisle Street, London W1V 6NN

Copyright © 1976 by George Malcolm Thomson

SBN: 436 52047 8

Printed and bound in Great Britain by
Morrison & Gibb Limited
London and Edinburgh
Maps by Cartographic Enterprises

Contents

v

List of Illustrations

List of Maps

Acknowledgments

I wish to acknowledge with gratitude the help I have received from the staff of the British Library Reading Room, above all to those in the Map Room. I am grateful too to the staff of the Admiralty Library for help in research, and, at the National Maritime Museum, Greenwich, to the officials in the Library, the Prints Department and the Photographic Section. In the National Portrait Gallery I have been given much courteous help in the Documentation and Archives departments. The search for a portrait of Prince Maurice was forwarded through the kindness of the Countess of Craven, the Courtauld Institute Photographic Library and others. Dr Finlayson of the Wellcome Museum of Medical Science gave me much valuable guidance on Prince Rupert's medical problems; Mr Price in the library of that museum helped to follow out the career of Antoine Choqueux. Mr John Cruesmann helped me on various German texts. The Librarian of the Royal Society is in my debt for allowing me to consult the Society's early records. Finally, let me thank Sybil Ray for the speed and accuracy with which she transformed my manuscript into a legible and comely text.

I

The Luck of the Palatines

'By virtue, first, then choice, a Queen.'

Sir Henry Wotton

His Highness, the Duke of Lusatia, who was also a Duke of Bavaria and Count Palatine, cried out in anger. He had awakened suddenly to find that he had fallen with a bump to the floor of a coach being driven on a road which zig-zagged steeply downhill. It was a disagreeable testimony that the circumstances of his life had changed sharply and for the worse. That was something, however, that His Highness was not yet able to understand. Later on, much later, he realised that the coach had been making its way hastily and clumsily down the steep descent that leads from the Hradschin to the city of Prague below. Although the Duke was well wrapped up for the wintry weather, the journey was uncomfortable. It had been hurriedly arranged in an atmosphere of panic. At the age of eleven months, His Highness could not be expected to understand that the Thirty Years' War, as it was later called, had just broken out and that he was one of the first of its countless innocent victims.

Little more than a year earlier, his father had been Frederick V, Elector Palatine, first of all the secular princes of the Holy Roman Empire, not a king certainly, but one of the most exalted princes in Christendom, the lord of a stretch of territory extending, with notable gaps in between, across two hundred miles of Germany including some of the richest and most pleasant land. 'In the Lower [Rhenish] Palatinate,' said a writer of the time, 'the Prince hath twenty-six walled townes, besides an infinite number of good and faire villages. The land is very fruitful of wine, corne and other comfortable fruits for man's use.'* Watered by the Rhine and the Neckar, favoured by sun and soil, producing enough from its vine-yards to be known as the Cellar of the Holy Roman Empire, the Rhenish

* See J. Nichols, *Progresses of James I.*

I

Palatinate could well be content with the lot that nature had reserved for it. There was another Palatinate, the Upper Palatinate, further to the east and not so rich, but under the same ruler.

Frederick V, in his capital at Heidelberg, could reflect that if he was not the Emperor or a king, he was an exalted dignitary of the Empire, supreme judge in lawsuits affecting the royal domains and one of the seven electors who chose the Emperor, when a vacancy occurred. He, like his subjects, could look on life with some complacency. He was young – twenty-two – handsome, an excellent horseman; he had a beautiful wife, daughter of the English king. Frederick was besotted with her, as she was with him. And Elizabeth, his wife? She had been born at Dunfermline and had come to England at the age of seven when her father, James I of England and VI of Scotland, ascended the English throne. She had an early experience of the vicissitudes of politics at the time of the Gunpowder Plot. The conspirators proposed to carry her off from Coombe Abbey where she was being brought up and make her queen, after a suitable change of religion. In the nick of time, Elizabeth was spirited off to Coventry by her guardian, Lord Harrington. The City Council of Coventry distributed pikes, bills, partisans and bows to the citizens for the girl's defence. The weapons were not, however, needed. The main objective of Guy Fawkes and his associates had already been frustrated. Elizabeth grew up to be a beautiful young woman, tall – a characteristic she had inherited from her Scottish grandmother – a favourite theme with the English poets of the time, who saw in the glorious tomboy, with her love of horses, dogs and hunting, a 'goddess excellently fair'. She was also a magnet for half the eligible princes of Europe – or at least for their questing ambassadors. Henry IV of France wondered if she would suit his son, Louis; and Elizabeth seems to have looked with some favour on a French match. 'I assure you,' wrote the French ambassador, 'it will not be her fault if she is not dauphine. She is handsome, graceful, well-nourished and speaks French very well.' Gustavus Adolphus of Sweden put in a claim, but, unfortunately, he was at war with Elizabeth's uncle, Christian of Denmark. He was followed by the Duke of Brunswick-Wolfenbuttel and Prince Maurice of Nassau, who was not thought to have a sufficiently exalted rank; the pretensions of two scions of the Howard family were dismissed with something like contempt – subjects! The Duke of Savoy suggested his son who was, as Sir Walter Raleigh said, poor and popish and could 'return no recompense of benefit to this state'; the King of Spain, left a widower, suggested himself a proposal much to the liking of the girl's mother, Anne of Denmark, a crypto-Catholic, but not at all to the liking of her father and even less to that of her brother, Henry, Prince of Wales, 'a great heretic' as the Spanish ambassador reported. And so, in the end, it seemed that the best prospect was for the marriage of Elizabeth and Frederick who, as Count Palatine was 'of reasonably eminent rank, and was certainly a Protestant'.

After some haggling, for Savoy was still in the market, and Frederick's uncle, the Duke of Bouillon, was a very cautious bargainer, the marriage treaty was signed. Elizabeth could worship by the Anglican rites and was assigned two dower houses in the Palatinate. Only Queen Anne was displeased. Frederick, after hastily brushing up his dancing, arrived in England with an impressive suite. His visit, after a brilliant opening, was marred by the sudden death of Henry, Prince of Wales, Elizabeth's beloved brother. This event was not simply mournful, it had also profound dynastic and political implications, for Prince Charles, now heir to the British throne, was a delicate youth. If he were to die, Elizabeth would be Queen of England. There must, therefore, be second thoughts about her marriage. However, everything went forward as was originally intended (and in the event Prince Charles' health improved). Frederick was given the Garter. The betrothal ceremony took place in the banqueting house in Whitehall and was followed by a splendid dinner which Queen Anne could not attend owing to an untimely attack of gout. The wedding was celebrated in the palace chapel on 14 February 1613. A bishop preached on the marriage at Cana and John Donne wrote a poem for the occasion:

> Be thou a new start that to us portends
> Ends of great wonder; and be thou those ends.

The City of London gave the bride a chain of pearls worth £2,000; from Scotland came a request that Elizabeth should be styled 'Princess and eldest daughter of Scotland', and Lyon King-at-Arms was given for the occasion a magnificent tabard on which the royal arms were quartered in the Scottish manner. The marriage cost the King £53,294, plus the bride's portion of £40,000. Against this, a levy-in-aid raised only £20,500. A sudden and necessary wave of economy swept over the Court and brought the festivities abruptly to an end. However, a month passed before Elizabeth and her husband left for Heidelberg.

She, probably, did not love her father and, almost certainly, detested her mother. But she was leaving a country of which she had been the spoilt daughter, surrounded by popular adoration. The brother she had loved above any man was dead. She was going, for the second time in her life, among strangers. The hour had the chill of departure to an unknown future. But it also had the frosty sparkle of adventure.

Elizabeth was a woman whose fabled charm did not spring from beauty alone. She had resilience and the gayest kind of courage. Later, when fortune had used her vilely enough, she confessed: 'Though I have cause enough to be sad, yet I am still of my wild humour to be as merry as I can.'

At that moment, in 1613, setting out on her unpredictable journey, Elizabeth was enchanting to others as well as to the husband whose adoration she returned. And it seemed that the worst dragons in her path were the Palatine officials who would soon be knitting their brows over her extravagant ways. It was a complaint she was to hear – and ignore – all through her life. She was, after all, a Stuart.

Frederick, her husband, had human weaknesses of which Elizabeth was probably unaware and which in an ordinary man might have passed unnoticed, such as bigotry, a weak character, bad judgment and a proneness to melancholia. Frederick was by birth no ordinary man, and the seventeenth century was no ordinary time. Looking at the combustible material, religious, dynastic and social, in Germany it required no great power of perception to predict that a vast conflagration could at any moment break out. It was Frederick's fate to light the match.

But, for a time, the young couple had only their own domestic happiness to think of, the children, Frederick Henry, Charles Louis, Elizabeth, who arrived regularly; the horses, the clothes, the jewels, the portraits of herself which Elizabeth ordered; the fabulous terrace garden which Frederick created at Heidelberg for Elizabeth's pleasure; the wild boars that they hunted together, even when Elizabeth's condition made it risky, and, of course, the groans of poor, worried Colonel Schomberg, Frederick's maître d'hôtel, about Elizabeth's improvident ways. 'Madame has no resolution, is too liberal to the unfortunate, which I call rather pusillanimity than virtuous liberality.' He laid down directions for the management of her household which, no doubt, were necessary for a girl of nineteen – 'Be generally more strict; liberty causes presumption; indifference in time spoils even the good.' And so on. Nothing seemed more remote than the disaster which was about to lay waste the whole Palatinate and drive its ruler and his family into exile.

Frederick acted with the noblest intentions in the world. He was a

Protestant, a Calvinist, much under the influence of his Chancellor, Christian of Anhalt, and even more under the influence of his chaplain, a fanatic named Abraham Schultz. But the moment was one in which it was extremely important for statesmen that ideological problems should not be seen through emotional spectacles. A crisis had blown up in the Holy Roman Empire.

The Emperor Matthias died in March 1619, six years after Elizabeth's arrival in Heidelberg. The Archduke Ferdinand, a Hapsburg, who was King of Bohemia, was elected as his successor. One of the votes that elected him was Frederick's. Simultaneously, the Bohemian Estates, dominated by Protestants, deposed Ferdinand from the Bohemian throne and offered it to Frederick. A question of appalling simplicity and gravity was, therefore, posed to the Elector Palatine: should he accept or not? He was tempted by the crown. After all, one of his ancestors had been Emperor. There was, too, another factor, the religious one. The path of Christian duty was pointed to him by his chaplain, Schultz. It led him, as a Protestant prince, infallibly to Prague. Christian of Anhalt advised him to accept. So did Frederick's relations of the House of Orange at The Hague.

On the other hand, his mother begged him not to go. The Union of German Protestant Princes was opposed to it. But the Archbishop of Canterbury thought he should accept. And another clergyman, John Donne, who had become chaplain to the English ambassador, preached before Frederick and Elizabeth at Heidelberg: 'It [the Bohemian Crown] is so general a business that even so low and poor a man as I have an office to do for it, which is to promove it with the same prayers as I present for mine own soul to the ears of Almighty God.'

No wonder that Frederick wrote to his uncle, the Duke of Bouillon, 'It is a divine calling which I must not disobey.' His father-in-law, James I of England, was appalled by the thought that the young man might throw himself into the morass of power-politics in central Europe over which hung the noxious gases of religious hatred. King James was very much of the opinion that his son-in-law, Frederick, was carried away by dreams of earthly grandeur and – which was even more alarming – might accept the crown in the belief that English armed force and money would help him to realise his dreams. Nothing was further from King James' mind. He was at that moment hoping to arrange a marriage between his son, Charles, and the Spanish Infanta. What made his son-in-law's behaviour even more irritating for the King was that the thoughtless, Protestant

5

people of England were manifestly on Frederick's side. If the foolish boy persisted on his course, so much the worse for him. As for his wife, James' daughter, Elizabeth, she must pay the price of her husband's ill-considered action. He, James, would bear his children's sufferings with stoicism knowing, as he reminded his son, Charles, in dedicating a book to him, that a king's crown is made up not of jewels, but, like Christ's, of thorns. So if Frederick was about to embark on a foolish and reckless policy, James was bent on pursuing a sensible and craven one. He did so at a time when popular feeling in England was running strongly in the opposite direction. Said one writer,* 'With what a great and general love Britain burned towards Frederick and Elizabeth I can scarcely describe.'

Meanwhile, Frederick's wife, Elizabeth, gave him advice which was, at the least, equivocal. While his alone must be the decision, were he to accept, she would follow the divine call whatever the suffering involved. More than that, she would pledge her diamonds for the cause.

One day in 1619, Frederick, Elizabeth, their children – by this time there were three – servants, soldiers, dogs, horses, set off eastwards from Heidelberg to Prague. There being no unfriendly states to bar the way, Frederick was duly crowned in the cathedral which stands on its hill beside the most romantic castle in Europe.

In the beginning of December 1619, just six weeks after Elizabeth was crowned, a son was born to her in the Hradschin, a dark-complexioned child, her fourth, for whose christening his parents made elaborate preparations. 'The king,' wrote Elizabeth, 'hath bidden Bethlen Gabor, the Prince of Transylvania, to christen this little boy. He is altogether of our religion.' It was necessary to say this because the common report ran that Gabor, who looked like a Tartar, was, in fact, a Moslem – 'half a Turk' as Elizabeth put it.

When King James, at supper in Whitehall, heard that once more he was a grandfather, 'he joyfully asked for a large beaker of wine. He gave his purse with all it contained to the gentleman who had brought the news, saying to him, "Run, and tell the good news to the Prince of Wales."' The King's jubilation as a grandfather did not, however, betray him into impulsive errors of statesmanship.

The christening took place on the last day of March, in St Vitus Cathedral. Gabor, who had at the last minute found that he could not come in person, sent a deputy, Count Turzo, a splendid if barbaric

* John Harrison, 'A short relation of the departure', 1619, London.

6

figure in Hungarian national costume wearing a steel helmet. It was Turzo who carried the baby to the font and uttered his baptismal name, 'Rupert'. The child was auspiciously named after an ancestor who, two centuries before, had been Emperor. After that, the representative noble ladies of Moravia, Silesia and Lusatia, one after another, took the child in their arms, while the Bohemian burgraves stood round, a gleaming, daunting array in full armour. The King conferred on the child the ducal title of Lusatia, a province of the kingdom. Bethlen Gabor presented him with a Turkish horse and richly jewelled saddlery. The Jewish community of Old Prague sent a deputation from their ghetto – 'the little city of the Jews' on the other side of the river – bringing a silver alms dish.

Feasting followed that lasted seven hours; dancing; a tournament; fountains flowing with wine; national costumes which the Queen found outlandish but undeniably picturesque – there was every sign of popular enthusiasm; everything, except any real belief that this outburst of Bohemian nationalism would last. For, of course, nobody in his senses would imagine that the resurgent Catholicism of the Counter-Reformation would willingly tolerate a Protestant revolution in Bohemia – or that the Hapsburgs would meekly submit when one of their princes, who was himself the Emperor, was deposed and replaced by a Protestant. It was simply a matter of time before the Imperialist counter-attack was delivered. When it came, Frederick neither foresaw its violence nor was ready to meet it. The battle of the White Mountain was lost while he was entertaining some English envoys to dinner in the castle at Prague a few miles from where his army was overwhelmed and slaughtered by the Imperialist forces. Although accounts of the battle vary, very few of the losers emerge with credit. Christian of Anhalt ran away. So did Count Hohenlohe, commander of Frederick's cavalry. His Hungarian troops fled in panic. It seems that the only unit in the Bohemian army which fought with courage was the Moravian infantry, the ranks of which were filled by Calvinist zealots. Although deserted by their comrades, they fell to a man, fighting round the strangely shaped Star Pavilion in the royal pleasure garden outside the city walls. It was a bizarre but decisive battle which gave Bohemia back to the Hapsburgs; it was followed by a massacre of the Czech nobility and by the enthronement of the Counter-Reformation in Prague. The city itself could not be defended. A few years earlier an English traveller had remarked acidly, 'Except the stench in the streets drive back the Turks, Prague

7

must fall prey to the infidel.'* It was equally vulnerable to a Christian onslaught.

Frederick had seen nothing of the battle. He seemed strangely remote from its events, almost as if it were happening on another planet instead of being only a few miles away. Now he occupied himself with arranging that he, his wife, family and retinue were hurriedly evacuated from the castle, across the river, past the Jewish quarter to the Old Town. In the last panic-stricken minutes of the evacuation, Baron Christopher Dohna, passing through the deserted, dismantled rooms of the royal quarters, came on a small forgotten bundle and threw it into a coach that was already on the move. In that way, Rupert, Duke of Lusatia, was rescued from his father's victorious enemies.

The royal fugitives spent the first night of their journey in an iron-merchant's mansion in the town; next day, they continued their flight to the east. When the convoy of 300 carriages reached the Powder Tower, in the ancient fortification of Prague, they were held up by citizens who thought, rightly, that they were being deserted by their sovereign. Frederick's nerves were shaken by the shrieks of the Bohemian women who feared that a worse fate would befall them. Only when officials assured the crowd that the King would soon be back, was the procession allowed to pass. A regiment of Moravian infantry covered the retreat. Next day, the first snowflakes of winter fell on the Winter King. The Queen's carriage broke down and was plundered by servants. Cool and composed, the Queen rode pillion for forty miles behind a young English captain, Ralph Hopton. Her grandmother, Mary Stuart, in an equally desperate emergency, had escaped from Holyrood House behind an equerry. In due course the refugees reached Saxony, where they had a chilly welcome, and Brandenburg, where the Elector looked on their arrival with alarm. It would be embarrassing for him to give them shelter but equally embarrassing to deny hospitality to the King and Queen of Bohemia. For not only was Frederick his brother-in-law, but Queen Elizabeth was once more pregnant and her time was near. The Elector could do no more than speak gloomily of the discomfort of their lodgings at Küstrin and hope that times would improve for them and him.

So ended in ignominy and discredit one of the most ill-considered escapades in history. The plot was badly planned, the cast was badly chosen, the curtain fell on an anti-climax and derision. In Vienna,

* Fynes Moryson, *Itinerary*.

jeering placards offered a reward for news of 'a king, run away a few days past, age adolescent, colour sanguine, height medium; a cast in one eye, no beard or moustache worth mention; disposition not bad, so long as a stolen kingdom does not lie in his way, name of Frederick.' For the most part, the chief actors in the farce came out badly. But not the Queen. She held her head high. More than that; before very long, she was able to see the comic side of her misfortunes. In this daughter of the Stuarts, there was something of her grandmother, the Queen of Scots, who had never enjoyed life so much, it was said, as when she was campaigning, dressed and armed like a man. Elizabeth's secretary said of her that she was 'the lady in the world that hath the least of woman in her'.

The opinion is, of course, a biased one and should not be misunderstood. Elizabeth was a downright, healthy young woman, outspoken, levelheaded, qualities which went very well with her Scots accent. But she was entirely feminine, although with nothing of the coquetry that, in the seventeenth century more crudely than today, was thought to be the most powerful weapon in a woman's armoury. She would sooner hear a dog bark, it was said, than hear a man swear that he loved her. She loved her silly husband to distraction. Her third son, Maurice, was born in Küstrin on Christmas Day, 1620, to the intense relief of the Elector of Brandenburg, Frederick's brother-in-law. The Elector could now say what he had wanted to say for a long time, that the time had come for the refugees to move on. But whither?

The problem was not at all an easy one. For, while the Imperialist Hapsburgs were running Frederick out of his kingdom of Bohemia, the Spanish Hapsburgs were over-running his Palatine Electorate. Frederick and Elizabeth were left without a country to call their own. The German Protestant princes were too frightened of the Emperor to give them shelter. The King of England, Elizabeth's father, had no desire at all to welcome his daughter to Whitehall, an event which, among other inconveniences, would have involved him in the need to receive Elizabeth as a queen. This would have upset the Spaniards whom he was courting just then. But what was the alternative? To deny her the title? This would have led to a family quarrel. 'Ye meaner beauties of the night, Who poorly satisfy our eyes.' To poor, infatuated, befuddled James, his daughter, who shone to others as the moon, was nothing now that the blazing sun of George Villiers had risen. Besides, he can hardly have been pleased when, in the flight after the battle of the White Mountain, the Garter he had bestowed on his son-in-law, Frederick, was found by looting imperialist troops. In Vienna, Munich and Brussels, Frederick's Garter was a source of endless ribald fun. The Doge of Venice drew a more serious political inference from King James' attitude. 'If,' he said, 'the king of England will do nothing in defence of his own daughter, others can hope nothing from him.'

In their predicament, Frederick and Elizabeth found a friend. Maurice, Prince of Orange, sent nineteen troops of horse to meet them at Bielefeld and put at their disposal a town residence at The Hague, the Hof te Wassenaer which had been a residence of a Dutch politician, now in exile. The exile's widow was allowed to occupy the less important rooms in the house and when, in due time, he was allowed to return, both families lived together in perfect amity. The wandering Palatines, homeless as a tribe of gypsies, growing year by year in numbers and with a long – if diminishing – tail of hangers-on, had found a shelter from the storm. Temporary it might be, but the fury of the gale would surely pass. Not so. As matters turned out, the pleasant brick-built house at The Hague, with its gables, towers, dormer windows, floors of stone mosaic, windows vivid with coats of arms, was for forty years their home.

There they lived comfortably enough on 10,000 guilders a month provided by the States-General, plus another £26,000 from the English government. The income did not seem too much for, to begin with, they brought with them from Prague a suite of two thousand. However, it was enough for modest comfort. And Queen Elizabeth had her famous ropes of pearls to give her the simulacrum of majesty, to be used when necessary to raise money for warlike purposes, and, in the end, to be bought from her son Rupert's estate by a celebrated English courtesan.

Elizabeth had, too, something which did not depend on her jewels, but which she won by her beauty and the exuberant charm and cheerfulness of her disposition, all the more appealing in the gloom of the family's fortunes. She had the devotion of chivalrous gentlemen, like Christian of Brunswick, Sir Thomas Roe, Sir Henry Wotton and Lord Craven (small, enormously rich, son of a former Lord Mayor of London). Such men were united in thinking her to be the most beautiful princess in the world. The Prince of Orange, speaking for many others, said that she was 'called by some the Queen of Hearts. But she is far more than that. She is a true and faithful wife and that of a husband in every respect her inferior.' Cheerfulness was not always easily attained. The Queen was much afflicted by preachers in the local English church who 'beat the ears' of the Palatine family with exhortations to support their affliction with patience. Mr Paget, a visiting minister from Amsterdam, went further; he made suffering an argument for happiness and prayed to God 'to increase our afflictions that thereby we might be known to be His children'. It can be imagined that the Queen's comment on this supplication was suitably tart. She was the most faithful of Anglicans, but with a clear idea of where sermons ended and impertinence began. Some of the Dutch clergy begged her chaplain to preach against her bare neck. 'I am not sent to tell Her Majesty how to dress,' retorted the chaplain, who clearly knew the character of the lady. Certainly, Elizabeth needed all her abundant high spirits to keep her husband from sinking through despondency into despair. Poor Frederick! In one respect, however, he was not a failure. Every year – or almost every year, thirteen children in eighteen years – the nursery in Hof de Wassenaer grew more crowded until, at last, it overflowed. Then the Prince of Orange lent the too prolific Palatines the Prinsenhof at Leiden as a nursery palace. There the younger Palatine children were brought up under the strict supervision of tutors and governesses, over whom was set an elderly nobleman from the Palatinate, named Wolrad von Plessen. They were carefully instructed in the Calvinist theology and soon were able to recite the Heidelberg Catechism 'without understanding one word of it', according to Sophie, the youngest daughter and the one with the sharpest tongue. They spoke English to their mother and French among themselves – French eked out with scraps of German and Dutch. It was only natural that they should be highly polyglot, although Rupert, the third son, and the most wayward of the brood, refused to learn Latin or Greek, pointing out that these languages would be of no use to him in his chosen profession, arms. However, his accent in Dutch and German was thought to be excellent and he spoke some Czech. Sophie, the youngest daughter, has left an unsentimental picture of a princess' life in the Prinsenhof. A plain little girl – the only one who lacked good looks – in whom the family ability had taken a satirical turn, she reports that the beautiful Queen of Bohemia preferred the company of her monkeys and lapdogs to that of her children. In this complaint there may have been some truth. Handsome mothers, as they become middle-aged, often find the presence of large, good-looking daughters a source of obscure irritation, especially when, as in this case, the girls have royal blood to limit the range of suitable husbands and lack of dowries to dampen the hopes of marriage.

There were good reasons, however, why the young Palatines should be sent to Leiden. They were growing up in Holland in the age of Dutch scientific and artistic glory. Some of it was likely to rub off on intelligent young foreigners making a protracted stay. For Rupert, whose bent was practical, who was an excellent mechanic by nature, the atmosphere was particularly congenial. And the University of Leiden was illustrious; nowhere in the world could young princes find a better education. In their different ways they made good use of it, although, as it chanced, it was one of the daughters, the eldest girl, Elizabeth, who grew up as the most learned of the brood, indeed as one of the most learned women in Europe. Discipline and deportment were by no means forgotten. The Palatines might be poor; homeless; living on charity; in debt to the tradesmen of The Hague – £140 to the milkman! – more heavily every year, for the Queen of Bohemia had inherited her father's utter fecklessness with money, so that, as Sophie said later on, there was sometimes more jewellery than food in the house – all that might be so, but the children would not, if the Queen could help it, disgrace their ancestry in any court in Europe.

Life in the Prinsenhof was ruled by Frau von Plessen, who had been Frederick's governess. 'From this,' says Sophie, 'you may judge her age. Her daughters looked older than their mother and were righteous in their dealings with God and man alike; they wept to one and never disquieted the other.' Dinner at the Prinsenhof was a highly formal business. Nine separate curtseys, Sophie remembered, she must make before sitting down – a deep one to each of her brothers, who were drawn up in a row in front of their attendants, one curtsey, not so deep, to the attendants, one to her governess, one when she took off her gloves, one when she took her place opposite her brothers, one when a gentleman brought her a basin of water to wash her hands, one after grace and, at last, one when she sat down.

However, mothers are apt to spend much of their time with their pets, tutors cannot always be in the nursery, and youth is youth. In spite of everything, the Palatine nursery palace at Leiden was a noisy household of clever, spirited young people, dressing up in their mother's cast-off dresses and – it was their favourite game – pretending to be staying in an inn. In this fantasy, they were on their way back to the town where the family's disastrous pilgrimage had begun. But Heidelberg, sacked and ravaged, was in enemy hands and years would pass before the Palatines saw it again. More misfortunes came. The eldest boy,

Henry, went with his father by boat to visit the Dutch warships which had returned after capturing the Spanish treasure fleet in Matanzas Bay in Havana. It was an historic coup; apart from the defeat of the Armada, the heaviest blow that Spanish maritime pride ever suffered. And it was of particular interest to the Palatines, for the Prince of Orange, by his will, had left them an eighth share in the company that owned the victorious fleet. On their trip to see the ships, the boat in which the boy prince and his father were travelling collided with a wine barge and overturned. The boy was drowned.

Three years later, it seemed that, at last, the luck of the Palatines had turned. The King of Sweden, Gustavus Adolphus, had invaded Germany. The war was going in favour of Protestantism and, therefore, it seemed reasonable to think hopefully of the fortunes of the Protestant martyr, Frederick, shadow King of Bohemia, exiled Elector Palatine. Frederick, who found The Hague an altogether tedious place, inhabited by people who were not at all on his social level, set off for Germany, hoping that Gustavus, after a final victory, would restore him. A great battle was fought at Lützen but Gustavus was killed before it was won.

A fortnight later Frederick died at Mainz of plague. 'It was the first time,' said Elizabeth, 'that ever I was frightened.' She lay, speechless with grief, in a shuttered room hung with black, while her brother, Charles, now King of England, begged her to come home. Eltham Palace was made ready to receive her. But Elizabeth, while assuring Charles that he was 'our sole resource', took advice and decided to stay at The Hague. She, who had always refused to learn German, remembered now that she was the widow of a German prince and – 'I must prefer the welfare of my poor children to my own satisfaction.' It is possible, too, that the queen had another reason for remaining in exile. In England, she would be only the second queen. It was not a position likely to be agreeable to 'Th' eclipse and glory of her kind'.

The Prisoner of Linz

'In England I have seen a country of great beauty and fertility and most rich in the soil and by its extensive commerce with all parts of the world.'

Foscarini, 1613

One day in December 1635, Prince Rupert, who had quietly dropped the title Duke of Lusatia, but was still a Palatine prince and a Bavarian duke, crossed to England. He was sixteen years old, exceptionally tall and impressively broad across the shoulders, dark in complexion, with that frowning look which some women find irresistible, especially in a younger man whom they have a motherly instinct to console. Considering the unhappy history of the family to which Rupert belonged – political disaster, exile, a prodigal fecundity, shortage of money – his severe good looks were thought to be exceptionally appropriate. Besides, the young prince had other qualities.

His manners might be *farouche*, as his mother warned the Queen of England, her distrusted sister-in-law, but they were formal, and he was well enough educated for a prince in the first half of the seventeenth century. The finer points of theology and literature he had left to his sisters, especially to the eldest, the grave and still beautiful Elizabeth; he spoke five living European languages, including Dutch, the tongue of the people they dwelt among, the 'canaille' of The Hague, as Rupert's father had ungratefully and snobbishly called them. In addition to these gifts, Rupert was a magnificent swordsman, as would in due course be proved on the duelling ground and the battlefield, a dead shot with the pistol and, from the age of thirteen, he had been able to go through the drill movements as smartly as any veteran in the Prince of Orange's household troops; he had even, a few months earlier, made his first campaign as a volunteer in the Prince of Orange's Life Guards, fighting the Spaniards in a desultory and unsatisfactory little war which, after a little, died of inanition.

When he stepped on to the vessel that was taking him to England, Rupert found that sea travel can have disagreeable surprises for young men. It was only a momentary weakness, as in due course he showed, but, passing or permanent, it did not weaken his determination to cross to England. Nothing in the world could have done that. To him, England had an altogether special magnetism. There his Uncle Charles was king, head of the most 'sumptuous and happy' court in Christendom. And was not England itself a wonderful base for a young man of spirit who wanted to make his way in the world? Rupert had somehow picked up the idea that it was. Perhaps it had been sown in his mind by devoted English friends of his mother's like Lord Craven and Sir Thomas Roe. At any rate, it could not be denied that Rupert who had not, strictly speaking, one drop of English blood in his veins, was English in sympathy before he set foot on English soil. Probably he did not realise that his arrival raised certain problems among his English relatives.

What was to be done with the boy? How was he to be assured of a career worthy of his birth and suitable to his talents if he should prove to have any? This matter was far from settled in 1635 and such testimony as was available, for instance the down-to-earth opinion of the boy's mother, was not altogether reassuring. An uncouth young man who might find his proper place in life as colonel of a regiment of horse? It seemed that the Queen of Bohemia would willingly have settled for something of the sort, with the proviso that no son of hers should ever sink so low as to become a mere mercenary soldier. But even to that, it seems, she would be willing to submit if a sufficiently dignified formula could be devised. The truth was, however, that apart from her anxiety to see Charles Louis restored as Elector, the queen was probably more worried about her girls than her sons. The Palatine princesses were growing up to looks – admittedly some of them were more beautiful than others – but not to marriage portions suitable to their rank. Another complication was the fact that the girls were Protestants by family loyalty as well as by belief. This was likely to bar them from some of the most prestigious marriage beds in Europe.

The King of England, feeling some responsibility towards his sister's children, took advice of the Archbishop of Canterbury, Laud. After due reflection, His Grace thought that Rupert and his younger brother, Maurice, that sombre shadow who followed Rupert through life, might in due course be found English dioceses. The plain truth was, however, that neither of the boys was likely episcopal timber. Their interests were thoroughly secular and their inclinations, so far as could be discerned, were military. This was not to say that Rupert had no religious opinions. On the contrary, day-by-day indoctrination by the chaplain at Leiden in the tenets of the Heidelberg Catechism had left a deep imprint. The brand of Christianity which the Catechism inculcated might not satisfy the strictest of Calvinists, although it had been inspired by Rupert's great-grandfather, the Elector Frederick III, in an attempt to weld together the more attractive elements in preceding Protestant Confessionals. It inclined, on the whole, to Calvinism; too diluted to please the tastes of the sterner brethren but strong enough to rouse the aversion of Lutherans. Be that as it may, it was unquestionably Protestant.

The outcome of its teaching was so manifest in young Rupert's character and demeanour that even King Charles' ardently proselytising Catholic wife, Henrietta Maria, did not suppose that there was any hope of plucking this lowering, half-German brand from the burning. One person was not so sure of young Rupert's steadfastness in the faith, his elder brother, Charles Louis, the titular Elector Palatine, who had arrived in England before Rupert and was watching, with some alarm, his brother's apparent readiness to enter into the refined but nonetheless dangerous diversions of the Queen's set. Somerset House where Henrietta Maria held her court was a haunt of Catholic priests as well as lovely ladies. There the fashionable cult was that of platonic love, a heady draught with an insipid after-taste; but the chapel was there too, alarming to Puritans and beguiling to unwary youth. Another ten days there, as Rupert told his mother later on, and he would have gone over to Rome.

Charles Louis, whose chief interest was to encourage his uncle to press by diplomacy for his return to the Palatinate, was concerned about his brother's spiritual future. Plainly, he regarded Rupert as a youth whose attainments were as modest as his fortune. A good marriage, he thought, would be the best answer to the boy's personal problems. It seemed, too, that a year or so before Rupert's English trip, the ideal solution had offered itself. The hand of M. de Rohan's only child, Marguerite, was offered, by approaches of the utmost delicacy. What could be better! Rohan was not only a French duke, head of an illustrious house, a man of great wealth, but he was also a Huguenot of the Huguenots. Indeed, as a brilliant soldier and the son of one of the bravest Calvinist leaders in the French wars of religion, he could be regarded as the first Protestant in France. What union could be more suitable for a Protestant prince than a marriage to his daughter? Rupert, a boy of thirteen when the project was first mooted, might not be of an age to give it serious thought; at the English court he found no lack of beautiful young women willing to dally with him, but the time would surely come when a rich marriage would interest a penniless youth of high degree. In the meantime, his elder brother, his mother and his uncle Charles, cautiously opened negotiations. As it turned out, however, a grave interruption in Rupert's career postponed any possibility of carrying the business further. Another and very different adventure was opened to the boy.

While Rupert and his brother, the far more cautious Charles Louis, lived agreeably enough in Whitehall, that royal enclosure on the banks of the Thames, an ambitious scheme was floated for an expedition to the island of Madagascar. The leading propagandist of the idea was a close and loyal friend of the King's, Endymion Porter. As leader of the expedition, destined, in due course, to be king of Madagascar, Porter picked Prince Rupert; Rupert's brother, Charles Louis, thought that no good would come of it. Not only was Porter too smooth and eloquent a talker by half, but he had a Papist wife as well! His circle was not at all suitable for a susceptible young man like Rupert who was already, at the court of Queen Henrietta Maria, with its flock of pretty women, its cult of music and the arts, only too likely to forget the duty he owed to the memory of his father, Frederick, the Protestant martyr-king of Bohemia, to say nothing of his brother, Charles Louis, who was, at that time, playing the Calvinist card for all it was worth as he manoeuvred to win back the Palatinate which his father had thrown away. So Charles Louis wrote anxiously to the Queen of Bohemia, who was inclined to believe all he said, and was equally prepared to believe any report of impulsive folly by her son, Rupert. 'Robert le Diable', as he was called in the family, was, it seemed, never out of the company of women and Papists and, as Charles Louis wrote from his apartment in Whitehall, 'is still in great friendship with Porter . . . I bid him take heed he do not meddle in points of religion among them, for fear some priest or other, that is too hard for him, may form an ill opinion in him.' The Queen, correspondingly alarmed, wrote deploring that any son of hers, 'still a little giddy' should become a 'knight errant', and clearly had no faith in the Madagascar scheme. 'Rupert's romance . . . sounds like one of Don Quixote's conquests.' She scoffed at the idea that the island with its vast natural riches, abundant vegetation, and agreeable climate, needed only colonisation to become an English possession as profitable as Peru had been for Spain. If it had been worth taking, the Portuguese would have taken it long before. Porter's proposal was that Rupert should sail as Viceroy at the head of a fleet of twelve warships and twenty-four merchantmen. After the island had been duly captured and its 'affable' inhabitants subdued and brought into King Charles' obedience, twelve ships laden with arms would go out every year and bring back the produce of its soil. Rupert, eager to go, accepted the post and named one Captain Bond as his lieutenant. Nor was Charles Louis forgotten in these colonial dreams which Porter was encouraging. The Elector Palatine would sail to the Caribbean and find a throne for himself there.

In the end, in spite of all Endymion Porter's eloquence, neither the Madagascar project nor the West Indian one came to anything. Rupert and his brother, Charles Louis, very soon were launched on a smaller, although equally misguided, enterprise than the conquest of Madagascar. In co-operation with the Swedes, they proposed to liberate the Palatinate from the Spanish yoke. They crossed from England to The Hague where Charles Louis waited until the King of England's contribution to the war chest was forthcoming. King Charles was down to back the venture with £10,000, as also was rich Lord Craven then, as always, a passionate zealot for the Palatinate cause. In churches throughout England, collections were taken up so that the good Protestant public of England would have the opportunity to take part in what was in the eyes of many of them little short of a crusade. Rupert was given £300 a year from King Charles' purse; which was increased later to become an annuity of £2,400 paid out of the proceeds of the subsidy on the import of tobacco. There was a delay occasioned by an attempt of the Queen of Bohemia to divert some of the money to her own purse so as to reduce the mountain of her debts in Holland. On this point, however, Charles Louis was adamant. First must come the restoration of the head of the family, himself!

While Rupert recruited an invading force, Charles Louis attempted to co-ordinate a plan of campaign with the Swedish Field-Marshal Banier. When this turned out to be a more protracted business than seemed reasonable, Rupert filled in the time by joining the army of the Prince of Orange which was, just then, besieging Breda. He took his brother Maurice along with him. Together, the young men, aged seventeen and sixteen, carried out a daring reconnaissance one misty night, bringing back news of an impending sortie by the besieged garrison. Warned in time, the Prince of Orange's Dutch troops were ready. A few days later, the Prince planned to storm a fortification commanding the town. Out of consideration for the anxious Queen of Bohemia, Orange hoped that he could persuade her two sons to stay out of the operation. Rupert, he decided, should remain by his side, as an aide-de-camp. However, it did not work as the Prince of Orange had hoped. Rupert galloped forward, bearing the order to attack, and, immediately afterwards leapt from his horse and plunged forward with the storming party. After bloody fighting, the fortifications were taken; many English volunteers were killed in the action.

Breda fell. Maurice was sent to finish his education at a French university. And Rupert, with his brother, Charles Louis, resumed the task of raising a force to win back the Palatinate. Their base was the town of Mepping, near Munster, which Charles Louis had bought from a Swedish general named Kniphausen, who had been given it by Gustavus Adolphus. With an army of three cavalry regiments, one guards regiment, two troops of dragoons (mounted infantry) and some cannon, they set off to defeat the forces of the Holy Roman Empire. Even if they had properly co-ordinated their operations with the Swedish troops in the vicinity, it was a remarkably hare-brained enterprise. However, craven doubts of that kind were far from the young heroes' minds. They were about to drive the hated usurpers from the sacred soil over which their dead father had reigned.

In fact, the young Elector Palatine had not concerted any plan with the Protestant princes; nor could he count on the help of Banier's Swedish army. Rupert, who was not yet twenty, commanded the vanguard of cavalry. Count Ferentz and Count Königsmarck, two German friends of the Palatine cause, rode with the little army. So did Lord Craven. Marching towards the Palatinate, they were joined by King, a Scottish general in the Swedish service. King was a professional soldier of some experience. He was also an Aberdonian, with all the caution of his kind. Maybe he thought that he should be the commander of the Palatine army. At any rate, he disapproved thoroughly of what was being done, not without reason. The original plan of campaign was to carry the little town of Lemgo by storm but the Palatine princes were curious to reconnoitre Rheine, a town where there was an imperialist garrison. Rupert, with three troops of cavalry, charged the enemy and drove them back into the town. After this heartening but trivial incident, the invaders rode on to Lemgo. No sooner had they reached it, however, than the alarming news came that the Imperialist general, Count Hatzfeldt, with a force much exceeding their own, was making his way across their rear towards the river Weser, which flowed on a twisting course fifteen miles to the north. Obviously, Hatzfeldt meant to cut off their retreat. Any thought of besieging Lemgo was at once abandoned. The problem that faced them was how they would slip through Hatzfeldt's clutches and reach either the nearest Swedish garrison at Minden or the Dutch border, where they would be safe. General King advised the move towards Holland, although it was known that Hatzfeldt was probably watching this route at a town called Vlotho. As it turned out, he was. Half a mile north of Lemgo, the Palatine force met eight regiments of armoured cavalry and a regiment of Irish dragoons. Nor was this all. Beyond the horsemen, they could see masses of Imperialist infantry. General King advised resistance on a stretch of rising ground, and went off to bring up the foot. While he was absent, the other Palatine generals decided that the high ground was too exposed for their liking. Led by Königsmarck, they awaited the attack in a deep valley. When the attack came, it swept two regiments of Palatine horse away. Königsmarck fled. Rupert, however, led his regiment in a charge and gained enough time for Lord Craven to come up with the Guards. However, their force was outnumbered and surrounded. In the meantime, his brother, Charles Louis, had left the scene in the company of General King. He had forced his horse into the Weser, meaning to swim across to the north bank. The horse went under but Charles Louis grasped the branch of a willow growing on the further bank and pulled himself on to dry land.

Rupert's fate was different. Before his last charge, he had bound a white feather to his helmet as a badge for his men to follow. Very soon, he found that he was surrounded by Imperialists, who were paying no heed to him. The reason was simple enough. The Imperialists had adopted white ribbons as their distinguishing badge and mistook him for one of themselves. He pulled his horse round, hoping to escape, when he saw a cornet of horse of the Palatine army defending his standard against several antagonists. At once, Rupert galloped to the officer's assistance. By this time, he was identified as an enemy by the Imperialists. There followed a desperate little skirmish in which he, Craven and Ferentz were all involved. When an Imperialist seized his bridle, Rupert slashed at the man's hand to free himself and put his horse at a stone wall. But the weary horse refused and, in a few minutes, Rupert was brought down and disarmed. 'What is your rank?' asked one of his captors,

Colonel Lippe. 'I am a colonel,' said Rupert. 'By God,' said Lippe, 'you are a young one.'

So ended the Palatine escapade of 1638. By the middle of November, the news had reached London that Rupert had been taken prisoner and was 'since dead of many wounds, having fought [as the Gazette says] like a lion'.* The truth was not so cruel.

Rupert, unwounded, but with two bullet holes through his cloak, was taken under guard to a house in Warrendorf not far from the battlefield. With him went Craven, who had two wounds, and Ferentz. Their keeper was an English colonel named Walter Devereux, who had already acquired a certain kind of fame. Four years earlier, he had murdered the great Wallenstein, with the help of the Scottish colonel, John Gordon. Rupert offered Devereux all the money in his pocket – five pieces – to connive at his escape, but the bribe was not big enough. However, Hatzfeldt seems to have got wind of the affair, because he now changed Rupert's custodian. When an English prisoner, Sir Richard Crane, was allowed to go home with the news that they were all alive, Rupert smuggled out a note to King Charles. After a time, the captives were taken, under escort, to Bamberg where Ferentz and Craven were ransomed (cost £20,000), and Craven offered to pay more to be allowed to stay with Rupert while Rupert, who was far too important a hostage to be exchanged for money, was carried off into Austria. His mother was more concerned about his religion than his life. While his fate was unknown, 'I wish him rather dead than in his enemies' hands,' she wrote, and later, 'All my fear is their going to Vienna. If it were possible to be hindered!' But soon there was comfort for the anxious mother: 'Rupert desired [Crane] to assure me that neither good usage or ill should ever make him change his religion or his party.' This promise the boy kept. Rupert fetched up at length in the castle at Linz, on the Danube, which was to be his home for the next two years. The Governor of Linz, Count Kufstein, was an old soldier, a convert from Lutheranism. He was determined to keep a close watch on his captive and was anxious to win him to the Catholic faith. Rupert was guarded wherever he went by twelve musketeers and two warders armed with halberds. He was allowed no male companions whom he might lure into plans for escape. But fortunately, the social picture was not completely dismal. Count Kufstein had a pretty little daughter of sixteen, named Suzanne Marie, whose heart was so touched by the good-looking, gloomy young

* *Calendar of State Papers, Domestic.*

21

prisoner, that she persuaded her father to allow the boy to visit the house, play tennis and receive visitors. In addition, Rupert occupied himself with sketching and, being of a scientific turn of mind, worked on perfecting an idea of Durer's for a device that would enable an artist to give correct perspective to a drawing. But a romance with Suzanne? No. For one thing she was a Catholic, for another, she did not have the rank to marry a prince of the Empire. Besides, Rupert was, all through his life, a difficult fish for marriage-makers to land.

After two tedious years of imprisonment, a new turn came in Rupert's life. The Emperor Ferdinand sent a message from Vienna offering to release him on three conditions: that he should become a Roman Catholic; that he should ask pardon for invading Germany; and that he should take a command in the imperial service against either France or Sweden. The first proposition, Rupert rejected out of hand. His not very loving and very distrustful mother had been certain that his captivity would lead inevitably to his conversion to Rome ('I did rather wish him killed'). But since then he had convinced her of the steadfastness of his faith. The imperial terms, like the wiles of the Jesuit fathers whom Count Kufstein brought in to the prison at Linz, were rejected with contempt. Nor would he ask to be pardoned for having made war in order to win back his brother's rightful heritage. As for the third suggestion, he would have nothing to do with it either. On the contrary, there were Swedish troops not far from Linz. And as everybody knew, Rupert's young brother, Maurice, was serving with the Swedish army. One of these days there might be a drive on Linz by the Swedes.

Maurice was one of four Palatine princes who were causing their mother disquiet at that time. With less than his usual circumspection, Charles Louis planned to recover the Palatinate in alliance with a near neighbour, Duke Bernhard of Saxe-Weimar. He travelled by way of Paris to join the Duke in Alsace. His brother, Maurice, who, by arrangement, was to have a high command in Bernhard's army, was already in Paris completing his education. So were two other Palatine princes, Edward and Philip. What the young Palatines failed to understand was that Cardinal Richelieu had no intention of allowing Bernhard's army to be used to liberate the Palatinate. The Cardinal, therefore, swooped on the four young hostages who had put themselves in his power. It was six months and more before the Queen of Bohemia saw her four boys again. Charles Louis crossed to England; Maurice joined the Swedish army fighting in Germany. Edward and Philip stayed at home. Amidst all this family turmoil, the Queen of Bohemia kept up her healthy way of life: 'I did hunt a hare last week with my hounds; it took seven hours, the dogs never being at fault.' She waited with composure for the return of the fifth of her missing sons.

In the crisis caused by the proximity of the Swedes to Linz, Rupert's guards were strengthened and the Emperor's brother, the Archduke Leopold, arrived in the city on his way to deal with the Swedish menace. He was a little older than Rupert, gentle and pious enough to be called 'the Angel'. He and Rupert met and became good friends as young men of opposing temperaments sometimes do. When he returned to Vienna, Leopold begged his brother, the Emperor, to set Rupert free. An intense controversy broke out at the imperial court. The aged Duke of Bavaria, arch-thief of the Palatine lands, told the Emperor that, if he released Rupert, he would be giving freedom to the most militant and potentially dangerous member of an aggrieved and embittered brood. Leopold retorted that, by kindness and patience, Rupert could very likely be made a Catholic. The Duchess of Bavaria threw herself on her knees before the Emperor, and implored him not to give way to Leopold's pleading. While the case hung in the balance, the Empress added her voice to those of Rupert's friends. Charles of England put in a word through his ambassador and Cardinal Richelieu decided that France's interest would be served better if Rupert were free to support his uncle Charles in England, where trouble was plainly brewing, than to have him kept a prisoner in an Austrian castle.

As a result, Rupert was put on parole. He was allowed to go visiting at country houses near Linz and he found time for some hunting. Liberty was granted him to shoot with a rifle, at which he was an adept. He agreed not to bear arms against the Empire but refused to sign a document putting the promise in writing. If his word was not good enough, so much the worse! After this, the formalities of release were quickly completed. By a well-contrived accident at an imperial hunt, Rupert killed a boar in the Emperor's presence and kissed the Emperor's hand. It was no more than a normal gesture of politeness by a vassal to his feudal superior, which in this case the Emperor certainly was. But it was held to be the symbolic end of the feud. Not long afterwards, Rupert began his journey home. He travelled by way of Vienna, where he failed to respond to the flattering attention of the ladies, to Prague, where he was born and which he had left twenty years before hurriedly, and in some discomfort. It was, by this time, an Austrian and, thanks to the zeal of the Jesuits, a Catholic city.

In Saxony, he puzzled the Elector by leaving a banquet before serious drinking had started. After that, he made his way to Holland. He stepped down from a post-wagon outside his mother's palace at The Hague. On a dark winter's night, he shouted a greeting to the British ambassador, Sir William Boswell. Then he went in to be welcomed by his mother with the warmth due to a returned prodigal. 'Not altered,' was Queen Elizabeth's verdict, 'only leaner and grown.' She had found it possible to bear her third son's captivity with a certain insouciance. 'I fear poor Rupert will not be set so soon at liberty,' she had written to her friend, Sir Thomas Roe, a few months before the son came back.

Now, the problem son had returned and all the old doubts about his character returned with him. 'What to do with Rupert I know not,' the poor lady complained to Sir Thomas. He could not in honour go to the war, having promised the Emperor he would not fight against him. He could not stay at The Hague in idleness. Trouble would, inevitably, follow. On the other hand, were he to go to England, things would hardly be any better. For the Queen of England, that dangerously seductive Frenchwoman who had already tried to win Rupert's soul for Rome, would certainly do all she could to entice him 'to the prejudice of the Prince Elector and his religion'.

Between the Queen of Bohemia and the Queen of England there was an ill-concealed rivalry. The mother was jealous of the aunt's supposed ascendancy over her son; with her charm and looks, she might tempt Rupert away from his Calvinist faith. That would be bad for his soul. And there was, too, a nearer source of anxiety. It would be damaging to the prospect that her son, the Prince Elector, might win back the Palatinate with the help of Protestant powers like England. And, as Rupert knew very well, in his mother's heart, Charles Louis, the Elector, their father's heir, came first. Before many weeks had passed, the emotional stresses in the family had grown more acute.

Meanwhile, in England, a political storm was blowing up. King and Parliament were quarrelling and, it seemed, the dispute was about to break out into an armed conflict. From The Hague, Elizabeth watched the situation with alarm. She was convinced that her sister-in-law, by flaunting her Catholicism in Whitehall, and, by giving King Charles dangerously bad advice, was leading the country and the monarchy towards a disaster: 'The Queen doth govern all the King's affaires,' she told her friend, Roe, 'you can guess the rest.'

The Queen of Bohemia was naturally concerned. She derived a great part of her income from England. If Parliament were to quarrel with her brother, that money might be cut off. Parliament might, indeed, be an unknown factor, bourgeois and Protestant – but was not she a Protestant, the revered lady of every conventicle between Nîmes and Edinburgh? On the other hand, she was a Stuart and, if the head of the family, her brother, Charles, were to be brought down, the whole Stuart position would be ruined. And, looking at matters from her neutral sanctuary at The Hague, she did not think that her brother, Charles, and his Parliament were equally matched.

For Charles, her brother, she had a protective love – was he not weak, sensitive, and rather stupid? Was he not, which was even worse, putty in the small, white hand of the Frenchwoman as he had been once before in the hands of the favourite Buckingham? Elizabeth's heart – clan sentiment being strong in that family which fortune had favoured and tragedy had haunted all the way up from Flodden and Fotheringay – her heart was with her brother. Her convictions, as might be expected of the mother of the Elector Palatine presumptive, were with the more Protestant of the two factions in England, that is to say, with the Parliament. The divergence of feeling in the Palatine family was expressed by the conduct of Elizabeth's two sons, Charles Louis, the Elector, and Rupert, his younger brother. The Elector took the English Parliament's side and its money. It was the businesslike thing to do, for not only did Parliament vote him a substantial annual income, but it was more likely than King Charles, his uncle, to put him back in his castle in Heidelberg. Rupert, as a younger brother, could not expect a fortune – any fortune. But he was a soldier, trained, thoughtful but so far unfavoured by fate. Now he could hear the trumpets sounding beyond the Straits of Dover. To do so did not require much imagination. And he had in his pocket his uncle's offer of a high command: General of the Horse! To a young man of spirit, who had lived through more than two years of captivity and frustration, the call was irresistible. Elizabeth tried to obtain for the boy a regiment in the Venetian service, which might have provided an outlet for his restless, adventurous spirit. There was talk of service with the King's forces in Ireland but the English Parliament objected. When that venture also failed, Elizabeth reconciled herself to the fact that he was determined to seek a post under his uncle, King Charles.

After spending a month with his mother, Rupert took ship to Dover, where he met his uncle. Charles had gone to the Channel port to bid fare-well to his wife who, at that moment, was about to accompany their

25

eldest daughter, Mary, on a journey to Holland when she would meet her husband, Prince William of Orange. Three days later, Rupert sailed back to Holland in the *Lyon* escorting the Queen of England and her daughter, his cousin.

Queen Henrietta Maria was not, however, making a visit to the Continent for pleasant family reasons alone. King Charles, late in the day, had realised that he was much inferior in financial and military power to his recalcitrant Parliament. In this matter, his wife was about to help him. The Queen of England had, that summer, planned to visit the Continent to drink Spa water, which would be brought to her at Utrecht or Amiens. Now she was going to Holland for a different reason. With the jewels and plate in her baggage, she was about to buy arms in Holland for her husband, the King, who, in the meantime, intended to capture Hull, the most important seaport of the North which was, at that time, in the hands of the Parliamentary party. Fifteen hours after leaving Dover, the Queen's ships were off Flushing. But the weather was hostile and the sandbanks outside the Dutch coast were dangerous.

Two ships in the Queen's fleet went down, taking with them the furniture of the royal chapel and a relic of the True Cross. Her retinue lost money and clothes. But the Prince of Orange was on the quay, primed to deliver a pompous address of welcome, which, among other extravagances, laid 'our royal sceptre at your feet'. By his side was his son, Prince William (aged fifteen), to greet his prospective bride (aged ten). After these courtesies, Henrietta Maria, who had suffered enough from the North Sea, set off by coach to The Hague. She was met outside the Dutch capital by Elizabeth of Bohemia, accompanied by her sons, Princes Rupert and Maurice, and two of her daughters. The Elector, Charles Louis, was, however, not one of the reception party. After all, most of his income came from England and, on the whole, he thought the odds in a struggle would be on the side of Parliament. It is unlikely that he looked further ahead at that stage. But if, by some tragic turn in events, King Charles were dethroned and his children deprived of their rights to the succession, there could hardly be any doubt who would be next in line for the throne of Britain – the eldest son of King Charles' widowed sister, the Elector Palatine himself!

The queens met with all the brittle amiability of two women who dislike one another. Queen Elizabeth's antipathy was, if anything, stronger than usual that day, because her Protestant eye had detected no fewer than four priests in her sister-in-law's entourage. However, principles and prejudices were ostensibly put aside and the two royal ladies, the Stuart and the Bourbon, drove together in a crimson velvet coach. Sitting opposite them were the two married children, Princess Mary and Prince William, while seated in the 'boot' there travelled four more royal personages, the Prince of Orange, Prince Rupert and two of his sisters, the Princesses Henrietta and Sophia. Youngest of the Palatine blood, Sophia was only twelve years old at the time but she had a cool, sharp eye and a retentive memory. She decided that Van Dyck, the painter, had taken some charitable liberties with the Queen of England's appearance. Her protruding teeth, the fact that one shoulder was higher than the other – the Princess noticed that these unimportant blemishes had been tactfully glossed over by the artist. After all, it is the duty of a Court painter to advance the prestige and further the political fortune of his patron rather than tamely to record her physical realities. And Van Dyck was a very great artist who knew exactly what was expected of him. With the Queen came her dwarf, Jeremy Hudson, whose hand was kissed by a courtly Dutchman in the belief that he was one of the Queen's sons.

Without loss of time, the Queen of England set about disposing of the jewels she had brought over from England. They were displayed, first of all, to dealers in the New Palace at The Hague where the gems excited considerable astonishment. After that, she moved on to Amsterdam where there was likely to be a better market for the more important pieces. Websters of Amsterdam gave 140,000 guilders for the Queen's rubies; other jewels went to the Burgomaster of Rotterdam, who paid 40,000 guilders, and to Fletchers of The Hague, 129,000 guilders. Agents of the English Parliament naturally insisted that the jewels were not hers to dispose of at all, being, in fact, the property of the State; they warned that anybody advancing money on them was dealing with stolen goods. However, in due course, and after tedious negotiations, the Queen raised the equivalent of two million pounds and set about turning the money into weapons of one kind and another.

III

A Rabble of Gentility

'Though we may know the beginning, no man can foretell the end and
consequence of an intestine war.'

Thomas Smith, *writing from York House to Sir John Pennington,
aboard the* Lyon *in the Downs, 29 December 1641*

After Rupert left Dover with Queen Henrietta Maria, six months passed
before he set out once more for England. In that interval, the English
political sky had darkened ominously. The gravest event had been the
defeat of the King in a struggle with the House of Commons over the
command of the City of London militia. The Lord Mayor, a King's man,
insisted that the right of veto over the appointment of a commander lay
with him. This was an incident in a wider conflict: Parliament, by a
Militia Bill, asserted its control over all the armed forces and, when the
King refused his consent, issued the Bill as an Ordinance of 'the High
Court of Parliament'. In other words, Parliament acted as a sovereign.
The King, who had by this time left London, was making his way to the
North while stubbornly refusing his consent to the Bill. England broke
in pieces around him and in London those who were too outspoken in
the championship of the monarch were hurried to the Tower.

From York, where he lived in state for a time, the King sent a message
to Parliament complaining of its distrust of him. All this was taking place
against the lurid background of a rebellion in Ireland which the authorities
seemed to be unable to master. While Puritan England – and Presbyterian
Scotland – waited with the gloomiest of forebodings for the arrival of an
army of marauding Irish papists, Charles announced that he would go to
Ireland in person to put down the insurrection there. But at the same time,
he was tactless enough to accept Catholic volunteers for the armed force
he was collecting in Yorkshire. Charles had a talent, amounting to genius,
for appearing by his actions to deny the meaning of his words.

In York, he held a chapter of Knights of the Garter at which Prince

Rupert, at that time in Holland helping Queen Henrietta Maria to raise volunteers, was elected to the Order. But the King's time was not wholly taken up with those ceremonial trivialities. His chief concern was to ensure that the arms obtained by his consort should be brought into England without mishap. For that he needed a port. He sent his younger son, the Duke of York, to Hull, and himself followed a day later. The Governor of Hull, Sir John Hotham, was in a dilemma. If he allowed the little Duke to enter the town, how could he refuse entry to the Duke's father? If the King came in, how could Hotham continue to be neutral as he had been hitherto in this great political quarrel? Sadly perplexed, Hotham gave admission to the Duke and his party, one of whom was Rupert's eldest brother, the Elector Palatine. The Elector had been in England all through the earlier stages of the crisis. Indeed, he alone had accompanied the King on his disastrous attempt to arrest the five members in the House of Commons. He had stayed on to watch developments, as he might well do, being Charles' eldest nephew. But when the King's party arrived and expected to be admitted, Hotham shut the town gates. Charles rode back to York in anger. It would now be necessary for the Queen to find another port of entry for her arms. One observer of the incident had no doubt about its inner meaning and further significance. The Elector Palatine quietly left the royal party and crossed to Holland. In doing so, his interest and his principles were in happy agreement. Parliament, which was the more Protestant side, was also the likelier to have money to spare for a dispossessed prince.

In England, confusion deepened and tempers rose. The Irish rebels suffered a setback but were not crushed. The Presbyterian grip on Scotland was strong enough to defeat an attempted movement in favour of the King. As the summer months passed, the rival English fronts hardened, although it was apparent that, whatever legal advantage the King might gain, for example, from his possession of the Great Seal, whatever he could hope from the help of the nobility, the balance of military power in the land lay with the Parliament. Above all, the King lost the loyalty of the Navy. When he hoped to win Hull with the connivance of its governor, Hotham, Parliament moved quickly enough to defeat the coup. In the middle of July, Lord Strange rode into Manchester recruiting for the King and was driven out again after what was hardly more than a scuffle. But shots had been fired, blows had been struck. The Civil War, so long hesitantly prepared, had, at last, half-heartedly, broken out. The King, still waiting for a shipment of arms from the Queen, heard the news at York. Rupert was at that time at The Hague, completing his preparations to sail to the prospective seat of war with all the weapons he could lay hands on.

His first attempt to reach England failed, thanks to the watchfulness of spies acting for the English Parliament. They suspected that the prince, who was proposing to cross the North Sea in HMS *Lyon*, which a few months before had brought the Queen to Holland, would if he reached England fight on the King's side, although they may not have known that he had just received his commission as General of the Horse from Queen Henrietta Maria. Parliament had no doubt at all that Rupert had too dangerous a reputation as a soldier to be given free passage to England at so critical a time. Captain Fox, commander of the *Lyon*, was advised on no account to bring him over to England. However, by the time the warning reached Fox, Rupert and his entourage were already on board and the *Lyon* was at sea. Fox, whose sympathies were with Parliament, was in an embarrassing situation. Just then a timely storm blew up and helped Fox in his quandary; the *Lyon* put back to the Texel and Fox was able to persuade Rupert to disembark, promising to pick him up again when the wind changed. After that, Fox put Rupert's baggage ashore and sailed off to join the Parliamentary fleet. Driven into the vilest of tempers by this trickery, Rupert was more determined than ever to join in the English war. His relative, the Prince of Orange, put a ship at his disposal. And Rupert assembled a nucleus of experienced officers and military technicians, including a 'fire worker', expert in the more devilish ingenuities of modern war. This time, he was joined by his younger brother, Maurice, aged twenty-one, who was determined not to be left out of the great adventure which was about to open in England, so exciting to young soldiers, especially to a young soldier who was sure of commanding all the King's cavalry. That the King possessed, at that moment, no cavalry worth speaking of was another matter altogether.

So the two Palatine brothers set out together for the war amidst the misgivings of many of the cautious Dutch who thought that they were putting at risk their mother's income from her property in England. There was really no occasion, thought those prudent advisers, for them to interfere in the quarrel between their uncle and his Parliament. The Dutch bourgeoisie had their own difficulties in resisting the political encroachments of the Orange family and were, for secular and religious reasons, inclined to side with the English Puritans. The Queen of Bohemia and her eldest son, the Elector, shared the doubts of these sceptics.

However, leaving Queen Henrietta Maria to soften the hearts of the Dutch States-General by reminding their High Mightinesses how much Holland owed to English sovereigns and how little – nothing at all – to English Parliaments, Rupert and Maurice set sail for Scarborough. As usual, Rupert suffered terribly from sea-sickness during the voyage, but he made an instantaneous recovery when they were challenged by ships of the Parliamentary fleet. When one of these vessels, the *London*, ordered them to heave to and be searched, Rupert staggered up on deck, put on a seaman's cap and, still white with sickness, ordered the guns to be run out. Two other English ships joined in the action but Rupert's ship was able to shake them off; he dropped anchor outside the bar at Tynemouth. There, the princes landed by boat while their vessel, after darkness had fallen on the sea, gained the harbour at Scarborough and landed its munitions.

Without waiting for a night to pass, Rupert and his brother took horse and rode south in the hope of reaching Nottingham, 200 miles away. There, or thereabouts, they knew King Charles was likely to be found. The royal standard might already have been raised! The first battle might have been fought! To warlike, impetuous young men, delay was not to be borne, especially when one of them had just been given his first effective command. In their hurry, Rupert's horse slipped and fell on an icy stretch of road; it was August, but the night was frosty. Rupert came down hard on his shoulder and dislocated it. A disastrous check. An infuriating setback to the impatience of youth. It turned out, however, that all was not completely black. Hammering on the doors of wayside houses, the two princes roused someone who knew that a bonesetter lived not far off. The shoulder was pulled back into place and bandaged. Rupert was on his way again within three hours. When the party arrived at Nottingham, he went to bed, worn out.

It turned out that the King was at Coventry, forty miles further south. What is more, His Majesty, much in need of a petard, had sent word to his friend and close adviser, Lord George Digby, to find one and despatch it to him. A petard? What, in the name of all the devils, might that be? Digby wanted to know. Such was English innocence of military ways on the eve of a bloody domestic war! Digby came to ask Rupert to explain. It was the meeting of two men who were destined to be deadly enemies in the months that followed as they were already contrasted in looks and character. Lord George Digby, son of the Earl of Bristol, was as blond as Rupert was dark, and as handsome, in a plump, easy-going way, as Rupert was frowning and saturnine. Digby, however, was more than simply an elegant sprig of the English aristocracy, a suitable model for Van Dyck to paint. He was quick-witted; words came easily to him. He was clever; conceited, inclined to be devious; in short, one who might in a situation made complex by emotion, by weakness and by ambition, be lured into treachery. To all that, it must be added that Digby was a man with the personal courage of his caste. That evening in Nottingham he came to ask the tall, dark-skinned new arrival from Europe about a petard.

This Prince might have a strange accent; his relationship with the King might raise problems which one could easily predict, even then, His temper might have all the roughness of which one had been warned. But he would certainly know what was this extraordinary object of which His Majesty had so urgent and inexplicable a need. A petard? Rupert knew, of course. He had seen many petards. So, to the relief of the flustered gentleman before him, he went without delay to rummage through the scanty royal arsenal for the bell-shaped metal instrument which, when filled with powder and fitted with a match, was useful for blowing in the doors of besieged houses. He found nothing that would serve the purpose. But he found an officer to whom from the beginning he took a liking. Captain William Legge was a professional soldier who had seen service on the Continent and was, in addition, an expert in ordnance matters. Now Legge improvised a petard out of two mortars and Rupert followed the petard when it was sent off to the King. From that time onwards, he and Legge were fast friends, bound by an affection of which, it may be said, Rupert was the chief beneficiary.

At Leicester Abbey the Prince met his uncle, the King, and assumed his command of the royal cavalry. It was impressive by quality rather than by numbers. The King could muster at that time well-mounted, high-spirited and daring young men. Rupert was bound to think, as his eye fell on them, that they were the raw material of a magnificent cavalry arm if only he could discipline them. If only he could discipline himself – a thought which probably did not occur to him! In becoming their commander, Rupert enjoyed several advantages: royal birth, important in an age when everyone was sensitive to social gradations; some knowledge of the science, as well as the practice, of war, unusual in a young man of his rank; an impressive and thoroughly martial appearance. Rupert was very much of a dandy, conspicuous in a scarlet coat, trimmed with silver lace. He was a fine horseman and, by repute, a formidable swordsman. He set the fashion for young men who watched how he dressed and copied him. Against him, were his youth – he was twenty-two – his impatience, an arrogant manner and – he was a foreigner. The arrogance was probably due, in part, to his awareness of the delicacy of his position as the King's favourite nephew. Basking in royal affection and family pride, he was likely to arouse envy and dislike in the jealous little circle of Charles' courtiers. Rupert was an immigrant, an interloper, a German – or, at least, not English – one whose arrival from the Continent disturbed the established order of precedence. Reserved and temperate, Rupert was a Puritan among the Cavaliers. In one sense, he was in the wrong camp. His brother, Maurice, without having his impetuous nature, had the same air of aloofness.

In the meantime, Rupert rode to Nottingham in his uncle's company and there, in the castle park, the royal standard, the oriflamme of war, was unfurled with all appropriate ceremony, and a royal proclamation was read by a herald. Later that night, the standard was blown down by a republican wind. This was thought by some to be an ill omen. At that time, there were many among the King's wiser counsellors who considered the appeal to arms a disastrous blunder and were quick to seize on any discouraging factors. Edward Hyde, for instance, had wanted Charles to retire to York and stay there, inactive. At Nottingham, on the day the standard was raised, Hyde met an old friend, Sir Edmund Verney, the King's standard-bearer, whom he was glad to see looking as jovial as usual. He begged Verney to cheer him up. 'My condition is worse than yours,' said Verney, smiling. 'You are satisfied that you are in the right and that the King ought not to grant what is required of him. But I don't like this quarrel and heartily wish that the King would yield. However, I have eaten his bread and served him near thirty years and will not do so base a thing as to forsake him. I am sure I will lose my life defending things which it is against my conscience to defend.' It is one of the classic expressions of the dilemmas which in times of ideological conflict can face loyal, intelligent men.

Rupert, who had come to England on the quest for glory and employment and out of a feeling of family solidarity, had walked into the bitter tangle of devotions and convictions out of which grew the Civil War. The men he met, those at least who were not simply thoughtless young sparks, had staked lives, families, estates on the struggle. For such men it was something more serious than an exciting military exercise, a promising adventure. Between them and Rupert there was inevitably some disparity of temper.

Looking at the military situation dispassionately, which few people in England in the late summer of 1642 were able to do, the King's cause could only be saved by something like a miracle. The City of London was against him, with all that meant in the way of money and resources. The main seaports were against him. The English Navy was against him. And, if it was true that a wide belt of agricultural England stretching from the North Sea to the coast of Wales was for the King, it was also true that London, the first port and incomparably the first city in the land, could supply itself from the farms and market gardens of East Anglia. It was not dependent upon what might be called Royalist England. More immediately relevant, London possessed in its trained bands the nearest approach to a militia of continental quality. These men were reasonably well-drilled and in good physical condition. Moreover, they were worked upon by Puritan preachers in the City; they would bring a certain ardour as well as the rudiments of military drill into their encounters with the Royalists. In addition, the main arsenals of the land were in the hands of the Parliament, the Tower, Windsor Castle, Plymouth and, very soon, Portsmouth. If Charles could count on the North, the West and Wales, he had no reserve of weapons to draw upon, not enough money to buy arms abroad and, it appeared, no ships with which to bring them into the country. The Queen's jewels, the silver plate of loyal supporters – what were they compared with the wealth of the merchants of London?

Finally, beyond the Tweed and the Cheviots there was a Scottish army, the Presbyterian Army of the Covenant, 21,000 strong. However, at the time the King's standard was raised at Nottingham and war was officially declared, the Scots were still hesitating about which was the wise course for them to follow: fight on the side of a king they did not trust, or on that of a Parliament in which there were all too many Independents and men who were hardly better than religious anarchists. In due course, the question would be settled by a mixture of John Pym's negotiating skill and the English Parliament's money.

That Rupert, a Palatine prince, was standing beside the King at Nottingham was something that the Puritans found hard to reconcile with their too-simple view of the world. One of their bitterest complaints against Charles, and even more against his father, James, had been that they had deserted the Protestants of the Palatinate. How deep was the disgrace of that betrayal! How miserable the contrast with the brave action of

34

Queen Elizabeth in resisting Spain and defending the Dutch! The pulpits had groaned over the cowardice and the treachery of King James who had not lifted a finger to defend his own daughter, that other Elizabeth, 'the Winter Queen', and now here was the son of that martyred Queen emerging as an active coadjutor of the faithless Charles who, if not a Papist himself, was the husband of a Papist, and was inordinately indulgent to Papist ways. It may be acknowledged that, shocked as they were by Rupert's arrival from Holland to join the King, the Puritan propagandists made a rapid recovery from the blow. These busy writers were admittedly adept craftsmen.

Their duty was, as that of propagandists usually is, to produce a handy demonology capable of rousing the fear and indignation of their readers. In the circumstances, this was a delicate task. Parliament was, paradoxically, making war in the King's name. So, on the one hand, they had to present the King as the unhappy, innocent victim of evil counsellors, while on the other, they sought to rouse a fighting spirit against the King's forces. Thus, they were without a target on whom could be directed the just anger and longing for vengeance of an outraged people.

Prince Rupert admirably supplied those needs. He was a foreigner. Very soon, he was pursuing an active military policy which might consist more in noise than in atrocity but this was a distinction not much noticed by peaceful villagers who were roused from their beds by an incursion of demonic young horsemen who came galloping down the High Street bawling, 'Damn us, the town is Prince Rupert's!' demanding provisions for themselves, fodder for their horses and money for His Majesty's war chest. The horrors of the late German war, the massacre of Magdeburg, the executions in Prague, the devastation of the Palatinate – all these remembered images of dread, with the quiet implacable activities of the Jesuits behind them, came thronging into the minds of the English when they were told of the reported doings of this desperate young man who had been imported from the Continent, presumably to give England a taste of what modern war could be. It was conveniently forgotten that Rupert's father and his family had been the first victims of the German war, that they had been exiled, stripped of their wealth, power and glory and forced through years of exile to live as the genteel dependents of a distant relative because of their improvident loyalty to the Protestant, nay, the Calvinist, cause. Yet it should not have been forgotten for the plight of the Palatine family was near to the heart of the British public. Only ten months before Rupert landed on British

35

soil, a solemn fast had been proclaimed in London, which had, as one of its several purposes, the imploring of divine aid for 'the affliction of the Palatine house', in other words, for Elizabeth and her children. In the meantime, in the neighbouring kingdom of Scotland, Parliament had decreed that 10,000 foot be levied and sent to Germany for the service of the Prince Elector. The English Parliament sought to divert 5,000 of these Scottish troops to service in Ireland, although some competent observers thought that the arrival of the Scots in Ireland was likely to incite the Irish rebels to a new pitch of frenzy, 'so great is the hatred the Irish bear to the Scottish nation'. In these circumstances, Parliamentary pamphleteers were careful to distinguish Rupert from his family. They laid emphasis on the fact that he was young, arrogant, violent, not a Papist, it might be conceded but, in all likelihood, a wizard with a familiar spirit, his white poodle, Boy, whom the Cavaliers promoted to the rank of Sergeant-Major General. In due course, Boy was one of the casualties of the war. In the meantime, he figured luridly in Roundhead propaganda. Rupert was suited by nature, and embellished by popular art, to fill the vacant place of chief villain of the English drama into which the figure of his uncle, Charles, could not easily be fitted. The London pamphleteers reflected in their own way a suspicion and dislike which Rupert found among his own colleagues in the royal army.

The royal army! The term could only be applied in compassion or derision to the woebegone little gathering in Nottingham. Some staunch country gentlemen, their servants and relations, some good horseflesh, a random sprinkling of weapons and armour – 'a rabble of gentility', as George Monck called it, which seemed to have equipped itself from some antiquarian museum of the arts of war. Fifteen years earlier, Sir Edward Cecil, a brave and experienced officer, had said, 'This kingdom hath been too long at peace. Our old commanders, both by sea and by land, are worn out and few men are bred in their places for the knowledge of war and almost the thought of war is extinguished.'*

Arms were as scarce as warriors. In particular, there was a shortage of cannon and firearms generally, although the importance of this could easily be exaggerated at a time when the rate of fire of a heavy cannon was twelve rounds an hour and the effective range of a cavalry pistol was five paces. If anyone thought that the old English longbow could make up for the absence of muskets, he had to reckon with the fact that in all the City of London only four bowmakers still practised their art. The age

* Charles Dalton, *Life of Cecil*, ii, 402.

of English archery was over. Surveying the troops he was called on to command, Rupert's heart may well have sunk within him. This was the meagre, untrained host with which the King of England was proposing to win back his kingdom! No doubt it was possible to overrate the miliary value of the 18,000 men of that half-trained militia, the train bands of London. It might be, as Thomas Venn said, that the officers of this force ate too much and that all the ranks drank a great deal: 'The god they worshipped was not Mars but Bacchus.' They might be prone to shut their eyes when they fired their muskets, as critics alleged. But they were the nearest thing in England to a trained and organised army. They were in the service of the Parliament. And they were more impressive to the eye of a soldier than the men who gathered at Nottingham to fight for their King.

Besides, imponderable forces were cast in the balance. Above all, the raw and strident power of Puritanism, loud of voice and pervasive of influence. Against it, what could Charles Stuart muster? Tradition. Inherited loyalty. A vague sense out of the feudal past that the state was a pyramidal structure with the Lord's anointed as its apex. And traditional religion which, in England, as in other countries, is subtler than any formulated belief and more local than doctrine. All these powers were present in Nottingham on that day. But they were not visible. And they were not likely to impress a visitor like Rupert. For their part, the Cavalier leaders looked on him with a highly qualified admiration. Having strong views, and some readiness to voice them, he was just the sort of youth that maturer men watch narrowly for signs of conceit and find what they expect. So the young foreign prince was not loved by the ring of courtiers round the King. This was sad, because, for his part, Rupert plainly loved England with the passion of one who could not call it his home, nor the English his fellow-countrymen. But, then, what *was* the home of a young man with a mother born in Scotland; his dead father a German prince; his upbringing Dutch, his usual language, French?

The Queen of Bohemia, with many misgivings, watched from a distance as her third son became active, indeed spectacular, in the cause of her brother, Charles. She had lived with a lost cause for most of her life, and her pessimism, which was so curiously allied with cheerfulness, was fed by gloomy reports about Charles' prospects from her canny eldest surviving boy, the Elector Palatine. There is little doubt, however, that when Rupert and his retinue arrived in the King's camp, he was where he wished most to be.

37

To the King, as to the Parliamentary pamphleteers, Rupert appeared as a godsend. He had just the qualities Charles needed at that time: youth, boundless energy, confidence in himself, belief that the royal cause could triumph. What an inspiring contrast he was to the loyal but dispirited counsellors with whom the King was surrounded! He could express himself with vehemence, too much for the taste of some. In debate over the Council table he was at his worst, abrupt in stating his views, contemptuous of the opinion of others; apt to subside into sullen silences. He had none of his mother's tempestuous charm or his father's impulsive weakness; basically, he was an intellectual, interested in the technical aspects of war. But he was also a young man of courage and resolution and Charles found in him something of the same robust qualities he had found in the lost, glamorous Buckingham. He cast his nephew for the role of man of action, and Rupert threw himself into the part with enthusiasm. By royal favour, he was entrusted with the task of conjuring a royal army out of nothing.

He was invested at Leicester as General of the Horse, which, in fact, meant that he was commander of a few hundred spirited, but lamentably undisciplined cavaliers from whom it would be his business to weed out the more obviously unsuitable and employ the better sort in the King's service. It would be prudent to give them something really active to do as soon as possible, something that would divert their minds from the more immediate pleasures of robbing the hen roosts of the neighbourhood, or sheathing their blades in one another. It would be better if they could have been trained to the standard Rupert had seen on the Continent before they were sent into action. But there was not going to be time for everything.

Rupert's cavalry were in action a bare month after he first set eyes on them on that August day, at Leicester. In the interval, making his headquarters at Queenborough nearby, he had given his troopers a smattering of mounted drill. In the nature of things, it could not have been very much. He had tightened their discipline. And, most important of all, he had lifted their morale. 'There was no more consternation in the King's troops now. Everyone grew assured.' Rupert had done more than that, however.

Finding the royal army deplorably short of supplies of every kind, he made levies on the houses of supporters of the Parliament that were within his reach. In the German campaigns, the armies of Wallenstein, Tilly and Gustavus Adolphus had grown into monsters, the appetite of which could not be fed by any civil authority so that 'frightfulness became a logistical necessity' (Piero Pieri). But a practice which might seem natural enough in war on the Continent, was by no means pleasing to free-born Englishmen. 'Robber Prince', 'Ravenous Vulture', 'Bloody Prince', shouted the pamphleteers who kept the London presses busy with their hair-raising accounts of Rupert's outrages. Yet these seem, by the standards of almost any war, to have been mild enough. However, their political value to the Parliamentary cause could not be doubted. And on one occasion Rupert went too far. He demanded £2,000 from Leicester, a city where political opinion was evenly divided, with most of the more substantial citizens supporting the Parliament. The Mayor paid £500 and, at the same time, sent a messenger to the King at Nottingham to complain of his nephew's conduct. Charles at once repudiated Rupert. The incident showed how completely the young, foreign professional soldier was out of touch with the average Englishmen's feeling about the war. It was hard for him to understand the anguish with which sensitive men of English birth watched their country shudder on the brink of a fratricidal, suicidal war. To him, it might be an adventurous service to which he was called by family affection and personal inclination. To them – to Falkland and Hyde and thousands like them – it was a horror in which their families and friendships would be divided, their homes burnt, their estates laid waste, in 'a war without an enemy', as Waller called it, but with uncounted victims, all of them English. In England nobody was eager to fight, least of all the King, who was willing to lower the standard he had just raised at Nottingham. If Parliament would withdraw the charge of treason against his adherents, he would do the same for them. But it was too late. Steps had been taken which could not be withdrawn. Things had been done which there was no undoing. Ancient loyalties, long dormant, now suddenly re-awakened, drew some men to fight. Pride influenced others: 'Unless a man were resolved to fight on the Parliament side,' wrote Lord Spencer to his wife, 'it will be said about a man that he is afraid to fight.' So Verney, a Puritan, was killed in battle, carrying the royal standard, as Falkland was killed, in a headlong charge of horse, both in a cause about which they were profoundly troubled in mind. But how could a newcomer like Rupert be expected to understand the melancholy involutions of the English conscience? The head of his mother's family had summoned him to the colours. For him that was enough.

IV

A Bible and a Winding Sheet

'Pox upon it, say we that would have peace; but the gentry so engaging on the Cavaliers' side, and the fury of some in Parliament, are like to hold on this business.'

Sir Robert Poynt, 1 June 1643

A month and a day after Rupert took over command of the royal cavalry he had his first brush with the enemy. In the interval, he had increased the strength of his mounted force from 800 to something over 2,000. He had found them horses, fodder and arms by methods that roused against him the execration of the plundered. In fact, there was no real difference between the exactions of either side, except that the King's men, being the poorer party, helped themselves more lavishly to other people's property, and were exposed and denounced by an indignant and effective press. But, having a purely military view of the war, Rupert had insufficient patience with the reluctance of prosperous English towns to hand over their cash contributions to a cause which he saw as indisputably righteous and lawful.

Rupert had also spent the September days of 1642 in improving the military quality of his cavalry. He did what could be done in a few weeks with good material: hardy, high-spirited young men whose brothers, cousins or uncles had fought overseas, who had fighting in their blood and who were well-mounted, if not well-armed. If he could not make of them a polished cavalry arm, he accomplished something which needed no more than a spark flying from one intrepid spirit to another, conveyed maybe by a single flash of an eye. 'He put spirit into the King's Army that all men seemed resolved,' said Sir Philip Warwick, who was there to see. 'Of so great virtue is the personal courage and example of one great commander.' In inspiring a meagre and makeshift host during the depressing days before fighting began, Rupert accomplished something more important than training and organisation. The Royalist horse might be a half-trained, badly equipped and undisciplined assembly, but they were eager to prove themselves in battle with an enemy whom they were prone to under-rate. The eagerness of the men was matched by the eagerness of their leader.

Rupert's first battle came about in a manner that illustrated how amateurish was the soldiering on both sides. While England was adorned in all its autumn beauty, blow after blow had fallen on the Royalist cause. Portsmouth, the last big seaport in the King's keeping, had been betrayed by Colonel Goring. The Earl of Northumberland had gone over to the Parliament and the Navy had gone over with him. In central England the armies blundered towards one another. Lord Essex with the main Parliamentary army was moving westwards from Northampton at a deliberate pace. Sir John Byron, finding that he was unable to hold Oxford against the Parliamentary forces, was retreating in a north-westerly direction to Worcester, taking a considerable treasure with him, including some silver plate which had been the property of Oxford colleges.

Farther north, the King was moving, first, westwards to Shrewsbury, then southwards in the direction of Oxford. Lord Northampton led a detachment to Banbury, a Puritan town, and then set about besieging Warwick Castle, held for Lord Brooke and for the Parliament by Sir Edmund Peto. Peto hoisted a Bible and a winding sheet on Guy's Tower, the highest point in the fortress. He would defend the Bible or fill the winding sheet. Faced with such fanatical resolve, Northampton pulled back to join the King.

At this juncture, on 20 or 21 September, Rupert was attending an election of town bailiffs at Bridgenorth, some miles to the west of Birmingham, where he advised the voters to choose men well affected to the King. At that moment, he received orders to march with a force of cavalry to Worcester, thirty miles farther south, in order to ensure that Byron and his treasure reached the King in safety. When he arrived at Worcester on the afternoon of 23 September, Rupert realised that the walls of the little cathedral city were too old and derelict to be defended. It was no place for him to be caught. By this time, Byron, taking a route farther north, was on his way to join the King. Before following him in that direction, Rupert and his cavalry rode some way to the south. Essex and the main Parliamentary army, lumbering westwards, might come into sight. He meant to find out. He had Charles' permission in writing to fight a battle if he thought proper. This had been followed by an amending instruction, even more liberal: Rupert could 'steer his own course'. Nothing could have pleased the young commander more.

The weather was warm. War and the enemy seemed far away. The late summer was at its most drowsy. Rupert and his force of horsemen dismounted and took their ease on the grass. Being on reconnaissance, they wore no armour. No patrols had been sent out. So it happened that they stumbled into trouble. Unnoticed by them, no more than the breadth of a field away, beyond a little stream and screened by trees, was a Parliamentary force of cavalry about twice as numerous as they were. However, their Roundhead commander, Colonel Sandys, was equally careless and confident. He had no scouts to warn him, no idea that Rupert was so near. He and his troopers rode down to the stream, crossed it at Powick Bridge and began to debouch out of a shady lane into a field beyond.

When the alarm was raised, the two bodies of horse were almost within pistol range. Rupert, it seems, was the first to recover from the surprise. He leapt to his feet, shouted the order to mount and, swinging into the saddle, put spurs to his horse. He rode straight at the enemy, sword in hand. He had a sublime confidence that his horsemen would ride after him. They did. They had the advantage of the afternoon sunshine at their backs. Sandys had just time to draw up his force in defensive array when he and his men were struck by the Royalist thunderbolt. An encounter between two forces of cavalry is not like the collision of two inanimate objects. Horses, faced by the imminent assault of an apparently determined assailant, shy, plunge and rear in alarm. In a split second they will turn tail and bolt. They must be held firmly by riders who are, at that moment, intent on parrying the slash of a hostile horseman's blade. The panic at Powick Bridge began among the terrified mounts of the Roundhead troopers before spreading to their riders.

Sandys and a handful of stout-hearted men fought manfully in front of the bridge until they were cut down. Sandys was wounded and taken prisoner. Most of the Roundhead cavalry did not make so creditable a showing. The sudden, alarming onset of the Cavaliers was too much for them. After the first impact, they made off over the bridge and streamed at top speed along the way they had come by. They were in lamentable confusion. Four miles along the road, at Pershore, they met Essex's Life Guards, to whom they gave so alarming an account of the clash that the Guards joined them in the flight. Together, they galloped to the Lord General's headquarters where their reception was understandably chilly.

Rupert did not pursue them far. His horses were tired and many of his men, without helmets or breastplates, were wounded. His brother, Prince Maurice, was bleeding copiously from a sword slash on the head. In fact, Rupert was almost the only officer to escape without a scratch. The legend that he could not be touched was established early. Sandys was not so lucky. He died that night at Worcester, tended by Rupert's chaplain. And – if Royalist propagandists do not lie – begging God to forgive him for rebelling against an anointed king.

It had only been a minor skirmish, a victory for quick-wittedness and the zest for action which was one of Rupert's gifts as a leader. The Royalist troopers, as they trotted off towards Worcester – pausing to give first aid to their wounded – had the setting sun on their cheeks. They knew that they had come well out of the incident and, as vainglorious young men are liable to do, were inclined to exaggerate the importance of the part they had played. Yet, in fact, they had done well enough – 200 strong – to rout a well-found cavalry force of more than twice their strength. In advance of them to the King's headquarters at Shrewsbury went the news of the action and a sheaf of captured standards borne by one of Rupert's secretaries. The Venetian ambassador in London sent a cautious but pious message to the Doge: 'It is a testimony that the Almighty, for the most part, is interposing His most holy hand in favour of the right cause.'

The Earl of Essex, no doubt, saw the incident in proper perspective, as an irritating but unimportant incident, best answered by improving the training of his troops. He had another matter to occupy his mind just then. Rupert had written him a letter – when is not certain, but it was probably before the Powick Bridge affair. In it, he suggested that the quarrel between the royal authority and Parliament's should be settled once and for all by a pitched battle between the two armies at Dunsmore Heath on 10 October. If that was too much trouble for Essex then, Rupert proposed, he and Essex should put the issue to the test by a duel, man to man. Essex, no doubt, remembered – and perhaps Rupert did too – that Essex's own father in the days of his youth and flamboyance, had challenged the Spanish Count Fuentes to a duel before the walls of Lisbon. The father's challenge had been ignored: the son now declined Rupert's. The letter to Essex finished on a bravura note: 'Now have I said all, and what more you expect of me to be said, shall be delivered in a larger field than a small sheet of paper; and that by my sword and not by my pen. I am your friend till I meet you next, Rupert.' Essex received the challenge gravely and gravely declined it. It was, of course, a preposterous notion, as even Rupert must have realised. But he saw some propagandist advantage to be gained from a challenge offered and declined. Rupert's little army joined the King at Shrewsbury two days after the fight. By that time Essex had arrived at Worcester, where his soldiers sacked the cathedral and tore down the organ.

Three weeks later, a series of manoeuvres began which, for a time, tilted the strategic balance in the King's favour. The Catholics of Lancashire joined him. A few hundred infantry came in off the Welsh farms where, by this time, the harvest had been brought in. These recruits brought with them no weapons beyond those that every peasant has always at hand. In this respect, the Welsh were no worse off than many of their English comrades in the infantry who had to be content with cudgels. The Welsh had no military training, no discipline, but were uplifted by the prospect of a fight and – why not? – the hope of good plunder in the rich towns of the Saxon. On a visit to Chester, Charles won the hearts of the people by some gracious public appearances and, more important, laid hands on the wagons and draught horses which Parliament had assembled in readiness for Lord Leicester's contemplated descent on Ireland of which he was Viceroy. Discouraged by the loss of these stores, Leicester postponed and, finally, gave up his expedition. He was not one of the most resolute Englishmen of his day.

One day, in mid-October, Charles gave the order to march on London. It was a bold and sensible move which he was emboldened to make since he had just been joined by Lord Forth, an old Scottish officer of the Swedish service. The King had neither as many men as Lord Essex nor were they as well armed. His quarters at Shrewsbury was farther from London than Essex's, who was at Worcester, but that was a handicap which a day's march could put right, and with any luck the King would be on the march before Essex realised what was happening. Rupert had passed the days in vigorously training his cavalry. Now his scouts fanned out to the west to watch for the Parliamentary army. Marching with a minimum of wagons and baggage, Charles passed south-east through Coventry and Warwick, twenty miles to the east of Coventry. By the time Essex, who was kept informed of the Royalist plans by a spy in Rupert's entourage, woke up to the danger, the King had already the edge on him in the race for London. The clash between the armies came as the result of a surprise. One of Rupert's patrols, probing about in the fog of war that enveloped both armies, went to seek billets for the night

in the village of Wormleighton, near Kineton, in the beautiful Warwick-
shire countryside not far from Stratford-on-Avon. They found that
Roundhead billeting officers were already there. Recovering from their
surprise, the Cavaliers gave battle at once and drove the enemy out.
More important, they took some prisoners whom they carried off to be
questioned by Rupert. Thus, ten days after the march on London began,
the King's General of Horse learned that Essex's main force was not
farther off than four miles to the west of him, at the village of Kineton.

He sent the news by galloper to the King's headquarters at Edgcott,
six miles from Kineton. Charles was awakened that night to hear it.
Until then, he had only a vague idea where the enemy was to be found
or what he was up to, apart from an uncomfortable suspicion that, like
himself, Essex was probably on the way to London. But where was he?
Farther north? Somewhere to the south? Charles had sent George Digby
on reconnaissance to Wolverhampton far to the north of the royal army.
There Digby had encountered a Roundhead force under Denzil Holles
and got more than he had bargained for. But of the main Parliamentary
strength the King had no information at all. In this respect, however, he
was no worse off than Essex. In spite of the Lord General's spy in Rupert's
household, he does not seem to have been aware of the location of the
King's army. For days two forces of some size – one of them near 20,000
men and one of them somewhat smaller – had been moving about
through the English countryside within a few miles of one another and
each had been oblivious of the other's whereabouts! Such was the
standard of reconnaissance among the inexperienced English soldiers of
1642! The veil was rudely torn across when Rupert's billeting party made
their discovery at Wormleighton.

The news which reached the King was good, but not good enough.
The royal army, billeted over a wide area and weary after ten days of
marching, was now between Lord Essex and London, the capital, the
great prize of the war. But Essex was only a few miles from the King's
right flank. Too near for comfort. The King's march on London could
not be resumed without embarrassment and possible catastrophe until
Essex had been encountered in battle and driven off. The tidings from
Rupert called for an instant reappraisal of all that had been planned. It
was carried out at once by the King's generals. Rupert's own opinion
was as clear-cut and emphatic as was to be expected: turn westwards, and
face the enemy. Early next morning – let the King march with the army
to the top of the rise known as Edgehill. There let him wait for Essex to

arrive and give battle. It has been conjectured that Rupert rode over after his messenger, to press his views upon his uncle, and that this was the occasion of a flare-up of bad temper between the Prince and the Secretary of State, Lord Falkland. Charles, it is said, sent his orders to Rupert by way of Falkland. Rupert, touchy as always and well aware of the envy and dislike that he roused among the King's English advisers, is reported to have said that he would take orders from nobody but the King. In Falkland he met a man as haughty and sensitive as himself.

'It is my business,' said the Secretary of State, 'to do what the King bids me do and Your Highness, in neglecting these orders, neglects the King who has done neither you nor the service any good by complying with your rough nature.' Here were hot words! It is certain that at some time or other during the campaign this exchange took place. Whether it was in Charles' quarters during the early hours of that Sunday morning is unproved, although it is, of course, possible. Rupert, being the head-strong, impatient man he was, probably did ride over during that cold October night to press his counsel on the King. After all, they were not many miles apart. In that case, he would have some reason to be annoyed that the King answered him through his Secretary. Nor was it merely a question of pride and pique. He did not have faith in the war-waging energy of the men around Charles. In any case, that question was soon settled. At four o'clock that morning, Charles sent off a note:

Nephew,
      I have given order as you have desired so I doubt not but all the foot and cannon will be at Edgehill betimes this morning where you will also find
Your loving uncle and faithful friend,
Charles R.

After that, the necessary orders were issued to the different units, snoring in their billets or shivering on the ground – it was a sharp night. Before it was dawn, the King rose, wrapped his ermine-lined cloak about him and rode towards Edgehill, his two sons, the Prince of Wales and the Duke of York, by his side. By that time, daylight had come and before long the church bells would be ringing. It was a Sunday morning.

V

A Night of Cruel Frost

'Seven things wherein England may be said to excel. First, a peaceable and quiet enjoying of God's true religion.'

Peter Mundy, 1639

'Keep trotting. When in doubt, gallop.'

Colonel A. D. Wintle

In the cold sunshine of that Sunday morning, Rupert and his horsemen stood on the crest of Edgehill looking on the valley below which stretched away towards the Avon. Under the steep ridge, the ground eased into open meadows broken here and there by rough tracts of heath. It was as beautiful and opulent a scene as can be found in all England, yet without too many hedges breaking it up which might have impeded the free movement of bodies of horse. While the sun rose and the day grew warmer, the two armies began to muster on the hill and in the valley below. Essex had been on his way to church when he was warned that the Royalists were to be seen, drawn up in strength about three miles away. As they stood between him and the main road to London, he was bound to give battle.

While Rupert watched from the hill top, the Parliamentary army gathered on the far side of the valley below, where the ground began to rise again about a mile from his position. They were a bizarre human patchwork – scarlet, purple, blue, green, expressing the taste in uniforms of individual commanders. One colour was repeated more often than any other, orange. It was Essex's family colour so that many of his officers wore orange sashes on their breastplates to show their allegiance. 'I never saw the rebels in a body before,' said the King, after a long, earnest inspection through his telescope. He would have found them, had he been able to compare the strength of the two armies, somewhat more numerous than his own, and much better armed. He noticed the gleam

47

of steel on breastplates, occurring more frequently than in the Royalist line, and particularly bright on the enemy's right wing where a cuirassier regiment was drawn up. Meanwhile, the royal army was being arranged in battle order – cavalry on either wing and the infantry units filling the ground between them. It was the conventional arrangement of the period.

Meanwhile, accentuated no doubt by the extraordinary tension of that period of waiting for the first large-scale battle of the war to open, the first battle between English armies fought on English soil since Bosworth Field one hundred and fifty-seven years before, a jealous quarrel broke out in Charles' high command. The elderly Earl of Lindsey resigned his post as commander-in-chief. He was, with some reason, annoyed because Rupert declined to take orders from him. For this, Charles was responsible, having failed to make clear when he appointed Rupert, that he, as general of horse, was subordinate to the general in command of the army. The truth was that the King had a greater respect for Rupert's military judgment than for that of most of his other officers. Rupert was for immediate attack with the cavalry in the forefront. Lindsey, who had served with Essex on the Continent, was for caution. When he lost the argument at the council of war, he ostentatiously put himself at the head of the Lincolnshire infantry regiment which he had raised. His son, Lord Willoughby, commanding a troop of cavalry under Rupert, dismounted and stood at his father's side. Family loyalty came before military discipline. The King gave the overall command to a professional, the veteran Patrick Ruthven, Lord Forth, who had recently joined him. Forth was a florid, corpulent man, famed in the Swedish army for his ability to drink enormous quantities of liquor and remain reasonably sober. Not long before, the King had made him an earl and a field-marshal. He and Rupert were apt to agree with one another on military questions. For some hours the two armies watched one another without moving. Essex had the greater incentive to take the offensive so that he could clear the road to London, yet he was conscious of one powerful argument in favour of patience. He knew that John Hampden was on his way to reinforce him with a force of three regiments of foot and eleven troops of cavalry. This might decisively turn the scales in favour of the Parliamentary army.

At three o'clock that afternoon, the King gave the order to advance. The most dilatory formations of the Royalist infantry had, by that time, been in position for two hours and their generals knew that Hampden could not be very far away. All in armour, with the Garter star on his breast, King Charles spoke a few kingly words to his followers: 'Your King is your cause, your quarrel and your captain.' If Charles did not actually use those words which have been attributed to him, he would certainly say something like them on an occasion so momentous and inspiring. As the infantry set off down the hill, one of the colonels, Sir Jacob Astley, prayed, 'Oh Lord, Thou knowest how busy I must be this day. If I forget Thee, do not Thou forget me.' Then, turning to the ranks behind him, 'March on, boys,' he shouted.

In the order of battle, Rupert was allotted the command of the cavalry on the right wing. But in the last minutes before the onset, he passed along the ranks of the Royalist horsemen on both wings to make sure that they understood the tactics to be followed. There was to be no firing of pistols or carbines until, with the sword, they had broken into the enemy formations. After that, every man could use his own judgment about what should be done. The first essential was to destroy the order and cohesion of the Roundhead cavalry. On the left wing was another division of horse under Lord Henry Wilmot, a self-seeking young Cavalier who, not long before, had promised a friend rich pickings from Parliament men after the Royalist victory. Wilmot was one of the Royalist leaders particularly detested by Rupert, who had known him as a soldier in the Dutch service. The infantry were strung out along the centre of the line in three divisions commanded by Forth, Lindsey and Sir Jacob Astley. The most impressively equipped of the foot were, naturally, put in the front line. And so the royal army surged down the slope below Edgehill towards the more level ground where cavalry could operate. The Parliamentary army was drawn up to receive them in a formation which conformed to their own – cavalry on each wing, commanded by two Scots professionals, Sir John Ramsay and Sir John Meldrum. Ramsay, on the left, would receive the first impact of Rupert's attack when it came.

In the preliminaries before battle was joined, Rupert had received a useful reinforcement. The King's Life Guard, wealthy aristocrats,* magnificently mounted and splendidly equipped, commanded by the King's cousin, Lord Bernard Stuart, had grown impatient with being sneered at by their comrades as a 'show troop'. They asked for the privilege of charging in the front rank of Rupert's cavalry. The King

* 'So gallant a body that the estate and revenue of that single troop might justly be valued as at least equal to all theirs who then voted in both Houses.' (Clarendon)

granted it. The Parliamentary artillery fired three rounds to which the King's guns replied. It was the signal for battle. When the downhill march was over and the lines had been brought back into some sort of order, the signal was given that released the Royalist horse in a walk

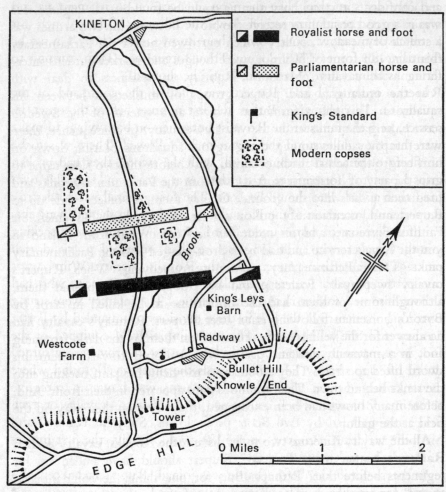

The Battle of Edgehill

which quickened into a trot. Minutes later, Rupert's sword was lifted in a signal. His trumpets sounded the charge. Wilmot's trumpets over on the left of the line took up the call. All the royal cavalry swept forward. Behind Rupert rode the Life Guard, the Prince of Wales' regiment, his own regiment, his brother's, and, some distance behind, the reserve cavalry under Byron. On the other wing rode Wilmot's own regiment, Grandison's, Carnarvon's, Digby's and Aston's.

In two separate blows, right and left, Essex was about to be struck by a force of 2,700 cavaliers, most of them untried in battle but mettlesome and confident, as good horsemen as could be found in all England. He was in a good position to receive the blow. Between the two armies was a stretch of meadow country which narrowed nearer the Parliamentary front line. In front of Wilmot, were hedges and market gardens interfering with cavalry operations. Ramsay, in readiness to deal with Rupert's onslaught, had posted groups of musketeers between his squadrons. This was a formation which, as a veteran of the Swedish service, he had often seen in the war in Germany. In consequence, there were empty saddles among the gorgeous squadrons bearing down on him before the actual shock occurred. Just before the two sides came to grips a party of horsemen trotted out from the Parliamentary ranks and fired their pistols into the ground. One of them, an officer, rode up to Rupert and ostentatiously pulled off his orange scarf. His chief, Sir Faithful Fortescue, and his comrades had come over from Ireland to join the King's service and had been press-ganged into the Parliamentary ranks. This mischance they were now remedying. When Rupert's cavalry swept past, Fortescue and his troopers fell in behind them, although some of them had the misfortune to be killed in error by Byron's horsemen following hard after Rupert. Ramsay's cavalry had no answer for the yelling horde unleashed on them by the dark, frowning and, in a moment, exultant prince who galloped towards them, his sword lifted to strike. They stood for a moment, hesitant, backing into the ranks behind them. Then ominous gaps appeared in their front. And, before many blows had been exchanged, they were on their way off the field at the gallop.

All the way to Kineton, two miles distant, the Royalist cavalry harried Ramsay's beaten men. Too far? Rupert should have pulled up his regiments before that? Perhaps. But, for one thing, he could not do so and, for another, it was necessary to make sure that the left wing of the Parliamentary army was really destroyed as a fighting force. On the other edge of the battle, Henry Wilmot had much the same luck. Musketeers, firing from the cover of hedges, brought an uncomfortable enfilading fire to bear on his squadrons as they moved into the attack. Wilmot dealt with this problem by sending his mounted infantry against them, flushing them out from their cover with well-timed

51

fusillades. By the time that Wilmot was at handgrips with the Parliamentary horse opposed to him, they were aware that their comrades on the Roundhead left wing had collapsed under Rupert's onset. They fled. Both of Essex's flanks had broken. But the battle was not over. Far from it.

Behind the infantry on the Parliamentary centre was a reserve cavalry division commanded by an experienced Scots officer, Sir William Balfour. Before him he saw opportunity beckoning and he had the cool-headed wit to seize it. The two main forces of Royalist cavalry had galloped incautiously off the field. They had left unprotected the King's artillery and the infantry of his centre. Balfour loosed his sabre-wielding horsemen first against the gunners and the gun-traces, then against the Royalist infantry, who by that time were exchanging short-range musket fire with Essex's foot and were about to come to push of pike with them. Balfour's horsemen intruded violently on the infantry battle, capturing the Earl of Lindsey who was wounded, and his son, Lord Willoughby, and coming so near to the King that Sir Edmund Verney, bearer of the royal standard, was struck down and the flag was snatched from him by the Roundheads. Balfour, along with other Roundhead cavalry officers, who included an MP named Oliver Cromwell, now turned his attention to the royal Foot Guards who disintegrated under the repeated onslaughts of the Parliamentary cavalry. But the centre of Charles' infantry line still held firm, the regiments commanded by Forth and Astley. The King himself, although besought to fly, remained staunchly in the fight. In the forefront of the enemy foot, the Earl of Essex fighting stoutly on foot wielded a pike like any other man in his line of infantry. For a little, there seems to have been a pause in the battle. By this time Rupert's men were beginning to drift back on to the field from the breathless business of pursuit. Rupert knew that there was no time to waste. He had caught sight in the distance of the green jackets of Hampden's force marching towards the fight. Meanwhile, Balfour's cavalry were re-grouping behind their infantry in preparation for the next phase. At that moment there was an incident which brought cheer to the royal ranks. Ensign Smith of the King's Life Guards saw the captured royal standard being waved exultantly by one of Essex's secretaries, Mr Chambers. Smith and Robert Walsh, an Irishman, put on orange scarves and rode in among the Roundheads. 'A scribbler like you has no business to carry such a standard,' said Smith to Chambers, snatching the flag from him and riding off back to the royal lines where he was instantly knighted by the King.

By this time, the light was fading. At first there was no sign of Wilmot's cavalry who, like Rupert's own, had been led too far in the manhunt after the routed Parliamentary cavalry. The Welsh of the royal reserve of infantry had disappeared. The King, surrounded by the remnants of his footguards and the infantry of the centre, was in the midst of a confused mêlée and in acute danger of capture. His Life Guards were not there to defend their sovereign. And now, Balfour's cavalry had come back into the fight. Essex put himself at the head of his infantry in beating back one of the last desperate onrushes made by the Royalist foot of Lord Forth and Astley. The Parliamentary commander thought he had lost the battle. He would take no quarter, he declared. Rather death than surrender! It seemed that the war was going as badly as he had expected from the beginning.

Like Essex, Charles was convinced that he had lost the battle. Meanwhile, the Secretary of State, Lord Falkland, who had charged into battle with Wilmot, was riding from one group to another of the horsemen of that wing, begging them to make one final effort against Balfour's dragoons. These were still comparatively fresh and were giving cover to Essex's weary pikemen. But when Wilmot's cavalry had been brought together once more, their commander refused to ask them for that last exertion. The riders were tired; the horses were drooping. 'My Lord,' said Wilmot to the Secretary of State, 'we have got the day. Let us live to enjoy the fruits thereof.' As for Rupert, he would collect only a handful of his troopers who, if they had charged, could have made no impression on Balfour's regiment. The fruits of the victorious cavalry actions would be hard to gather and enjoy.

Night was falling on the fields under Edgehill. The fury had drained away from the fighting. Men had no longer heart to continue the slaughter, even if they had the strength, even if they had been able to see where to strike at the enemy or where to parry his strokes. In the fading light, the two armies pulled apart, tending the wounded as well as they could and leaving the dead to be stripped by the ghouls who, after every battle, emerge from nowhere and carry out their beastly offices. That night they had rich pickings.

The English Civil War had begun reluctantly, as if men on either side could hardly believe that they were about to murder their fellow-countrymen. But, battle had been joined and the outcome was grimly impressive. When the untrained English were at last surprised into killing one another, they took to the work with some thoroughness. There had

53

been something between thirty and forty thousand men in the fight at Edgehill. Five or six thousand men lay dead or wounded on the ground. The Earl of Lindsey was carried to a cottage by his Roundhead captors. Balfour went to see him and was cursed as a traitor and a rebel until he went away. Lindsey died before daylight. From the slope down which he had led his cavalry, Rupert, wrapped in his riding cloak, watched for long over the double line of bivouac fires that marked the space between the armies. But there was no sign during that night of any fresh activity from the Parliamentary host.

It was a night of cruel frost.

Next day, in the early-morning hours before dawn, Hampden arrived with 3,000 reinforcements; the green-clad men whom Rupert had seen the night before. Hampden urged Essex to renew the fight. On the other side, the Royalist army was in a state of wild confusion. The King had spent the night in reasonable comfort in his coach wrapped in his ermine cloak. But when morning came, he was not eager to begin the slaughter again. He had been shaken by the casualties his army had suffered and the suffering he had witnessed: his own cousin, Lord d'Aubigny, mortally wounded; Sir Ralph Verney, his standard-bearer, killed; Lord Lindsey, badly wounded and in the enemy's hands, his fate still unknown; sixty dead bodies wearing the uniform of the Royal Guard lay in heaps at the place where Charles' standard had been snatched; in the end, neither army moved during that day. The King contented himself by sending Clarencieux King-at-Arms over to Essex's lines with a proclamation offering free pardon to all the rebels. When the herald reached the Roundhead outposts he was forbidden to utter a word until he had been led, blindfolded, into Essex's presence. The Lord General listened, asked him about the King and took good care that no word of the royal offer reached his soldiers. Clarencieux brought back to the royal camp the news that Lord Lindsey had died. It was the only positive result of his mission.

In the evening, Essex withdrew with his army to Warwick ten miles to the north. He was harried as far as Kineton by Rupert, with a mounted force. The village street was choked with baggage and the houses crowded with sick and wounded. A party of Parliamentary dragoons escorting plate, money and correspondence belonging to Essex, were overwhelmed and among the documents found were letters from Rupert's treacherous secretary, asking for an increase in his pay as a spy. The secretary was later hanged in Oxford. After that a fog came down, compelling the Prince to give up his pursuit of the enemy. There was now, however, a question more urgent and acute than Essex and his troops, the question of London. The battle of Edgehill had ended with the tactical honours equally divided. But, strategically, it was a Royalist victory. London lay at the end of a road eighty miles long, and that road was open. If the King's army attempted to reach the city, it would no longer be threatened by any substantial Parliamentary force. March on London and end the war at a blow? The temptation to do so was almost irresistible.

Rupert urged it and Lord Forth was of his opinion, as usual. But the elders of the King's Council were against it, and the King was against it, too. Enemies were busy whispering about the Prince. Could it not be argued, for instance, that by allowing his cavalry to run riot after smashing Essex's left wing, Rupert had thrown away the victory at Edgehill? There was no lack of critics to whisper just such doubts and to see that they reached the ears of the King. But the main argument against an immediate drive on London was not military or personal. On the morrow of Edgehill, men looked appalled on a reality from which they had always shrunk and which had turned out to be even bloodier and more tragic than they had imagined. Could not another armed collision at least be postponed and, perhaps, averted? The King clung to that hope and found many to encourage him in doing so. Too doctrinaire to be a statesman and too sensitive to be a soldier, Charles distrusted himself and gave his complete trust to nobody else; a feminine strain in his character led him to seek strength in some stronger and more assured personality; ironically, he found it in his wife. His intentions were honest but his procedures created around him an atmosphere of duplicity. As the Kaiser said of Nicolas II, 'The Tsar is not treacherous, but he is weak. Weakness is not treachery, but it fulfils all its functions.'

The King took the decision not to decide. His army was raw, even the best of it. Its discipline, as Edgehill had proved, was a brittle thing. Its training was incomplete. There was a great shortage of military stores and, above all, of artillery. The cavalry arm, regarded as the best part of the service, would be at a disadvantage in the enclosed country on the outskirts of London. The arguments against bold action were strong. The arguments for doing nothing, for patience and diplomacy, were tempting, and delusive. A forced march on London in the days that followed Edgehill might well have failed. But, as was proved in due course, it was the King's best chance – perhaps his only chance – of victory.

Finally, and most substantial of all the arguments against Rupert, any force attacking London would soon have Essex breathing down its neck. If London's defences were not swamped by a torrent of Royalist cavalry, if the trained bands, fighting from house to house and street to street, were able to check the attack for a day or two, then the King might find himself caught between two fires. And one of the disconcerting facts was that nobody seems to have known exactly where Essex was. There was, therefore, from the strictly military point of view, a case to be made for the policy of caution. Even so, on balance, Rupert's dynamic strategy should have carried the day. It was dangerous. It might have failed. But how else could the King win the war save by striking the rebellion down before it had time to organise its potentially overwhelming power.

However, this was not a war like other wars, a fact which Rupert, that dedicated professional, never seems to have understood. It was a quarrel among Englishmen which had passed from bitter debate to blood spilt on English soil. Forty thousand men in a fight and six thousand dead or wounded. Could not this senseless fraticidal quarrel be brought back to the conference table, which it should never have left? Was there any need to put London, by far the richest city in the land, to the risk of war? If Rupert entered the city, said old Lord Bristol, he would probably give it over to the flames. Danger to life! Danger to property! Both were detestable to the cautious elderly men round Charles' council table, and many of the younger ones, too.

So the King took refuge in prevarications and, as such men do, made the worst of both worlds. He took Banbury and a thousand prisoners, entered Oxford in triumph and advanced to Reading. By that time, eleven days had passed since the clash at Edgehill.

In Oxford, the social atmosphere was agreeable. The charming ladies of the court flocked in, to brighten the quadrangles with their silks and dazzle the young cavaliers with their glances. There was, for instance, the beautiful Duchess of Richmond, of whom Rupert was, in due course, enamoured. He had rooms in Christ Church, although he had established his military headquarters at Abingdon a few miles to the south of Oxford. There, fretting over the pause in the war, he worked off his energies by carrying out a series of raids on the country houses of known Parliamentary supporters in search of weapons for the King's soldiers and fodder for their horses. Needless to say, the London pamphleteers took full advantage of these partisan operations. Meanwhile, in Oxford, Rupert's severe younger brother, Maurice, had succumbed to the bright eyes of Mrs Kirke. The elder brother, the Elector Palatine, still trimming his sails between King and Parliament, found time to exchange a few shots with 'fair Mistress Watt'. Lord Hawley was said to be the victim of Kate, the widow of Lord d'Aubigny, who had fallen in Rupert's charge at Edgehill and whose funeral at Oxford was one of the sumptuous spectacles of that season. It was even said, for this sickness is catching, that the virtuous King had become aware of the charms of Lady Isabella Thynne.

The appeal of Oxford and the dilatory inclinations of the King admirably accorded with the reactions of the Parliamentary leaders to the result at Edgehill. They had been considerably shocked by the success of the Royalist cavalry. They were not at all disposed to under-rate the military efficiency of the young Prince and the force he was training. Cromwell, who had taken part in the battle, told Hampden, who had not, that the fury of the Cavaliers called for a higher degree of morale and discipline than anything the Parliamentary army had so far been able to produce. He saw what was needed and went off to his own East Anglia to create it. John Pym, a political tactician of genius, kept the King talking while he laid the foundations of a treaty with Scotland, which was neither humiliating to England nor dishonest, although it might have different meanings to different readers. But its practical effect was not in doubt. It brought into the field against the King an army as formidable as that which Essex had commanded at Edgehill.

VI

London Saves Itself

'London: a nation, not a city.'

Disraeli, Lothair

A great city rises to the height of a great emergency. Paris in 1590. London in 1940. Leningrad in the months after September 1941. And London in the early November days of 1642. In each case a defeat in the field was followed by a rapidly developing threat to a key centre of population and civilian life. Gloom, defeatism, even panic were the most likely sequels to the danger. Although London was predominantly on the side of the Parliament, it had its supporters of the King who, in their taverns, could be heard bellowing – or humming, as circumstances indicated – Royalist songs. What if these partisans rose in arms at the crisis of an attack on the City by the army of the terrible Prince Rupert and, in that desperate emergency, struck London's valiant defenders in the back? Nothing seemed more probable. The danger was one which could only be beaten off by a combination of civic nerve and military energy. When they looked at their maps the Parliamentary leaders were bound to wonder anxiously whether what must be done could be done quickly enough or at all. For after Edgehill, Essex had pulled his shaken army back north-west to Warwick. The King's army was between the main Parliamentary force and the capital.

Only some miracle of strategic ineptitude, it seemed to London's inhabitants, could save London from an attack which on any reasonable expectation had a chance of success. Rupert had seen what a good soldier ought to do, which, in truth, was obvious enough. He proposed to push on with the horse and 3,000 foot, to seize Westminster and the rebel part of the Parliament and occupy the Palace of Whitehall until the King should come up. Although it is likely that Rupert would have needed to put more weight behind his thrust, the general conception was sound enough. Speed, speed! Before Parliament and London could recover from the shock of the setback at Edgehill! But, instead of speed, there was debate and delay. Time passed and opportunity dwindled. Rupert, controlling as best he could his impatience over the way the war was being carried on, requisitioned in the neighbourhood to provide for necessities of the court. The farmers and villagers of Berkshire grumbled and blamed the 'robber' prince, and the court, which consumed the proceeds of his forays, was quite content that he, the foreign intruder, should bear the odium of them. However, he did not spend his time in foraging only. He was a restless and, as it seemed, an ubiquitous leader.

Among the young bloods of the King's party he had become a legend. 'He was,' as the son of one of them said later,* 'the greatest hero as well as the greatest beau, whom all the leading men strove to imitate, as well in his dress as in his bravery.' Even the way he had his hair dressed was watched and admired. When he tied a lace handkerchief round his neck on a cold morning, he launched a fashion for lace cravats. And to serve under him was a coveted distinction. 'I have neither desire nor affection to wait upon any other general.' ''Tis not advance of title I covet but your commission.' To young men like that even a defeat for the King was hardly of greater consequence than to lose their hero: 'If your Highness shall be pleased to command my attendance, I will break through all difficulties and come to you.'† Such hero-worship carried a double threat to the young man who was its object. His judgment of men and affairs might be impaired by it. And his enemies might work against him all the more bitterly because of it. Both dangers were realised in Rupert's case. Although he was a straightforward man, he was apt to fall in with the opinion of those who liked him and to form parties with them against his rivals.

In the autumn of 1642, he was busy with those flashing, stabbing cavalry raids in which the adventurous youth of the Royalist party longed to take part. On 1 November, only a week after Edgehill, he had the worst of it in a tussle at Aylesbury, twenty miles from his base, with a Roundhead force led by his opponent at Edgehill, Sir William Balfour. The scene of his next exploit, which occurred six days later, was thirty miles distant and in a totally different direction. He tried to carry Windsor Castle by surprise. If it had succeeded, it would have been an important coup, for the castle, apart altogether from the prestige value of its capture,

---

* Sir Edward Southcote.
† Louis Dyves.

was one of the chief arsenals in the country. Rupert had brought along with him a few cannon which he placed in the grounds of Eton College to pound the castle. Meanwhile, his troopers were set to work digging trenches as near to the castle wall as they dared. However, their heart was not in the business. They were harassed by gunfire from the castle. After a time they protested to Rupert that this was no work for cavalry. The attempt on the castle was abandoned.

All this was trifling stuff compared with the advance on London which Rupert had urged, and which, when at last it began, the King combined with some singularly maladroit diplomacy. Whereas, until then he had taken the initiative in seeking peace talks, now, with the new turn in the fortunes of the war, the first move came from Parliament's side. On 3 November, that is, three days before Rupert's attack on Windsor, a message from Westminster reached the King at Reading. Would he be willing to receive commissioners bringing proposals for a treaty to end the war? Charles agreed, provided that none of the commissioners had been named by him as a traitor. Two peers and four members of Parliament were therefore selected. But on the day after Rupert's repulse at Windsor, Parliament learned with indignation that one of its nominees, Sir John Evelyn, had been denied a safe conduct, on the ground that the King had, a few days earlier, proclaimed him a traitor. While Sir John begged his colleagues not to allow the issue of peace and war to turn upon the exclusion of one man, Lords and Commons alike decided that this was an act of bad faith which proved that the King was not to be trusted. The truth was that Parliament could now afford to be indignant.

While the King's Council hesitated, and his army dallied on the way to London, waging desultory warfare in the Thames valley, Lord Essex had not been idle. He was a surprising son for Queen Elizabeth's daring and disastrous lover – if lover is the proper word. The second Essex was ponderous, grave and reliable. He was staunch and pessimistic. He had brought along with him to the campaign his coffin and winding sheet and the escutcheon for his funeral as an earl. There was a reason for these dismal preparations. Not only might he be killed in battle, but he might be captured, in which case he was likely to share his father's fate as a rebel. It was his good fortune, in the days after Edgehill, that he was pitted against the one man in England who could outmatch him in slow-motion campaigning, Charles Stuart. While the royal army seems to have had no idea where he was and did not even trouble to look for him, Essex stayed in Warwick long enough for his shaken regiments to recover – shedding thousands of deserters in the process. Then he moved eastwards round the shoulder of the Chilterns into Bedfordshire. And he rode into London from the north on the day that Charles' rejection of Sir John Evelyn as a peace commissioner was known. His arrival made it certain that Parliament's reply to the King would be one of defiance, although London was not depending for her defence on Essex's battered legions alone.

The Venetian ambassador, Giovanni Giustinian, plainly impressed by what he saw, sent back to the Serene Republic a graphic account of the city as it stood at bay. All the streets were barricaded with heavy chains; every post was guarded; trenches and earthworks were constructed at the approaches. Women and children worked at them alongside the men; cannon commanded the main streets with the gunners standing by with their matches burning ready. Shops were shut. The trained bands were mustered, armed ships were brought up river, passing through London Bridge. It was intended that their cannon should give cover to the Houses of Parliament. Apprentices who deserted their masters in order to enlist would, by law, be indemnified.

The hackney coachmen of the city furnished horses for the gun-teams of which, later on, they were to remind Oliver Cromwell.* By the time Essex arrived in the city, 9,000 young apprentices had assembled on Finsbury Field, where the Lord General picked the best of them to fill his depleted ranks. One scrivener's son, although of military age, was driven not to arms but to verse:

> Captain, or Colonel or Knight-in-arms,
> Whose chance on these defenceless doors may seize,
> If deed of honour did thee ever please,
> Guard them, and him within protect from harm.

When he had completed his sonnet, John Milton fixed it to the door of his house.

Meanwhile, the royal army crawled towards the city. Rupert had been

---

* Among the State Papers (Domestic) of 1654, there is a Petition of the ancient Hackney coachmen of London and Westminster to the Lord Protector. 'We have from the beginning of the wars been ready to serve with our horses in the artillery train under Lord Essex and others for which large sums are due to us . . .'

They go on to complain of the unfair competition they suffer in their business from interlopers of one kind and another, in consequence of which 'parishes are much burdened with the wives and children of Hackney coachmen who die and break and the useful trade of watermen is much discouraged'.

61

beaten off at Windsor, but by 8 November his patrols were approaching Kingston, and the King's foot were at Staines. Riding down from Westminster, Lord Brooke told the City Fathers how dire was the peril. 'When you hear the drums beat, say not "I am not of the trained band" nor this, nor that, but doubt not to go out to work and fight courageously.'

London's resistance had two main nerve-centres, Parliament and the Guildhall, and many lesser ones, the pulpits of the City churches from which Puritan divines spread the warnings of danger, the calls to greater zeal, the assurance of heavenly aid. And from one outpost to another rode Parliamentary emissaries, grave, armed politicians, to knit the City's endeavour into a united whole. Meanwhile, the cloud in the west loomed slowly nearer. If it were slow, the fault did not lie with Rupert, riding at the head of the royal horse, his famous scarlet cloak floating in the autumn air, his ill-humour and vexation at the hesitancy of it all plain in his frown.

The King's army was at Staines one day and outside Kingston the next. There, a trusted spy failed Rupert. Sent out in disguise to find out how strong was the enemy, the spy was recognised and taken prisoner. Kingston was, in fact, held by a strong force of trained bands, men pulled in from Berkshire and Surrey. Faced by this obstacle, Rupert did what could be expected of him; he led a furious attack, streaming ahead of his troopers on the far right wing of the assault. In a minute or two he and his horsemen were engulfed by the garrison, but after some hot and bloody work with sword and pistol, the Cavaliers cut their way through and crossed to Maidenhead.

At this moment, the King excelled himself in rousing Parliament's distrust. He had moved forward from Maidenhead to Colnbrook where he met the Parliamentary Commissioners and suggested Windsor as a suitable place for negotiations. Thinking, reasonably enough, that a truce was in the making, Parliament sent word to Essex to refrain from any provocation and on the next day, 12 November, despatched a messenger to the King asking for a ceasefire. That morning, with heavy mist hanging over the Thames valley, Rupert made a thrust at Brentford. Danger was ten miles closer to London.

A pair of businessmen were pulled in by Royalist scouts a few days before. Soon after, they found themselves in Rupert's bedroom to be interrogated. The Prince was in bed, fully dressed and not in the best of humours. Pointing to the ribbons in one man's hat, he said, 'None of the King's colours here.' 'No, they are our mistresses' favours,' said the captive Roundheads. Rupert grinned and handed the hat back. Not long afterwards, the two saw Rupert in passionate talk with the King while they walked to and fro on Hounslow Heath. It was apparent to them, from the way the Prince wore his hat that he was bitterly disappointed with the way things were going.

To what extent his advice was responsible for the attack on Brentford can only be guessed. To a soldier conducting a military operation, it would seem no more than common sense. But Charles at that moment was dealing with his frightened and suspicious Parliament, as well as fighting it. When he let Rupert off the leash, he was taking a risk with his own reputation and his diplomacy. The gamble had better succeed! On the foggy morning air, the Brentford defenders picked up the sound of a body of horse moving at the trot, unmistakable, and coming nearer. Who the unseen riders might be was a matter of doubt up until the moment when, through the mist, Rupert loomed up with, behind him, a dark blue cloud of horsemen and the glitter of steel. He was riding at the head of the Prince of Wales' regiment, a crack formation of the King's army, which Rupert himself had trained. Instantly, if belatedly, trumpets sounded the alarm, and Brentford's garrison rushed to arms. They belonged to one of the best Parliamentary formations, Denzil Holles' Redcoats, who had been in the fight at Edgehill. The advantage of surprise lay with Rupert but Holles had artillery to sweep the streets and barricades to bar them. In a few minutes it was plain that the storming of Brentford was going to be no job for cavalry. Rupert rode back to bring up the infantry. In the van, as it chanced, was a Welsh regiment commanded by Colonel Salisbury. Rupert dismounted and put himself at their head in an assault on the barricades, while his cavalry hung back waiting for the moment when the Redcoats were driven out of their shelter. Then they rode in to harry the retreating men. But the Redcoats fought back with spirit. After three hours, although they had been evicted from the town, they were still holding on to the outlying houses. At that moment, relief arrived, Lord Brooke's regiment in purple coats, John Hampden's in green. By then, however, it was too late to save Brentford from looting by the Welsh, or its defenders from Rupert's cavalry. Some were killed, some driven into the river. Most of them retreated in admirable order. When the King arrived in Brentford with the main army, his nephew was able to show him a dozen captured cannon, some colours and a few hundred prisoners.

Early that afternoon, Lord Essex heard the news in the House of Lords.

He mounted and rode westwards with all speed. He was going to make a last stand before the capital at Turnham Green – ten miles to the west. All through the night and all next morning, while the church bells rang – it was Sunday, as it had been on the morning of Edgehill – and the preachers harangued their flocks, the young manhood of the city streamed out to fight. Food by the cartload and wine by the cask rumbled out after them. The kitchens and cookshops had been mobilised to fill the bellies and raise the spirits of the defenders. When the time came for Charles' commanders to look out to the east, where the sun was up and the mist had vanished, London had assembled an army of 27,000 men between the King and his capital. It was not, perhaps, a very good army. Few in its ranks had fought before and not many of them knew a great deal about fighting. But they were well fed and in excellent heart. They had heard warm words from Essex and General Skippon to inspire them, and the sight of many members of Parliament to convince them that they were not being called on to perform a duty from which the politicians flinched. They were well positioned for defence behind hedges and ditches. And they numbered twice as many as those who stood on the western verge of Turnham Green, no more than half a mile away, in the King's ranks.

In due course, the King and his generals realised that it would be madness to attack where everything favoured the defence. The royal army withdrew behind a screen of cavalry which Rupert commanded with nonchalant courage. London had saved itself.

VII

This Scribbling Age

'Calomniez! Calomniez! Il en restera toujours quelquechose!'

Beaumarchais

Socially, the winter of 1642–3 was brilliant. The attempt on London having failed, through the energy of London itself, the King pulled back to Oxford there to await the coming of spring. The Great Seal was with him, while Parliament and the Law Courts stayed in Westminster. England was divided but, somehow, across the lines drawn by the armies, the national life went on. Rupert, having nothing better to do, was for the first and last time in his life, stung into answering the pamphleteers who, from their headquarters under St Paul's, were pouring out a stream of vicious propaganda against him. These publications had some success; they had even infected men on his own side of the great political divide. Men like Lord Bristol. It was perhaps of these men that Rupert was chiefly thinking when he wrote: 'I shall repute it with the greatest military victory in the world to see his Majesty enter London in peace, without shedding one drop of blood; where I dare say (God and his Majesty are witnesses that I lie not) no citizen shall be plundered of one penny or farthing.' He had been accused of allowing his troopers to commit outrages: 'I openly dare the most valiant and quick-sighted of that lying faction to name the time, the person or the house where any child or woman lost so much as a hair of their head by me or any of our soldiers.' As for the charge that he was a Papist in disguise, 'The world knows how deeply I have smarted and what perils I have undergone for the Protestant cause.' On the other hand, he did not deny that, when members of the King's Council were arguing in favour of an accommodation with the Parliament, he had swung the debate towards an attack on London. His purpose was to win the war for God and King Charles, 'a cause full of piety and justice'. It might seem strange, he said in conclusion, to see him in print, 'my known disposition being so contrary to this scribbling age'. With that single, indignant retort, Rupert went back to the business of making war.

In this business, he had rivals. After the first effects of the King's failure to take London had worn off, the Royalist cause revived, especially in the North. In Lancashire, the Royalist champion, Lord Derby, was in the ascendancy. In Yorkshire, the Earl of Newcastle had so many successes that Lord Fairfax groaned to Parliament, 'The enemy is mighty and master of the field.' Farther south, at Hereford, the Parliamentarian Earl of Stamford was driven back to Gloucester. A strategy was emerging. The heart of Parliamentary strength lay in the clothing towns: were these cut off from their supplies of wool on the one hand and from their market in London on the other, a shrewd blow would be struck at the economic power of the Parliamentary movement. With this purpose in mind, George Digby and Henry Wilmot, neither of whom loved Rupert, struck at Marlborough, thirty miles as the crow flies south-west of the Royalist headquarters. They took it, and plundered it of cheese, cloth and money. What was much more important, they could now interrupt the wool traffic from Wiltshire to London.

This was not the only purpose of the Royalist commanders. The military situation was promising enough. The North was mainly the King's; Wales was his. In Cornwall, Sir Ralph Hopton was winning battles for him. Hopton had last appeared in Rupert's life when the Queen of Bohemia rode pillion behind him on the snow-bound roads leading from Prague. But it was essential to knit those dispersed efforts together in a coherent plan.

The Royalist strategists proposed, therefore, that while Essex was kept pinned down at Windsor, the Earl of Newcastle would march south from Yorkshire through Lincoln and Cambridge and break into East Anglia, where at that moment Colonel Cromwell was training the cavalry later known as the Ironsides. At the same time, Hopton would march his west-country troops into Kent. He and Newcastle would then reach the opposite banks of the Thames estuary somewhere between London and the sea. With Hopton on the south bank and Newcastle on the north, London would – it was hopefully assumed – be cut off from the sea. If, in addition, the King could interfere with the river traffic to the west, London would be strangled. It was a plan, or at least, an idea, holding great possibilities, if only it could be carried out. But it called for a remarkable degree of correlation between the various elements in the

Royalist strategy, and for a standard of staff work which they had not yet displayed. And Parliament enjoyed the advantage of interior lines.

Rupert's part in the scheme was important. His first task was to clear the King's communications with Hopton and the Welsh by opening a way through Gloucestershire. He decided to aim at Cirencester and, with that purpose in mind, reinforced his cavalry at Abingdon. In the process, his officers had a great deal of trouble with the new arrivals, a rowdy undisciplined batch of recruits who beat up the quartermaster and raided the regimental stores for food. Infantry poured in from Wales and were ear-marked for the assault on Cirencester, while Rupert with the cavalry was to prevent help reaching the Cirencester garrison from the solidly Roundhead city of Gloucester. After the failure of an attack on Cirencester in the first week of January, when Lord Hertford arrived late for the battle, there was a successful assault three weeks later. The fiery Welsh drove the Roundhead garrison from a farm they were holding outside the town. Seizing the opportunity afforded by this success, Rupert urged his cavalry forward so that they rode into the retreating Roundheads before they had reached the gates of the town and entered it along with them. A handful of determined men held out in the marketplace for an hour. After that, Cirencester was in Royalist hands. An important part of the Royalist scheme had been realised, to the great satisfaction of the King who was, at that moment, negotiating with Commissioners from the Parliament. The Commissioners, for their part, were witnesses of the arrival in Oxford of the wretched survivors of the Cirencester garrison. Cirencester was, in fact, an important gain. From the region around it came money, horses and supplies for the royal army. Less than a month later, the Queen landed at Bridlington.

Rupert's thrust towards the west was followed by a more ambitious movement towards the north. Its purpose was to link up with Lord Newcastle's force coming down from the north. There was, too, a call for help from Charlotte de la Tremoille, Countess of Derby, who had known the Palatines at The Hague and who was hard pressed in Lancashire by Parliamentary forces: 'Ayez pitié de mon mari, mes enfants, et moi.' In the first weeks of April, Rupert set off from Oxford with George Digby and Lord Denbigh, an elderly man who had volunteered in the King's Horse Guards. All told, Rupert led a force of twelve hundred horse and six hundred foot. His dragoons are reported to have carried a musket in front and an Irishwoman behind. Less fortunate, the infantry were equipped with pikes, halberds, hedging-bills, Welsh hooks, clubs, chopping knives and the like. In addition, the force dragged in its wake half a dozen light guns – drakes and sakers. With this nondescript army, Rupert approached Birmingham, famed for its 'hearty, wilful, affected disloyalty to the King'. When he was ten miles distant, the more timorous citizens were seized with alarm. The minister of Birmingham begged the local defenders to abandon any idea of resistance. The officers were willing enough to oblige him but the rank and file – 'the middle and inferior sort of people' – insisted on fighting. In fact, they were able to keep the Royalists out of the town until the thatch was alight on some roofs.

After that, the cavalry broke into the town through the fields behind the houses. Old Lord Denbigh rode in front of the raiders, singing as he went. However, a troop of Roundhead horse under a brave commander named Captain Greaves rallied and launched a counter-attack. In the fight that followed, Denbigh was knocked off his horse and left for dead in the street. While he lay unconscious, he had his pockets picked. He died a week later. Covered by Greaves' resolute action, the Birmingham infantry slipped out of the clutches of Rupert's soldiers who fell to the congenial tasks of plunder and blackmail.

Needless to say, the raid on the town was seized on by the Parliamentary propagandists. An appalling picture was painted of Birmingham, stronghold of the Puritans, given up to the flames and at the mercy of drunken, dissolute revellers, terrifying the good women of the city and, most devilish of all, drinking the health of Prince Rupert's poodle, Boy. Birmingham was left as a woeful spectacle to behold, a thoroughfare for thieves and plunderers. So, at least, the excited Parliamentary war correspondents alleged.

The Royalist account of the incident was less colourful. Birmingham, it was said, was not a peaceful little Midland town. Not only had it sent 15,000 swords to Lord Essex's army but it had stolen valuable plate belonging to the King and had carried it off to Warwick. What was more, when Rupert's force approached, the Birmingham people had called them cursed dogs, Papist traitors and other expressions likely to irritate even the most equable of soldiers. As for the firing of houses, it was not done by Rupert's command. On the contrary, he had given orders that the fires should be put out, but unfortunately the wind was too high. Typical of the special poignancies of a civil war, Denbigh's son was on the Parliament side and when he came, under a flag of truce, to see his father, he arrived too late. 'You were carried away by error,' wrote Lady Denbigh to him. 'The last words your dear father spoke was to desire God to forgive you.'

Rupert's raiding force moved on to an attack on Lichfield. Here regular siege operations were needed. While he waited for the mine to be prepared, Rupert received a letter from the King ordering him 'to wait patiently for the Divine opportunity to comfort the distractions of our kingdom and by no means seek to anticipate Divine revenge on our subjects'. In besieging Lichfield, the matter immediately on hand, Rupert was to have a particular care of spilling innocent blood. Charles was aware of the fiercer side to his nephew's temperament. No doubt, he had seen it at work during the Edgehill fight. And, no doubt, he was aware of the use that enemy propaganda was making of it. But Lichfield turned out to be a tougher nut to crack than Birmingham had been. The Parliamentary garrison, commanded by Colonel Russell, was resolute and was skilfully posted in the Cathedral close. Rupert's cannon, light pieces, could make no impression on the walls. The weather was not on his side, for heavy rain made the Royalist trenches untenable. Lord George Digby, up to his waist in mud, was hit in the thigh and put out of action. Now there was urgent need for a decision. Essex was besieging Reading, a key town in the Thames valley. Letters came from the King at Oxford, stressing the need for a quick result at Lichfield. In this situation, Rupert sent one of his officers, Colonel Hastings, to mobilise the Cannock miners, 'as skilful as any'. Hastings immediately recruited fifty and promised a hundred more a day later. They duly arrived bringing their pickaxes with them. Helped by officers and volunteers from Rupert's troopers they set to work, sapping the walls of Lichfield Cathedral close. The moat was drained and two light bridges were constructed for the assault party to use.

When the mine was ready, Rupert sent by his trumpeter a final offer of surrender terms. Colonel Russell answered by clashing the Cathedral bell in defiance. Next day the mine was sprung. A great gap was torn in the defences. The storming party rushed forward with Colonel Usher at their head. They were met by a heavy fire and Usher's men were driven back. Rupert's guns were brought into use to overcome the garrison's resistance. After the surrender, Rupert congratulated the Roundhead commander as he marched out at the head of his troops, colours flying, trumpets sounding. Then, as soon as he had installed a Royalist garrison in the town, Rupert rode off in the direction of Oxford. Time was running short. If he had ever doubted it, a letter from the King's Secretary arriving at that moment made the matter plain. 'It is the opinion here that if Prince Rupert come not speedily, the town of Reading will be lost.'

The Prince at once gave up any idea of linking up with the Royalists in the north. He knew as well as anyone in the Royalist camp how important Reading was to the King's strategy. The town stood on the main Oxford–London road. It commanded the Thames and the valley that ran to the north between the Chilterns and the Berkshire Downs. In recent months, he had urged that the fortifications of Reading should be strengthened. He had urged in vain. So he needed no letters from Oxford to tell him that a major crisis threatened to engulf all the tenuous hopes of the King's cause. He increased the pace of his column on its way to the scene of action. At Caversham, not far north of Reading, he fell in with the King's main army. After a few minutes' talk with his uncle, he realised that Reading could not be saved. At best, its garrison of 3,000 men and twenty guns might be rescued from falling into the hands of Essex if an attack were delivered on the besiegers' lines. At the King's side, Rupert rode forward in threatening weather to see what could still be done. In fact, they had arrived too late. Sir Arthur Aston, commanding the town for Charles, had, from the start, taken the most pessimistic view of his prospects. This was hardly surprising, since the whole military weight of the Parliamentary army was directed against him and he was running out of ammunition. Accident put a swift end to his doubts and fears. A tile from a chimney hit by a chance Roundhead shot fell on his head and, not perhaps without relief, Sir Arthur handed over to his second-in-command. This was Colonel Richard Fielding, a son of Lord Denbigh who had fallen at Birmingham. He sent emissaries to Essex. The sound of musket fire came to Fielding's ears. He heard the shouts of the advancing Royalist vanguard. 'Go out and join them,' Fielding was implored by his officers. But no, he said. He had opened negotiations with Essex. Honour demanded that he should go through with them. The punctilio may seem somewhat strained to modern ways of thinking. But it is not the only respect in which that war seems strange and remarkable to a later and less fastidious age.

While Rupert was covering the Royalist retreat from Caversham Bridge, in the midst of a tremendous storm of rain and wind, he was followed by a Roundhead officer who was riding far ahead of his men. At length two of Rupert's companions swung their horses round and charged the intruder. The Roundhead waited calmly and put a pistol bullet into the thigh of one – who chanced to be Daniel O'Neill, commander of Rupert's Horse Guards – and knocked the other Royalist out of his saddle. Then he rode back to join his men. Rupert, a witness of this exploit, was so impressed by it that he sent a note to Lord Essex asking for the name of this intrepid antagonist. Essex made diligent enquiries but could not identify the man. Fearless himself, Rupert admired daring in others.

In due course, the negotiations for the surrender of Reading were completed. The garrison marched out with drums beating and colours flying. The Roundhead besiegers wanted very much to attack them as they passed and were with difficulty restrained by Essex who promised each man twelve shillings if they refrained. He could not, however, prevent his troops from plundering Fielding's wagons. In the town, the victors found the butchers' stalls full of meat and the taverns flowing with beer. The King rode back to Oxford where he sent the luckless Fielding to face a court-martial which condemned him to death. All appeals for reprieve were rejected. The King was particularly outraged by the fact that Fielding had surrendered to the enemy not only Reading but all the Roundhead deserters who had come into the town. In this painful situation, Rupert came to the rescue, remembering perhaps how bravely Fielding's father had fought at Birmingham. It is possible, too, that he had some sympathy with what Fielding felt as a moral dilemma. At any rate, he prevailed on the young Prince of Wales to intercede with his father for the condemned man. Fielding was pardoned and served throughout the war as a volunteer in the Royalist army. The net result of Rupert's operations in the West Midlands and Essex's on the Thames was deeply depressing for the royal cause. The King was still divided from his forces in the north and west, where he suffered some local setbacks. Rupert's main force was pinned down to the defence of Oxford which was under constant threat from Reading. If matters were not as catastrophic as at first they seemed to be, it was only because, as often happens in war, the other side, too, had its troubles. Essex should have attacked Oxford at once, by all the textbooks of war. But his soldiers were unpaid and were swept by sickness. He remained inert at Reading as the spring of 1643 warmed into summer.

Rupert sent out raiding parties of his cavalry to forage in the villages of Buckinghamshire or levy contributions on unwilling towns. These operations may have had little military significance but they kept up the morale of his troopers and they interrupted the traffic of food to London, which was beginning to suffer from a shortage of draught horses, wagons and, especially – Newcastle being cut off from the sea – supplies of coal.

In the middle of June came an incident which has become better known than the rest of Rupert's adventures of that period. A Roundhead deserter named Colonel Urry brought the news to Oxford that a valuable consignment of gold was about to be moved from London to Thame to pay the arrears of pay owed to disgruntled Roundhead soldiers. It would, he said, be worth £21,000. Obviously, it would be a prize of exceptional value for the King, who was even more short of ready cash than his opponents. Rupert needed no prompting as to what should be done and who was to do it.

At four o'clock one afternoon he rode out of Oxford, passing over Magdalen Bridge. He led a force that was mainly cavalry, with some dragoons and 500 infantry in light marching order. They numbered about 1,700 men in all and included some of Rupert's special comrades-in-arms: Daniel O'Neill, recovered from the wound he had got at Reading; Sir Richard Crane, Will Legge, a close friend of the Prince's, and, in command of the foot, Colonel Lunsford, already so redoubtable in the eyes of Parliamentary pamphleteers that he was supposed to be a cannibal. Riding south-east from Oxford in the darkness, the raiding force swung on an arc to the north through Tetsworth, ignoring the fusillades of the enemy patrols. At daybreak, they arrived at Chinnor where the advance guard – the 'forlorn hope' – under Legge made prisoners of 120 surprised Roundheads roused from their billets. They also captured the Roundhead standard, five yellow Bibles on a black ground. But they had not found what they were looking for, the £21,000 of bullion on its way to Essex, although, in the silence, they heard the rumble of distant wheels. But the road ahead of them when they paused outside Chinnor was empty in the golden light of that summer morning. It was infuriating. The alarm had been given. The treasure had been tucked away into safekeeping in the depths of some forest. And it was not a time to loiter. Already, the Parliamentary troops were stirring. Rupert gave the order to ride back to Oxford. He used every possible device on the way to entice Round-heads to follow him in the hope that they would be trapped into fighting at a disadvantage. It was a dangerous game because, although the boundaries dividing one side and the other might be shadowy, Rupert's force had certainly penetrated some distance behind Essex's outposts. It might find itself cut off from Oxford.

Riding to the west, at Chalgrove Field, a few miles from a bridge which crossed the River Thames, Rupert paused and turned on his pursuers who, by this time, were as numerous as his own force. He set out his cavalry in a cornfield while his infantry manned the bridge behind them and dragoons lined the road that led to it. All in all, it was a neatly arranged little battle plan. The Roundheads had only to come on hard and Rupert would lure them towards the bridge. On the way, the dragoons would sweep them with an enfilading fire; the infantry would hold the bridge and – up to a point, it worked out, more or less like that. Until Rupert, retreating as was arranged, felt himself incommoded by Roundhead snipers who came too close for his liking, firing from too near. Unable to endure this insolence, the Prince turned his horse and put spurs to it. Then he drove it at the hedge behind which the enemy musketeers were lined. He was followed by a handful of his Life Guards who were quick-witted enough to follow their leader. He had given them no command, but by this time they were accustomed to his ways. The Roundhead dragoons, taken by surprise by this audacious attack, ran back to join their cavalry. Rupert waited only for a cluster of his horsemen to gather behind him. Then he ordered his trumpeter to blow the charge. The Roundheads, although Rupert did not know it, had been joined by the famous John Hampden who had been roused from his bed by the noise of the Royalist incursion. They beat off the first assault. Then Rupert went in on one flank with his Life Guards while Daniel O'Neill swept round the other flank. Will Legge, who had been captured in the first onset, was rescued when the enemy broke under Rupert's impetuous attack. After a few minutes' fighting the Roundheads rode from the field, taking John Hampden with them, bowed over his saddle bow with two carbine bullets in his shoulder. He was dying and knew it. His only anxiety was to reach his father-in-law's house at Pyrton where, first, he had loved and married. But the pursuing Cavaliers were in the way. Hampden turned back to Thame where, six days later, he died.

Rupert, on his way back to Oxford, crossed the Thame at Chisel-hampton and spent the night there. By this time, his horsemen were weary after fourteen hours in the saddle. He reached Oxford at noon the next day. He left two of his prisoners with a surgeon to look after them. When the men decamped, Rupert sent a protest to Essex who sent two Royalist prisoners in compensation. Relations between the two leaders were on a high level of courtesy. When Essex caught Rupert's falcon and his hawk, he sent them back with a polite note. Rupert had not intercepted the treasure but he had ridden fifty miles, won a small battle, taken some prisoners and caused a great deal of confusion behind the enemy's lines.

And now the war was going to take on a new dimension.

The Queen had brought her consignment of arms to England, escorted by a Dutch warship commanded by Van Tromp. She had landed the arms and herself at Bridlington in spite of bad weather and the attempt of a Roundhead squadron to interfere. The commander of the Parliamentary warship which harassed the Queen on that occasion was felt, even in Roundhead circles, to have gone too far. He narrowly escaped a vote of censure in the House of Lords. Such was the confused state of public feeling in England at that stage of the war. Four months after coming ashore with her warlike cargo, the Queen was able to make her way southwards. First, she went to York, escorted by 2,000 horse and foot. With her went 250 wagons, artillery and treasure. She was a woman of spirit and vivacity and, as a Frenchwoman, daughter of the first and best of the Bourbons, was utterly unable to grasp the political and religious complexities of her too devoted husband's problem. She saw only disobedient subjects, a rowdy and insolent Parliament, a nation divided both in its loyalty and its religion. As the daughter of the man who had won at Coutras with the help of the dour Huguenot squires, she should have realised the strength of one strand that bound together Charles' antagonists, the strand of religion. But this she does not seem to have done. Over the King, she exercised a powerful and fatal influence. Meanwhile, she marched at the head of her little army southwards to York, styling herself 'Majesty and She-Generalissima'; picnicking by the roadside in sight of her troops and, generally, behaving with the high spirits suitable to her soldierly ancestry. As her unloving, distrustful sister-in-law, Elizabeth of Bohemia said, she was by far the stronger of the English royal couple. Elizabeth's son, Rupert, waited for the Queen's arrival at Oxford to put new energy into the war. She did not come quickly. At York, she tarried; then she moved on to Newark on the Trent, through country infested by Parliamentary troops who, at any moment, might have coalesced to fall on her convoy which, at that moment, was by far the richest military prize in England. The Queen was aware of her danger. 'Have a care, dear heart,' she wrote to Charles, 'that no troop of Essex's army incommodate us.' From Newark she aimed diagonally across England towards the Cotswolds.

At that moment, Rupert was mobilised to bring the precious cargo safely home. He set off to the north with the intention of imposing a barrier between Essex and the Queen. For some days his patrols harried the Roundhead outposts in Buckingham, constantly on the move, darting in to attack and sheering off when a large force of Essex's cavalry was drawn in. Thus, he kept the Parliamentary horsemen occupied at a time when they might have captured the Queen and seized her convoy. While he was shaving early one morning in his quarters at Buckingham, he heard shouting and the clash of steel. A patrol of Essex's was attacking his outposts. With one side of his face still unshaved, Rupert rushed out to his horse, helped to drive off the intruders and returned to finish his toilet. After some days of this enjoyable and dangerous warfare, Rupert gave up his diversionary activities suddenly and rode westwards to the Avon valley where he knew that about this time the Queen would be arriving. The two, Queen and Prince, met at Stratford. After that, there was no more need for alarm. Their joint forces moved towards Oxford.

Under the slope at Edgehill, still grim with the debris of battle, they met the King. But on that beautiful summer's day it was easy to forget the tragedy in which they were leading actors. At Woodstock, farther on, came the news of two fine victories for the royal cause. Lord Newcastle had defeated the Fairfaxes in the north while, in the west at Lansdowne, Sir Ralph Hopton, Lord Hertford and Rupert's brother, Maurice, had beaten Sir William Waller. Not long afterwards, Maurice himself arrived, demanding reinforcements of cavalry. Waller, he reported, would have been destroyed at Lansdowne if only the Royalist army had possessed better cavalry and more of it. Rupert spared him 1,500 of his own horsemen and, a sacrifice still more grievous, agreed that they should be commanded by Henry Wilmot, between whom and himself a bitter animosity had grown up. At Devizes, the force met Waller's cavalry which broke under their charge, leaving the Roundhead infantry unprotected and filled with an urgent wish to flee. It was the end of Waller's army. The news cheered the royal party at Woodstock on the day before they rode in triumph into Oxford, where the Queen was lodged at Merton and Charles at Christ Church. Oxford was gayer and more fashionable than ever. On college lawns were scenes of dalliance. Silk was the only wear. Music was in the air. All over England, it seemed, the royal cause had triumphed. All over England? Except that Essex was still in the Thames valley and that, in the south-east, the army of the Eastern Association had pulled back and was crouching at St Albans.

VIII

Washington's Breach

'Soldiers with swords in hands,
To the walls coming.
Horsemen about the streets
Riding and running.
Sentinels on the walls,
Arm, arm, a-crying.
Petards against the ports
Wild fire a-flying.'

John Forbes, Cantus, 1662

The arrival of the Queen complicated life for Rupert in more ways than one. In her train was a lady of dazzling beauty; one who was witty, lively, charming. She was Mary Villiers, daughter of the Duke of Buckingham, who had been the 'Steenie' of King James I and the bosom, dominating friend of his son, Charles I. Mary Villiers had been married to Lord Herbert but, to her relief because she had detested him, he had died when she was only eleven. By this time, Mary had become an orphan, so that the King adopted her and brought her up with his own children. At court she was known as 'Butterfly', because she was pretty, because she was flighty, because of any one of the reasons that cause girls to be called 'Butterfly'. In due course, she was married to the Duke of Richmond, who was very grand, rather solemn, a cousin of the King's, and head of the Franco-Scottish military family of Stuart d'Aubigny. He was also – which is very much to the point – a devoted friend of his relative, Prince Rupert.

When Rupert met the Duchess, she was a bewitching twenty, he a severe, handsome young general of twenty-four, with the glamour that attaches to soldiers in the midst of war. Victorious, they are overweening; defeated, they are tragic; wounded, they are irresistible. But in the case of Mary Villiers and Rupert, exceptional factors were present. She was not the kind of young woman to lose her heart easily. And he was a young man with strict notions about his personal honour, mindful that the Duke of Richmond was his close friend. So, while the two sauntered through the Oxford quadrangles, the Prince's manner, although attentive, was notably sombre. When one of his best officers, Daniel O'Neill, teased him about the lady, Rupert flared up angrily and stripped O'Neill of his

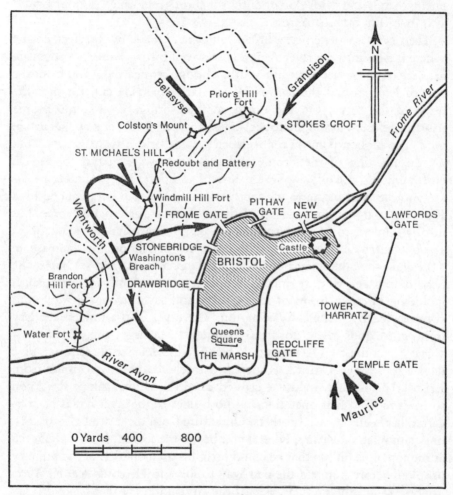

The Siege of Bristol

command. From a frustrating association, Rupert was snatched after a few days by the call to battle.

Bristol, second English city and second English seaport, was the most important Parliamentary stronghold in the West Country. To win it for the King would be something more than a resounding climax to the military successes of the western army led by Hopton, Hertford and Prince Maurice. It would give the Royalist forces an outlet on the sea through which – if the Parliamentary cruisers allowed – they could bring arms, supplies and reinforcements from the Continent. With Plymouth in enemy hands and with Portsmouth lost through Goring's action, Bristol was more important than ever.

The city was situated on a broad spit of land made by the river Frome where it runs into the river Avon. It was well fortified and had adequate artillery. Approached from the south, a bridge crossed the Avon from the suburb lying round the church of St Mary Redcliffe and led into the heart of the town. On the north, another bridge crossed the Frome towards houses outside the town, beyond which were forts and a curtain wall. The highest point in the fortified area of Bristol was Brandon Hill. At the junction of the Frome and the Avon were quays, roperies, a customs house and other appurtenances of a seaport. The ground immediately to the west of the town was marshy. Bristol was commanded by a Roundhead governor, Colonel Nathaniel Fiennes, believed by some, but not by Rupert, to be a determined officer. The garrison was made up of 1,500 infantry and 300 horse, with ninety-eight cannon great and small.

Leaving the allurements of Oxford behind him, Rupert set out at the head of fourteen weak regiments of infantry and two brigades of cavalry, including his own troop of Life Guards and seven troops of dragoons commanded by Colonel Washington. There was also a modest artillery train, eight guns in all, not nearly enough for a siege, and certainly far weaker than the guns Fiennes could bring to the defence of the town. Five days after leaving Oxford, Rupert had reached a point two miles from Bristol. His brother, Maurice, crossed from the south bank of the Avon to meet him, so that operations on both sides of the river could be concerted between the two brothers. Under fire from the nearest Bristol fort, only a musket-shot away, Rupert climbed to the tower of Clifton Church at the top of its hill, so that he could form his own opinion of the military problem before him and the best way to solve it. He could see the Avon flowing round the southern side of the city and knew that beyond it lay the Royalist western army which had just beaten Waller. On the near side of the river the outer fortifications of Bristol ran to the east over hilly country, and at last swung in towards the Frome. These defences were stronger than was usual with English cities at that time, for Colonel Fiennes and his garrison had worked hard to improve them.

Strung out along the perimeter were substantial forts, the strongest of which, Brandon Hill Fort, was immediately opposite Rupert as he consulted with his staff on the church tower. He could see that to capture Bristol was going to be a formidable task, although it was comforting to notice that the ditch under the city wall was only a few feet deep. Next morning, Monday 24 July, Rupert paraded his army on Dudham Down in full view of the Bristol garrison while on the south bank of the Avon, Lord Hertford put the western army on show. Thus, the defending troops were given ample opportunity to see how powerful were the forces brought against them. As the day wore on, there was a constant rattle of musketry at close range with cannon joining in after nightfall. It was, as one enthusiastic eye-witness put it, 'a beautiful piece of danger to see so many fires incessantly in the dark'. On Tuesday morning, Rupert slipped across the Avon to plan the assault on the city with his brother and Lord Hertford. The Cornish officers of the western army argued against an immediate attack. On their sector of the front the ground was unsuitable for sapping operations. They would be forced to cross the river and advance against the town wall over marshy ground.

Rupert rejected the case for delay. Sapping took time. They had no time to spare. Besides, he said, Fiennes, governor of the town, was a notorious coward. If they broke through the curtain wall, resistance at Bristol would collapse. It was arranged that green would be the colour used to distinguish the storming party. And two cannon shots, fired at the orders of Lord Grandison, general in command of the infantry, would give the signal for the attack which was to be launched simultaneously north and south just before daybreak. That was the plan. The battle was different.

The Cornishmen, who had been so anxious to postpone the assault, now opened it on their own account before the signal to attack was given. Rupert heard the noise of fighting across the Avon and realised what was happening. He sent off word to Lord Grandison to fire the signal gun. In the meantime, the Cornish infantry were attacking with more dash than forethought and, in particular, without the faggots that were to help them across the ditch in front of the town wall. They suffered heavy losses, especially among their incomparable officers. Slanning fell, Trevanion fell, both mortally wounded. Stricken by such losses – and there were many more – the Cornishmen fell back in disorder. Maurice went from one regiment to the next encouraging the soldiers and spreading the news, untrue at that moment, that Rupert's men had broken into the town. Grandison, on the northern sector, sent his storming parties against the curtain wall with pistols, picks and hand grenades. When that attack was beaten off, he led them against the fort that was nearest to him, Prior's Hill Fort. Here, too, the attack was delivered before it had been properly mounted. There were no scaling ladders to help his men over the wall. When a ladder belonging to the defenders was found, it turned out to be too short. The Royalist troops, their ranks thinned by musket and cannon fire, began to lose heart and drift away. Grandison, riding up and down the line to put new courage into his men, was wounded, and rode off to the Prince's quarters to have his wound dressed. But it was mortal. The attack died away, after an hour and a half. On the immediate right of the Grandison attack an attempt to storm Colston's Mount, led by Colonel Belasyse, was defeated Thus, it seemed that, north and south, the day was lost. But just then Colonel Legge brought Rupert the good news that Lord Wentworth, attacking on the far right of the northern sector, had broken into the city between two forts. It had happened in this way.

Colonel Washington of the dragoons had found himself in dead ground, invisible from either Windmill Hill Fort or Brandon Hill. With a handful of companions, he had crept up to the curtain wall and, with a timely shower of hand-grenades, had frightened off the defenders. Then, reinforced to a total of 300, he and his men had swarmed over the wall, low at that point, and begun to make a breach in it, using hands, halberds and partisans as levers. A Roundhead troop charged them and might have driven back Washington's pikemen. But this counter-attack was beaten off by muskets and firepikes, a form of defence which the horses could not face.

The Royalists had established a foothold in Bristol.

On hearing Legge's report, Rupert hurried off to regain control of Grandison's disheartened soldiers. Rallying them, he put one of his colonels, Moyle, at their head and sent them forward in a new attack on the outer defences of the town. Then he rode back to bring forward the cavalry. At that moment, his horse was killed under him, shot through the eye. But Rupert continued on his way on foot as if nothing had happened, to the wonder and admiration of all who saw. By this time 'Washington's breach' as it was called was swarming with Wentworth's infantry who were soon joined in the town by the men under Colonel Moyle. As they advanced more deeply into the streets of Bristol they were fired on by snipers shooting from the windows. They lost heavily, the officers in particular. Colonel Moyle was killed; Colonel Lunsford was killed; Colonel Belasyse was wounded. Although the town's main defences were carried, savage fighting went on through the afternoon in the streets. The fighting spirit of the garrison was extraordinarily high and Rupert, running from one sector to another, had his work cut out to maintain the morale of his troops.

While the issue still hung in the balance, he sent a message across the river to his brother, Maurice, asking for 1,000 Cornish foot. He said that he had broken into the suburbs. Maurice sent over 200 and, later, came over himself with 500 more. But by that time the town was taken. Rupert decided to use the reinforcements in storming Brandon Hill Fort, which dominated the battlefield. He told his explosives expert, Hendrick, a Dutchman, to blow open the door of the fort with petards. But at that moment a drummer came out from Fiennes asking for a parley. Rupert agreed for a two hours' truce, provided men of substance were sent out. By trumpet, the command was given for a ceasefire. The defenders were by that time weary and disheartened men – a hundred foot left out of fourteen companies. Somebody in their camp suggested that the town could be set on fire and a retreat made to the Castle. This was voted down. The Castle was not big enough to hold them all and, being short of powder and match, they could not hope to hold it for more than two or three days. The parley took place about five in the afternoon in a garden house in the city wall. It was agreed that the officers of the garrison should march out with arms, horses, bag and baggage; that the infantry should not have arms and the cavalry only their horses and swords. Prominent Roundhead citizens were also given permission to leave. Bristol had fallen.

The handover was, unfortunately, accompanied by some disorder, the blame for which, in the excitement of the moment, was placed both on indignant townspeople and on Royalist soldiers smarting under the ill-usage they had received from Essex's troops after the surrender at Reading. A Roundhead was accused of shooting a Cavalier in the street. Some of the departing garrison were said to have sneaked out their pistols in their cloak bags. In short, there were all the customary excuses for breaking a ceasefire. Rupert was furious enough over the business to set about the more blatant offenders among his troops with his sword. To him, any breach of an agreement he had made was a blot on his personal honour, to be violently resented. However, he had some difficulty in appeasing the discontent of troopers in his own regiments who were annoyed because they had been ordered out of the town before the work of pillage began.

More important than all this was the outcome of an interview before the storming between Rupert and a Bristol merchant, Mr Fitzherbert. This made it certain that, when the town fell, merchant ships in the harbour would come over to the King's obedience. The transfer of allegiance was signalled by the firing of ships' guns, answered by artillery from the besiegers. Apart from its usefulness to shipping, the strategic value of the city was obvious – command of the Severn and of communications with Ireland and Wales, from both of which a flow of reinforcements for the army could be expected. Then again, useful military stores were available in the town, 700 barrels of powder, sixty brass cannon, and twenty-two ships. Finally, £140,000 was paid 'by way of composition to save the town from plundering', in other words, a respectable form of blackmail.

It was a fine victory, but it had been dearly bought. King Charles' finest troops had been the Cornishmen, and now they had lost some of their most inspiring leaders in the heroic, premature attempt to carry by assault the southern defences of the town. In return, the King had won the only English seaport that could be compared with London. Bristol had resented his policy of favouring its rival; now it came into the sunshine of royal benevolence. By charter, it was made the staple seaport of the great companies of merchants which flourished in London – and which were controlled by strong Parliament men. When the King came to Bristol, exulting in his nephew's hard-won triumph, he was greeted by bonfires and loyal cheers. He faced a minor but tiresome problem.

Rupert and Maurice had fought the battle for Bristol very much as their own personal affair. It was obviously an advantage that an assault by two separated forces should be co-ordinated by two commanders, each of whom was likely to know the other's mind. But it involved the risk of appearing to slight other generals who were not members of the Palatine family. And Rupert and Maurice were not the most tactful of young men. Above all, Lord Hertford, Maurice's superior officer in the western army, an elderly peer, felt that the princes had carried matters off with altogether too high a hand. Rupert, in making the truce with Fiennes, had not even had the good manners to consult his fellow commander, the leader of the western army. Hertford's *amour propre* suffered accordingly, and the wound was made deeper when Rupert insisted on brushing aside Hertford's nominee, Sir Ralph Hopton, as governor of the town and taking the post himself. Charles solved the problem by summoning Hertford to his Council at Oxford and appointing Hopton as the deputy – the effective – governor of Bristol. Maurice took Hertford's place as Royalist commander in the West.

The capture of Bristol was a feat of arms for which Rupert received the chief glory. He deserved it. He had been the chief co-ordinating mind behind the desperate fighting outside the north wall of the town. His determination and tactical insight had been, as was conceded by all, the decisive factors which ensured that the good luck of Colonel Washington's breach of the wall was fully exploited and that a losing battle was turned into a triumph. Thanks to Rupert, the royal cause had reached its highest point of fortune since the outbreak of war. The ports on the Dorset coast came over to the King; the Channel Islands and the Scillies were his; the French allowed his ships to use the Breton harbours. The Parliamentary navy could not prevent Irish and Cornish pirates from swarming in the Channel. Charles seized the occasion to proclaim an offer of pardon to his rebels. At Westminster, Parliament learned with alarm that armed Royalist risings had broken out in Kent – Kent the traditional nursery of English revolt! There were, too, troubles affecting the high command of the Parliamentary army. Waller, who had lost the West to Hertford and the Cornishmen, was acclaimed as one who had been betrayed by the lethargy of Essex. In reply, Essex demanded that his troops should be paid. He asked why the Queen with her important convoy had been allowed to march down through the Midlands from York. Where was Fairfax? Where was Cromwell? The questions were reasonable enough. While they went unanswered, Essex lost soldiers by desertion. Graffiti on London walls showed him as an idle tippler. The peace party in the Commons grew. Noisy demonstrations outside Parliament demanded that the war be brought to an end. In this crisis, the resolution and energy of one man saved the day for the Parliament: John Pym.

He saw that one thing which he had long been urging must be done without any more delay; if the King was to be beaten, Parliament must now make an alliance with the Presbyterians of Scotland. The Scots had an army of 21,000 men, horse, foot and artillery. It was commanded by officers of experience. Almost all its lieutenant-colonels, who were in real command of the Scottish regiments, had seen action on the Continent. It was organised in territorial regiments and squadrons. Scottish soldiers of fortune, hardened – and enriched – in the ferocious fighting in Germany, had poured back to their native land at the earliest whisper of a conflict in Britain. In each case, the nominal command of the units was given to some nobleman or magnate – Cassilis, Tullibardine, Crawford, Coupar, Loudoun, Maitland and so on – who in that feudal country were traditionally at the head of the levies of their district. Thus the Army of the Solemn League and Covenant, as it came to be called, married professional expertise with the ancient structure of Scottish society. It had an additional advantage, ideological unity. It was a Presbyterian army. Each regiment had a minister and elders – a kirk session – to ensure that all the army thought in the right way, that is to say, thought alike. Although the shortage of ministers was sometimes a cause of anxiety, there does not seem to have been any real failure in spiritual sustenance. The staff of the general in command were able to call at need on the prayers and admonitions of nine chaplains. In theory at least, the Army of the Solemn League and Covenant was the Kirk of Scotland in arms.

From the point of view of the English Puritans, there was, of course, one difficulty which could not be brushed lightly aside. The Scots were unquestionably Protestant – Calvinist in doctrine and ecclesiastical government, imbued for three generations with the simple, strenuous philosophy which John Knox had brought over from Geneva. But if they regarded Episcopacy with suspicion, they were not in the least enamoured of English Protestantism, which was altogether too casual for their liking. At this moment, events played into Pym's hands. At a time when Scotland was quaking with reports of an impending Royalist rising, an Irish Royalist, the Earl of Antrim, was captured. On him was found a letter planning an invasion of Scotland by his clan, the Macdonnells. Here, indeed, was occasion to freeze Scottish blood! The Presbyterian leaders set about raising a Scottish army to fight off the Irish, after which it would be available to England. They offered the chief command to an attractive and brilliant Presbyterian soldier, Montrose. Then a new cause for alarm arose. Montrose disappeared.

It was not certain where he had gone but many believed he was on his way to join the King, carrying dangerous information with him. The Scots were suddenly aware that their danger was acute. Simultaneously, the English Parliament was plunged into gloom by the military situation in the South. Out of the twin fears of Parliament in Westminster and Presbytery in Edinburgh, Pym welded the Anglo-Scottish alliance which transformed the military picture.

IX

Let the Old Drum be Beaten

'The women kiss his charger and the little children sing:
  "Prince Rupert's brought us bread to eat,
    From God and from the King".'

Davenant

In the meantime, the hard-won victory at Bristol had raised fresh problems for the Royal strategists. Should there now be a swift, determined
thrust at London, a thrust of the sort that Rupert had suggested after
Edgehill? Or should there be a more cautious advance on the capital?
The Queen, more powerful than ever in the King's councils since she
had, not without risk, brought the arms over from the Continent, was
shrilly in favour of the first course. She looked to Rupert for support
but Rupert was never seen to advantage in discussion round a table.
Unable, or unwilling, to express himself with fluency in debate, he was
liable to take refuge in shrugs and sneers. And, after Bristol, his intoler-
ance of other mens' opinions was greater than ever. Now when the
Queen looked to him for support, he annoyed her by casting doubts on
the London project which she and her friends had espoused. In fact,
there were substantial military arguments in favour of caution.

The Royalist forces could hardly be called an army; they were essenti-
ally local levies loosely grouped together, reluctant to move outside
their own shires and more concerned to drive the Roundheads out of,
say, Hull or Plymouth, than to march through strange counties and
conquer the distant capital. This was a main factor in the military situation
of which Rupert had become aware as a commander in the field. In
particular, he had trouble with the Welsh. They did not fancy advancing
on London so long as Gloucester, a fanatically Roundhead city on the
borders of Wales, was held by a strong garrison under a determined
commander, Colonel Edward Massey. Massey was twenty-three years
old, in other words, he was the same age as Rupert. He was a staunch

Presbyterian from Chester and, for that reason, was held in some suspicion by the Parliamentary army where the Independents were more and more in the ascendancy. Rupert, for reasons of his own, shared the reluctance of the Welsh to march on the capital. He had advanced on London once, a year before. Then he had been compelled to retreat at Turnham Green. What if the same situation arose once more? He might find himself carrying out a difficult withdrawal while Massey from Gloucester operated behind him. During the King's visit to Bristol, the decision was taken: Gloucester was to be reduced before the advance on London began. The King's councillors thought that Gloucester would quickly fall, if, indeed, Massey fought at all. Messages were coming out of the city which suggested he was ready to change sides. But as it turned out, Massey fought. More important, Gloucester fought.

Rupert advised an immediate attack on the city. When the Council rejected his proposal, he refused the command of the siege and retired to Oxford, where the Queen glowered on him from her rooms in Merton. He was, she had decided, the ringleader of those who were trying to destroy her influence with the King. An incident now happened to strengthen her suspicion. Two defectors from the Roundhead camp, the Earls of Holland and Bedford, turned up at Oxford, having stolen away from London. These two noblemen did not have a very high reputation, either morally or politically. What was to be done with the pair? Charles asked his Council and his Council answered: Let them stay in Oxford but otherwise let them be ostracized. It was stupid advice, making an insignificant point in morals and losing the political advantage which this flight of the earls might have offered. Properly handled, they might prove to be the first of a stream of deserters. Rupert, dour as he might be and impetuous in action as he certainly was, had developed a vein of realism. He went out of his way to be agreeable to the fugitive earls and escorted them into the King's presence. Because of this, the Queen was furious with him to the point where Rupert's relations with her lady-in-waiting, the Duchess of Richmond, were jeopardised. At Oxford, the court, although it was within the bounds of England, was apt to behave like a court in exile, afflicted with the intrigues and jealousies that go with exile and frustration.

The siege of Gloucester went on day after day with no sign of a break in the morale of the defenders and certainly with no sign that Massey, whatever his intentions may have been in the first place, was ready to deal with the King. He walked about the streets of the town, a young soldier of middle height, brown-haired, red-cheeked, cheerful, spreading confidence in the idea that Essex would come in time to raise the siege. And as it had become clear that, after all, Gloucester was going to hold out, the Parliamentary chiefs in London roused themselves from despondency. Gloucester, they resolved, must at all costs be saved. Five new infantry regiments were raised and 1,000 cavalry; the trained bands were brought up to strength. Essex marched north-west at the head of a respectable force of 12,000 men. Keeping clear of Oxford, he bore to the south-west, after he had passed through Aylesbury. By the time he approached Gloucester, on 5 September, reinforcements had brought his strength up to 15,000. When he was within sight of the town, he fired four cannon shots to let the garrison know that relief was at hand. The King had decided that he should allow Essex to reach Gloucester and then cut his return road to London, thus forcing him to fight his way back to his base. However, this was not so easy to achieve. Essex had a choice of routes: he could turn north-about through Warwick or take the road by Newbury, leaving Oxford well to the north. He moved with some agility. First, he marched to Tewkesbury; then he turned about and headed for Cirencester. There luck was with him, for he captured forty wagons loaded with food and ammunition intended for the royal army and left unguarded through some failure in staff work. Rupert, with 6,000 cavalry, hovered about his flank, but Essex, by adroit manoeuvres, eluded him for a time. When, at last, the Prince located the Parliamentary army he sent a request to the King for permission to pursue. By that time, darkness had fallen. Receiving no order, he rode off across Broadway Down, with one companion and a groom. At last, he saw a light in a cottage and looked inside. There he found the King playing piquet by the fire with Lord Percy. Looking on was Lord Forth, commander-in-chief of the royal army. Rupert, with his accustomed forcefulness, put the case for immediate action. Essex should be brought a battle before he could link up with another Parliamentary army under General Waller which was believed to be marching out from London. He, Rupert, had his cavalry all ready to move and not many miles away. They would harry Essex until the King came up with the main army. Forth and Percy were opposed to the plan – far too dangerous in the darkness. But when Rupert insisted, the King gave way and ordered 1,000 musketeers to follow the Prince. Rupert rushed out of the house, mounted his horse and galloped off.

A night and a day later, after hours of hard riding, he was told by a scout further east that Essex was not far off, passing south-east towards Newbury. Not long afterwards, riding hard at the head of his cavalry, Rupert himself caught sight of the enemy. He had come up with the Roundhead rearguard. Without losing a moment, he attacked, over the noiseless Berkshire turf, keeping his trumpets silent until his squadrons rode in for the final impact. There was a fierce little engagement, in which plump Lord Jermyn, the Queen's favourite, was wounded. A French volunteer, the Marquis de Vieuville, was struck down. When he was offered quarter, he answered, 'Vous voyez ici un grand marquis mourant.' Later, Charles ransomed his body for 300 crowns. As a result of Rupert's surprise attack, Essex pulled his wet and weary troops back to Hungerford, and the King, urged on by Rupert's friend, the Duke of Richmond, reached Newbury, and was therefore between the Parliamentary general and London. It seemed that, after all, the Royalists were victors in the war of manoeuvre. The King had won the race, thanks in large measure to Rupert's exertions. He was in an excellent position, in which he could afford to wait for Essex to attack. Rupert urged him to do just that, pointing out that much needed supplies of ammunition were still on the way to them from Oxford. The fiery young Palatine, usually the prophet of incisive war, was on this occasion an advocate of the defensive. Charles rejected his advice.

Next day, 20 September, the two armies fought on ground south of the town of Newbury where the King had slept the night. Essex, leading a tired and hungry army, 15,000 strong, was first on the move, trying to by-pass Newbury to the south. There, Rupert and the Royalist cavalry were drawn up on the left of the King's front. They faced an enemy who were better placed than they were. Towards one flank of Essex's line was a small hill, overlooking the whole of the front which the King had chosen for his army. The ground between the two lines was much broken up by hedges and ditches which made it hard for Rupert to use his cavalry and which provided good cover for the Roundhead musketeers. Rupert tried to overcome this disadvantage by outflanking the enemy. It looked for a little as if the London trained bands were going to break before the furious onslaughts of his horsemen, but Essex rode over, conspicuous in a white hat, and appealed to them to stand firm. He was popular with those Londoners and they responded. Their pikes made a hedge that Rupert's mounted swordsmen could not pierce. Their musket fire took a terrible toll of the royal ranks. Being short of ammunition, Charles' infantry could not answer in kind, and after a time, they began to drift disconsolately back towards the town.

After twelve hours of heavy fighting, the right wing of the Royalist army held Essex in check; in the centre, the Roundheads made progress over cultivated land until they reached open country where they were attacked and driven off by Royalist cavalry. But the mounted men, in their excitement, pursued the enemy into a narrow lane where the horsemen were at the mercy of lurking musketeers. Many saddles were emptied. On the Royalist left wing, Rupert rode at the head of his horsemen, so eager for a fight that many of them had thrown away helmets and doublets and rode into action in their shirt sleeves. But for all their gallantry they could not break the obstinate front of the London regiments. As the light failed, the fighting died away. Before it was over, a Roundhead colonel of horse, Sir Philip Stapledon, rode up to a group of Cavaliers. Among them was Rupert, whom he took pains to identify. Aiming coolly, he fired his pistol in the Prince's face. Miraculously, he missed, and rode off pursued, but unharmed, by Royalist pistol-shots.

The two armies reeled sullenly apart and drew back from the battle-field.

The King had, before the fight began, been in a mood of despondency and indecision. That night his depression had something to feed on. Men he knew well, noblemen who had been ornaments of his court, were killed in the bloody fighting among the ditches of Wash Common outside Newbury. Lord Sunderland was killed. Lord Carnarvon was run through and carried off fatally wounded. The King sat mourning at his bedside until he died. When the battle was at its hottest, Lord Falkland, young, brave, hating the war and now despairing of peace on any terms he would find tolerable, spurred his horse through a gap in a hedge. It was a moment when his troopers, reining in their horses, hesitated in the face of a hail of shot. Courting death and maybe seeking it, Falkland was lost in the turmoil of the frantic battle. When it was all over, in the darkness of the night that followed, Rupert, tireless after a day that would have been exhausting to most men, sent a note to Essex asking if he had news of Falkland, alive or dead. Essex had news. Falkland was dead, killed by a musket shot. 'So fell that incomparable young man in the four and thirtieth year of his age,' wrote his friend, Lord Clarendon, years afterwards, when the time had come to sum up in majestic prose those great and sorrowful events, 'having so much dispatched the true business of life that the oldest rarely attain to that immense knowledge and the youngest enter not into the world with more innocency.'

The Roundheads lay down to sleep in the open air. The King pulled his troops back into Newbury. It seems that Rupert alone, with his iron frame, remained awake and active. Before first light the busy ghouls were startled in their horrible gleaning by the apparition of the dark, tall figure of a rider at the head of a troop of horse. It was Rupert, looking for men fit to be saved, looking, above all, for Falkland, who had disliked him. In the morning, still in the saddle, he heard from his scouts that Essex had slipped past on his way eastwards to Reading. He overtook the Roundhead rearguard, near Aldermaston, and coaxed his troopers into delivering one last charge. There, many London apprentices lost their lives; many were captured. But this was the last spasm of the battle. Rupert's cavalry were utterly exhausted. He alone, it seems, after three days and nights on horseback, was ready for action. In physical strength and fighting spirit, the dark-visaged Palatine was an extraordinary man.

As for Essex, he pressed on towards Reading. On the whole, his army had come off the better in the muddled clash at Newbury. More important by far, he had relieved Gloucester and had fought his way back to London. It was a considerable feat of generalship. In Oxford, bonfires blazed to salute the King's victory at Newbury. In London, Essex's soldiers were cheered as they marched through the streets, wearing laurel leaves in their hats. Parliament voted £1,000 to Colonel Massey, the hero of Gloucester.

Much more worthy of note was an event that took place in St Margaret's, Westminster, just five days after the battle: Members of both Houses of Parliament signed the Solemn League and Covenant with the Scots. This was something more than a military alliance against the King. It involved a promise by the English to bring the churches of England, Scotland and Ireland into conformity with one another, 'according to the Word of God'. To the simple Scots this could only mean one thing – acceptance of the Presbyterian system of church government. It is unlikely, however, that all Scots Presbyterians were equally persuaded of the theological efficacy of the treaty. Certainly many of them were of the opinion that, when their unfortunate English brethren had, with the aid of the Scots army, defeated their episcopalian, quasi-papist opponents, then Scotland would be in a position to impose her own religious preferences on the grateful English. It is possible, however, that a few of the more intelligent Scotsmen took a less rosy view and were inclined to doubt whether the English, notoriously a pragmatical people, would be swept into Presbyterianism at a time when they would no longer need the support of Presbytery's Scottish champions. All this lay in the future. What mattered in those tense September days of 1643 was that, while Scotland was threatened by an incursion of the Irish, 'those idolatrous butchers', the English Parliament had narrowly escaped total defeat by the royal army and was in a state of deep anxiety about the future. It was not a time to worry about doctrinaire treaties.

The Army of the Solemn League and Covenant was formed, 'considering the danger imminent to the true Protestant religion, his Majesty's person and the peace of this kingdom by the multitude of papists in arms in England'. It marched down to the Border on 29 November in wintry weather. It was a well-found force of 18,000 foot, 3,000 horse and 1,000 dragoons. It was equipped with sixty-four cannon and eighty-eight lighter guns. These were provided by one of the best artillerists of the period, Sir Alexander Hamilton, known as 'Dear Sandy'. After working with Gustavus Adolphus on the development of field guns, he had set up his own gun foundry in the Potterrow of Edinburgh 'upon hope of bloody war'. It seemed then that the Covenanters had in no wise neglected technology while they were cultivating, by spiritual means, the morale of their army. They had put down a major new piece on the chess-board of the war.

The army that crossed the frozen Tweed in the early days of 1644 in its short-sleeved, grey duffle coats and its blue ribbons, singing psalms as it went, was always conscious of the stern eyes of the ministers and elders who marched in its ranks. It was a highly moral force, or at least, severe to any prostitutes who might audaciously intrude on the ambulant Tabernacle of the Lord. (If married, the doxics were executed; if not, they were married by order, prior to being scourged out of the army.) This army was, in its own opinion, bringing Christian doctrine to a weak and, it was to be feared, errant sister land. It might have indifferent horse-flesh (as shrewd, but biased, Oliver Cromwell was to think); it might have in its ranks a contingent of 'Redshanks', wild, tattered figures from the glens and the islands, many of whom were armed with nothing better than a broadsword and a bow and arrows with which, however, they could bring down 'a deer at his speed'. But the guns of the Scots army were plentiful, its leadership, reared under the great Gustavus, was professional. It was a formidable instrument of war. To counter it, the King prepared to send his nephew, Rupert, to the North.

Rupert had been worried because his brother, Maurice, an unsmiling young man to whom he was devoted, was for a time ill at Exeter.

Maurice had won a series of encouraging successes in the West Country until Plymouth proved too hard a nut for him to crack. Then he was struck down with influenza and a report about his condition was sent to Rupert, signed among others by William Harvey, who had become illustrious earlier as the discoverer of the circulation of the blood. To Rupert's anxiety about his brother were added other troubles. He was annoyed because the endless intrigues at court seemed designed to thwart his plans. In this, he was probably right; Rupert had a talent for making enemies among his uncle's cronies. In particular the Queen resented his influence over her husband. In February, he had been made President – in effect, Viceroy – of Wales with his headquarters at Shrewsbury. He was also a peer of the realm as Duke of Cumberland. The Welsh office had brought him many cares, although a young man of his bustling energy was well able to deal with the problems of the marches. He even found time for one of his favourite sports, for one April day he wrote to the Marquis of Ormonde, the Irish Lord Lieutenant, for 'a cast of goshawks'. Away from Oxford, he felt himself more than ever at the mercy of the incompetence and the factions of the court. Meanwhile, as spring wore on, he was aware that the separated armies of the enemy were stretching out their arms to one another and that the Scots were already at Morpeth, 14,000 strong. Very soon, the town of Newcastle would lie under their siege guns and the barrier of the Tyne would be in danger. The Marquis of Newcastle, the magnate to whom the King had entrusted the defence of the North, cried out for help and was dissatisfied with it when it came. Farther south and more acute, was the problem of Newark. This town on the Trent, so long as it was in Royalist hands, prevented a link-up between Lord Fairfax's Roundheads in Yorkshire and Lord Manchester's forces in the Eastern counties. Now it was sorely beset.

Rupert left Shrewsbury on 13 March on a mission of rescue. A week later, he paused, twelve miles from Newark, accompanied by a force of respectable size which he had bundled together by borrowing soldiers from various Royalist garrisons. Characteristically, he set off again at two o'clock in the morning, accompanied only by his cavalry. A full moon lighted the way. As his brigade circled round the town before making a final swoop, a galloper arrived from Nottingham at the headquarters of the besieging general, who was a Scottish professional named Sir John Meldrum, last seen at Edgehill. He brought the news that Rupert was in the neighbourhood and was likely to attack. Meldrum at once suspended his leisurely siege operations and pulled back to a fortified position called The Spittle. Rupert for his part had been able to get a message through to the officer commanding the town, who was also, as it chanced, a Scottish professional, Sir John Henderson. The message was in a crude and fairly transparent cypher: 'Let the old drum on the north side be beaten early on the morrow morning.' Henderson took the hint and made preparation to break out next day. Soon after nine that morning, Rupert appeared on the high ground above the town at the head of his cavalry. Without a moment's hesitation, he ordered his trumpets to sound the charge. There followed a fierce encounter with the Roundhead cavalry who were far more numerous than the troopers who had arrived with the Prince. But the core of his force were cavalrymen of exceptional quality, a chosen band of 400 strong, drawn from his own Life Guards and the Prince of Wales' Regiment. Rupert himself, riding far out in front, was set upon simultaneously by three Roundheads. One he killed with a swordstroke. The second fell to a pistol shot by Mortaigne, a French soldier of fortune who was seeking adventure in the Prince's service. The third, a powerful man, took hold of his collar in an attempt to pull him out of the saddle. Just then Daniel O'Neill, an officer in Rupert's Guards, galloped alongside and slashed the Roundhead's hand off at the wrist. A few minutes later, the mass of the Royalist horse arrived on the scene and the Roundheads fell back in some disorder. At that moment, the Newark garrison made its sortie.

Caught between two enemies, Meldrum decided that his position had become hopeless. He sent over a ceasefire proposal by Charles Gerrard, a friend of Rupert, who had been wounded and captured. After the briefest of parleys, Rupert allowed the besieging force to march off without their arms or baggage. He had captured 4,000 muskets and thirty cannon, and had made some converts to the Royalist cause. His victorious cavalry then rode in, meaning to plunder the disarmed enemy. Nothing was better calculated to enrage the Prince than such indiscipline. Rupert beat off the looters with the flat of his sword. Someone had taken a standard from one of the Roundhead officers. Rupert snatched it from the thief and handed it back. It had not been captured in battle, and, therefore, belonged to the officer who carried it. On these matters of military punctilio, Rupert was strict. The relief of Newark – the swift dash across England, the trumpets sounding in the dawn, the sudden attack by a force of modest size and high mettle – it was a magnificent feat of war. After it, Rupert's reputation as a soldier was higher than ever, and his opinions were stronger. 'This is no less than the saving of all the North,' the King told him. Richmond asked for 'leave to dilate now upon my particular joys'. Even Digby was ecstatic.

At this stage, Rupert had, in all likelihood, no illusions about the war or of his uncle's chances of victory. He had fought harder than any other commander on either side. It had brought him successes and set-backs. He had kept the trust and affection of the King but had won only the coolest and shortest lived praise from the King's advisers. He thought – and he had never the ability to conceal his views – that the war could not be waged successfully as a kind of occasional dangerous interlude in a round of balls and tennis parties at Oxford. It was a grave national crisis and it could become a disastrous one. The courtiers – men like Digby, who had succeeded Falkland as Secretary of State – thought that Rupert was altogether too violent in action, rough in manner and forthright in speech.

He was a Prince of the Blood. That could not be denied. He was fearless; a fine athlete; handsome; a gentleman, although not an English gentleman. In addition, Rupert had friends outside the immediate circle of the King's Council. They were soldiers like himself, taking a soldier's view of the war and liable to betray their impatience with what seemed the lackadaisical, namby-pamby policy of the court. For the most part, however, these officers with their regiments were quartered in villages at some distance from Oxford. They had not the ear of power. More serious for Rupert was the fact that the Queen's influence was in the ascendant, and that the Queen had become his opponent. Henrietta Maria was an intensely jealous woman, determined to hold the power which her courage and her feminine charm had, after years of neglect in the early part of the marriage, given her over her husband. She was suspicious of the urgent young Palatine who had once had the audacity to oppose her and who was the son of her husband's sister, a woman whose antipathy to her on grounds both personal and religious she did not doubt.

After his triumph at Newark, Rupert returned to Wales in the hope that he could build up a new army capable of making some impact in the North against the Scots. He believed that in Wales he could expedite a flow of reinforcements from Ireland which could counterbalance Parliament's Scottish allies. He was, as he told Ormonde, 'mightily in love' with his Irish soldiers. He was less than pleased, then, to be summoned back to Oxford and ordered to see that the Queen, who was in the family way, reached the south coast in safety. This was the sort of mission that seemed to betray a basic frivolity in the whole attitude of the court to the war. He broke out in fury, made all the more violent by a proposal to make the Prince of Wales, aged fourteen, titular commander of the army of the west. The war seemed to him to be too serious for that kind of triviality. Besides, his brother, Maurice, was commander in the West.

He can hardly have doubted too that, short of some prompt and decisive stroke, the royal cause was in danger of catastrophe. The Scots were in the North, held in check with some difficulty by the Marquis of Newcastle. The Fairfaxs, father and son, were safe in Hull. From the territory of the Eastern Association there were reports – there was good evidence – that the Earl of Manchester and Colonel Cromwell had conjured up out of the dour nonconformist yeomanry of East Anglia a cavalry force, disciplined, devout and determined. If those three coalesced – and already Cromwell had made contact with Fairfax – then the Royalists would be in greater danger than at any time since the standard was raised in Nottingham. At the end of April, Rupert went to Oxford to concert action with the King and his Council. In the interval the military situation had worsened. The Marquis of Newcastle had fallen back on York and was preparing to be besieged there by the Scots. The Earl of Manchester, commander of the forces of the Eastern Association, was on his way north to join Fairfax and the Scots. This would be a supremely alarming conjunction of forces. Rupert asked that the little army with which he had taken Newark should not be dispersed to the various garrisons from which he had borrowed it. With it, he would march northwards while the King remained at Oxford on the defensive. Not everybody in the King's entourage favoured the plan; for instance, Digby was against it; but, for once, Lord Jermyn, the Queen's favourite, was on Rupert's side. And the Prince himself, for once, used all the gifts of a courtier. When the general scheme was accepted, the Prince went to his headquarters at Shrewsbury and from there rode at the head of 8,000 men into Lancashire. Among them were his own infantry regiment, three English regiments, some Welshmen and four or five weak units from Ireland. As he passed Chester, he was joined by Byron with 6,000 men. On 28 May he was once more on the move, this time against Bolton, a stronghold of the Roundheads. When he had secured the town, he turned aside to relieve Lathom House nearby. There, the Countess of Derby, the indomitable Charlotte de la Tremoille, had been holding out for three months in the absence of her husband. Against her was a superior force commanded by a local lawyer named Rigby, an ardent Parliamentarian. Lathom House, however, had some advantages. It had thick walls; it was surrounded by a moat beyond which the ground rose so steeply that cannon could not be brought into play by the besiegers without the gunners being exposed to the musket fire of the defence. Rigby brought a mortar into use, doing a great deal of damage to Lord Derby's house but making no dent on the garrison's morale. Indeed, one day, they sallied out and captured the mortar. On 23 May Lady Derby received a final summons to surrender to the mercy of the Parliament. 'The mercies of the wicked are cruel,' she retorted, tearing up the summons. 'Go back and tell that insolent rebel he shall have neither persons, goods nor house. When our strength is spent, we shall find a fire more merciful than Rigby.'

Two days later, Rupert approached and Rigby pulled his besieging troops back into Bolton. Posted among the houses outside the town, they threw back the first Royalist wave of attack. One unfortunate Irishman whom they captured was hanged exultantly from the walls of the town. This barbarity drove Rupert into a frenzy. Leaping from his horse, he put himself at the head of the second assault. Very soon, his infantry had opened the way. The cavalry went in. They were in no pleasant mood. Lord Derby, in the van, met one of his servants who had deserted to help Rigby aim his mortars at the places where they could do most harm. Derby dispatched the turncoat with his sword. After that, there was a massacre in Bolton in which 1,600 men were slaughtered. In addition, the town was thoroughly looted. The hanged Irishman was amply avenged by his comrades whom Rupert, in a rage over the original atrocity, for once did not restrain.

Already, at Nantwich, he had some experience of the ferocious animosity of the Roundheads against those they thought were Irish Papists and who, quite often, were Protestants serving in Irish regiments. Thirteen of his Irish troopers, captured in battle, had been executed by the Nantwich garrison. Rupert had gone to some pains to capture fourteen of the enemy. Thirteen of them he hanged. The fourteenth he sent to Lord Essex with a message, saying that for every Royalist who was executed, he would hang two Roundheads.

After the beastly business in Bolton was over, there followed something more agreeable. Twenty-two stands of Roundhead colours were taken to Lady Derby by officers who gave her Rupert's homage on her courage. After Bolton, Wigan was Rupert's for the asking. The citizens strewed rushes on the streets to welcome him. Liverpool followed, where he fought his way into the town while most of the garrison fled by boat. On 11 June, he was joined by Lord Goring with 5,000 cavalry and 800 foot. Goring was a man whom Rupert knew and disliked. He was good-looking and his manners were exquisite. While he was serving the Prince of Orange at The Hague, he had been an intimate of the Palatine family and, it was said, the lover of Rupert's sister, Louise. He was clever, brave and untrustworthy. He heartily returned Rupert's antipathy. But now a new crisis of the war had blown up.

Three days after Goring's arrival, the King wrote to Rupert in some agitation. The letter should be reproduced at length:

Nephew,

First, I must congratulate with you for your good successes, assuring you that the things themselves are no more welcome to me than that you are the means. I know the importance of the supplying you with powder, for which I have taken all possible ways, having sent both to Ireland and Bristol. As from Oxford, it is impossible to have any at present. But what I can get from Bristol, you shall have.

But now I must give you the true state of my affairs which, if their condition be such as enforces me to give you more peremptory commands than I would willingly do, you must not take it ill. If York be lost, I shall esteem my crown little less; unless supported by your sudden march to me, and a miraculous conquest in the South before the effects of their Northern power can be found here. But if York be relieved and you beat the rebels' army of both Kingdoms which are before it, then (but not otherwise) I may possibly make a shift upon the defensive to spin out time until you come to assist me.

Wherefore I command and conjure you, by the duty and affection which I know you bear me, that all new enterprises laid aside, you immediately march, according to your first intention, with all your force to the relief of York.

But if that be either lost or have freed themselves from the besiegers, or that for want of power you cannot undertake that work, then you immediately march with all your strength directly to Worcester to assist me and my army. Without which or your having relieved York by beating the Scots all the successes you can afterwards have must infallibly be useless unto me. You may believe that nothing but an extreme necessity could make me write thus unto you. Wherefore in this case I can no ways doubt of your compliance with

Your loving and most faithful friend

Charles R.

The letter was dated 14 June 1644 from Tickenhall in Worcestershire. It came into Rupert's hands at Liverpool, four days after it was written. He read it as a desperate cry for help and an order from the King which admitted no question. How else could it be read? 'Peremptory command'; 'extreme necessity'; 'I command and conjure you' – what did words like these mean, if they were not to be dismissed as simple and panicky emotion? And there was reason to think they were more than that. Already there had been signals of distress from York. On two nights in succession, a beacon had been seen burning on the top of one of the minster towers which was answered by an answering signal from the walls of Pontefract Castle, twenty-six miles to the south. York was in dire straits. The worst was to be feared. It is doubtful, however, if the effect of the letter was fully realised by the man who wrote it. Lord Culpepper, who was in the King's retinue when the letter was written, read it and asked the King if it had been sent. When he was told that it had, he cried out in alarm, 'Then, before God, you are undone, for on this peremptory order, he will fight, whatever comes on't.' The story is Culpepper's, but it is probable enough that he said it. What indeed else was to be expected, even if the young man to whom the letter was written had not been the aggressive cavalry leader that, in fact, he was? On receiving it, Rupert began the march to York.

X

The Rebels' Army of Both Kingdoms

'We want money, men, conduct, diligence, time and good counsel.'
Duke of Richmond, writing to Rupert, 9 June 1644

For two months York had been invested. Then, after 5 June, the city had been more closely besieged by three allied armies, the Scots, the Northern Parliamentary Army under Fairfax and the Eastern Association commanded by the Earl of Manchester. The Scots had at their head a veteran soldier, the Earl of Leven who, among other distinctions, had successfully defended Stralsund against Wallenstein. He held the rank of field-marshal in the Swedish army. The Scots covered the west side of the city on the walls of which, four and a half miles in circuit, they must have looked with awe. York was, after London, the most imposing city in England. To the north were the forces of the Eastern Association which included a body of heavy cavalry who would very soon be known as the Ironsides. Oliver Cromwell, who had trained them, was their lieutenant-general. To the east were the Yorkshire Roundheads led by Lord Fairfax and his son, Sir Thomas Fairfax. In all, the allied army numbered about 25,000 men, of whom about half were Scots. Against them, Rupert was marching over from Lancashire with 13,000 men.

Within the walls of York was the Marquis of Newcastle, no expert in war but a popular nobleman, immensely rich and completely devoted to the King. A dilettante in the arts, the owner of great houses like Bolsover and Welbeck, Newcastle's passionate interest was in training horses, in dressage, the art of *haute école*. In this, he had no superior in Europe. As well as he could, he had held the North for Charles with the help of a Scottish professional soldier whom Rupert had met once before in Germany, General James King, now Lord Eythin. Eythin remembered Rupert as a foolhardy young pup in his teens who had

been deservedly punished for his rashness by a long spell in an Austrian gaol. Rupert probably thought of Eythin as somebody who had deserted him in an hour of danger.

When the allied generals heard that, against all likelihood, Rupert was hurrying eastwards over the Pennines with a substantial force of horse and foot, they broke off the siege of York and withdrew Lord

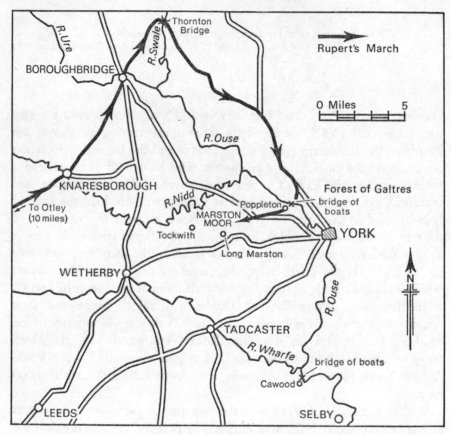

The route followed by Rupert before the Battle of Marston Moor

Manchester's army to the west bank of the Ouse. The allied army assembled near Long Marston, a village seven miles from the city. They knew that Rupert had been at Knaresborough and they reasoned that he would be compelled to pass near Long Marston on his way to York. There, they would be ready for him while they waited for reinforcements from the south. But, in a war of movement, Rupert was a cunning practitioner, capable of electrifying changes of speed and direction. At Knaresborough, he turned abruptly to the North and reached Borough-bridge. From that moment he had a river between him and the allies, and a clear run into York, twenty miles to the south-east. His swift circular march had been a brilliant success. Nothing stood between him and the city on that side since Manchester's troops had crossed the river by a bridge of boats which the Scots had built at Poppleton, and which was guarded by a detachment of dragoons. Accordingly, there was some slight danger that the bridge might be used to bring the allied army back to the east bank of the river. To make sure that this did not happen, Rupert sent a party ahead to drive off the guards and seize the bridge.

On 1 July, the Prince saw the long line of York city wall like a streak of yellow chalk above its mound. His march was over. He and his men had covered twenty miles that day. Against all the odds he had carried out the King's order or, at any rate, the first part of it. He had 'relieved York'. But he had still to 'beat the rebels' army of both kingdoms'. On this point, the King's letter was composed with some ambiguity, a defect that is often found in the instructions dictated by a distant commander-in-chief to a general in the field. But it seemed to impose on Rupert the duty, not only to bring the siege of York to an end, but also to defeat the allied forces which had been investing the city. How else could York be said to be 'relieved'? The letter spoke of relieving York and beating the Scots as if it were a single operation. Only if the dual task were accomplished did the King think that he could spin out his defensive in the South until Rupert came to his help. There might be a slight suggestion of hysteria in the letter. Rupert could not be expected to be a judge of that. He had been given an order. He would carry it out if he could. He had made the long march eastwards from Lancashire at a time when he would have preferred to make that county safe for the royal cause. When that had been accomplished, he could march on York with 20,000 troops. But the King had spoken to his nephew of the need for 'punctual compliance', that is immediate obedience, and Rupert had assumed that the case was, indeed, urgent. He hurried to York and, having reached it, he proposed to bring the allies to battle without further delay. In one respect he had suffered a disappointment. He had asked the Scottish Royalist, Montrose, to join him. Montrose had raised a Royalist force in Cumberland and had marched with it over the border into Dumfries where he was held in check by a larger army of Coven-

anters. Now he was unable at once to answer Rupert's summons owing
to disaffection among his troops.

Newcastle asked for time. He knew, and Rupert did, that they were
outnumbered. Rupert would have none of it. He had the King's letter.
Besides, he was aware that Sir John Meldrum, the vanquished Parliamentary commander at Newark, was on his way from the South to
join the allied army. In the early hours of 2 July, Rupert led his cavalry
over the Poppleton bridge of boats with the July sun warming his back.
He marched westward out of the city to a stretch of rough heath sloping
down to a ditch and rising on the far side to a low ridge on which a
crop of rye was growing. It was called Marston Moor. It had just been
evacuated by the allied infantry, although a strong rearguard of cavalry
still lingered there, numerous enough to discourage anything short of
an attack in force. Rupert reluctantly resolved that he must stand and
fight where he was. Waiting for the arrival of Newcastle's troops, he
picked the spot where he meant to establish his command post and
ordered his personal standard to be planted. It was an imposing heraldic
banner, fifteen feet long from mast to tip, in four colours, black and
gold for the Palatinate, blue and silver for Bavaria, with a red St George's
cross in the middle.

After the event, it seems quite clear that only something like a miracle
of military genius on the one side or gross incompetence on the other
could win the day for the royal army. The odds against Rupert and
Newcastle were too heavy, even if they were not as great as the traditional
figure of 17,000 men against 27,000. Sir James Lumsden, present that day
as an infantry general in the allied army, sent the Earl of Loudoun, in
Edinburgh, a report containing a map of the military dispositions which
suggests that no more than 22,000 men were in the allied units. Even so,
the disparity in numbers was so great that it could only be counter-
balanced by some extraordinary difference in the quality of the troops.
No doubt, Rupert's cavalry were outstanding in reputation and experience. But Newcastle's infantry were mutinous. And, on the other side,
the Scottish lancers on their nimble little horses were not to be despised.
They had their own traditional role in war. Before the harvest moon
rose over Marston Moor that night, they would play their part. Finally,
there were the austere troopers whom Oliver Cromwell had trained in
the country round Huntingdon and who had already won a reputation
for themselves. Anybody who watched them file on to the hillside above

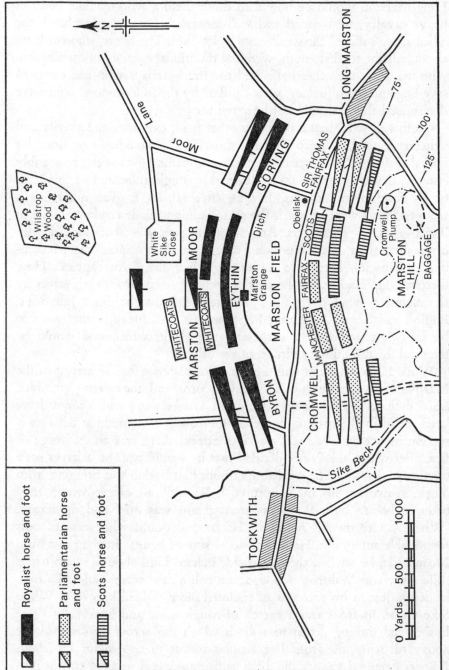

The Battle of Marston Moor

Legend:
- Royalist horse and foot
- Parliamentarian horse and foot
- Scots horse and foot

Map labels: LONG MARSTON, Moor Lane, GORING, SIR THOMAS FAIRFAX, 75', 100', 125', Obelisk, FAIRFAX, SCOTS, Cromwell Plump, BAGGAGE, MARSTON HILL, White Sike Close, MARSTON MOOR, EYTHIN, Ditch, Marston Grange, MARSTON FIELD, WHITECOATS, WHITECOATS, MANCHESTER, CROMWELL, BYRON, Wilstrop Wood, Sike Beck, TOCKWITH

Scale: 0 Yards 500 1000

Long Marston would be bound to think them a workmanlike body of heavy cavalry, well-armed and well-mounted. On the other hand, the allied army suffered the weaknesses of its kind. The Scots, who made up about half the total strength, were the traditional enemies of the English, who made up the other half. And the Presbyterians who had come to save England from prelacy, were disliked by the Independents who were determined that it should not be saved for presbytery.

Cromwell who, better than any other man, expressed the gravity and vehemence of the Nonconformist ethos, said he would as soon draw his sword against a Presbyterian as against a Royalist. He thought, reasonably enough, that the war should be directed by Englishmen and not by Scots or by foreign mercenaries. It was, after all, an English quarrel. His troopers, who were of much the same opinion, made crude jokes about 'Priest-haters' – Presbyters. And for their part, the Scots looked with dogmatic horror on the emotional excesses of the Independents. Muddle-headed fanatics, hardly to be distinguished from Anabaptists! How fortunate England was to be on the brink of rescue from such errors by the cleansing wind sweeping down from Edinburgh! On 2 July 1644, English and Scots, Anglicans, Presbyterians, and Independents were to be thrown together in a desperate struggle in which one would be thankful for the military virtues of the other.

While Rupert waited with no excess of patience for the arrival of the Marquis of Newcastle and his second-in-command, the recently ennobled Lord Eythin, he made a tentative effort to take a hill which might have been useful in the coming battle. In the course of something between a reconnaissance in force and a serious attack, there was an exchange of fire, after which the Prince decided that he would wait on a larger scale operation, for which he needed the troops that Eythin was bringing from York. However, his men captured a Roundhead officer whom they brought before him. Rupert's interrogation was brief and significant. 'Where is Cromwell?' he asked. He had no doubt who was his most formidable antagonist. He wished to be sure of being pitted against him. Meanwhile, he studied the battlefield. Behind him, about a quarter of a mile away was Wilstrop Wood, about half a mile across and half a mile in depth. Just at his rear was an enclosed piece of land known as White Sike Close. In front was a stretch of rough moorland broken by gorse bushes and sinking down to a ditch which ran across the front about 400 yards from the front line Rupert meant to choose for his army. Rupert intended to sow the ditch with musketeers so as to turn it into a stronger obstacle to an advancing army. On the far side of the ditch, a country road ran parallel to it, joining the hamlets of Long Marston and Tockwith. Beyond that, the land rose to a modest eminence where there was a group of trees which is known today as Cromwell's Plump. Here, it seems, the elderly allied commander-in-chief, Lord Leven, made his observation post and from it he departed in some haste before sunset.

XI

'Wae's Us! We're All Undone'

'Et j'ai toujours connu, qu'en chaque événement
Le destin des états dépend d'un moment.'
Quoted by Napoleon on the eve of Leipzig, 31 August 1813

The two armies assembled during the morning and afternoon. The sound of psalms rose from the fields in which the allies were gathering. Newcastle received a cool reception when, about nine o'clock, he greeted Rupert. 'My lord, I wish you had come sooner with your forces,' said the Prince, 'but I hope we shall yet have a glorious day.' In fact, Newcastle had not brought all his troops with him. Five hours passed before Lord Eythin arrived with 3,000 infantry. They were in the sullen humour natural to soldiers who have been too long without pay. That morning there had been disorderly scenes in the streets of York. Rupert, an abstemious young man, noted with displeasure that some of them were drunk on arrival at the battlefield. These were the famous Whitecoats, north country soldiers raised by Newcastle, who, drunk or sober, before the day was done, were to show themselves fighting men of the most stubborn courage.

When Newcastle met Rupert, he renewed the arguments against fighting that day; he wished to wait for reinforcements which he expected to arrive from Cumberland under Colonel Clavering. But the Prince insisted that he had the King's order to give battle. Faced by this, the Marquis gave way. However, by the time Eythin arrived, it is clear that the opportunity to catch the enemy before they were in battle array had passed. With the aid of a sketch map, Rupert showed the Scots general how and where he intended to dispose the troops. 'It is too near,' said Eythin, who probably meant that Rupert was drawing his front line too close to the enemy's. The allies came into line on the ridge after the commanders of their rearguard, Fairfax, Cromwell and Sir

David Leslie, had sent word to Leven, then on his way to Tadcaster with the main strength, that Rupert, against all expectations, had come out to fight. Thereupon, the allies retraced their steps and made ready to give battle. In his discussion with Eythin, Rupert, for once, kept his temper and offered to pull the troops back. 'No, sir,' said Eythin. 'It is too late.' He was in a disagreeable mood and, at one moment in the argument, reminded Rupert that, 'Sir, your forwardness lost us the day in Germany where yourself was taken prisoner.' But Rupert had his own ideas about what had happened in Germany.

It was nearly seven o'clock when Rupert decided that there was going to be no fighting until next morning. He retired to eat his dinner near his sumpter horse while Newcastle entered his coach and lit a pipe. The army relaxed. Troopers lay on the ground beside their mounts, one hand on the reins. It was just then, with the day already far advanced, and sunset less than two hours away, that the picture abruptly changed. From his eyrie above the moor, Leven enjoyed an excellent view of the Royalist army which had come out from York and was drawn up across a mile and a half of open country. The Royalist order of battle was, as at Edgehill, with the cavalry drawn up on either wing, Byron in command of the right wing, Goring the other, with the infantry filling up the centre. It was exactly the formation Leven himself had adopted. Looking down at the Royalist array, he picked out the Bluecoats of Rupert's own regiment of foot, and the Whitecoats of Newcastle's regiment, commanded by Sir Francis Mackworth. A mass of green colour showed where the infantry stood which Henry Tillier had brought over from Ireland. He noted how groups of musketeers broke up the lines of pike-men in the manner that the great Gustavus had approved. He could distinguish the officers by the extra showiness of their lace and their sashes. Behind the centre of the line, near his great standard, was Prince Rupert himself, an unmistakable figure – 'kenspeckle' as the Scot Leven would put it – tall, dark, with glossy black ringlets, a dandy wearing a coat of brilliant scarlet. Over the royal host there fluttered a multiplicity of standards of various sizes and many colours. Many were heraldic but some of them bore a slogan which had some religious or political significance. There was, for instance, a yellow cornet which showed a mastiff from whose mouth, as in modern cartoons, proceeded the words on a balloon, 'Pym, Pym, Pym, how long will you abuse our patience?' As an army trickled on to the field of battle in those days, it somewhat resembled a procession in a modern city preparing to enact a political 'demonstration'. There was no lack of evidence, however, that on this occasion the demonstration would be a violent one – the dark sheen of breastplates, the countless strokes of light reflected from swords, the dark plantations of pikes eighteen feet tall.

Leven had assigned to his major-general of horse in the Army of the Covenant, Sir David Leslie, the task of marshalling the allied host for battle. It was something that Leslie, the younger son of a Fifeshire laird and an experienced colonel in the Swedish cavalry, could efficiently perform. On the right wing, he placed Sir Thomas Fairfax's mounted regiments with three Scots horse regiments behind them – Balgonie's, Eglinton's, and Dalhousie's. The centre, three-quarters of a mile in length, was taken up by the infantry, drawn up in three lines. Four Scots regiments held the right of the front line and another eight manned the whole length of the middle line. The foot regiments of Lords Manchester and Fairfax made up the rest of the centre. On the left flank was Oliver Cromwell, at the head of his cavalry, already much talked about and soon to be famous. On the extreme tip of the line was a regiment of Scots dragoons under Hugh Fraser; they were reckoned to be the best mounted men in the Scottish service. Behind Cromwell, Leslie posted himself with three regiments of Scottish horse, riding 'light little nags', capable, however, of doing useful work if properly handled.

As seven o'clock approached, Leven thought that his men were sufficiently rested after their march. He had been watching the enemy closely, perhaps through a telescope, although that would not be necessary. He had observed the symptoms of slackened vigilance. Now he decided that the moment to attack had come. If it were done without warning, the whole business would be over before dark. In this respect, the old soldier of Gustavus, the veteran of thirty years of military service, was cutting things rather fine. But his decision, at the moment he took it, was rational enough. It was, in fact, one of the crucial factors in the battle that followed. Suddenly, without warning, the whole of the allied line surged down the slope towards the ditch below, cavalry moving at a quick trot, pikemen running as quickly as they could with their long and cumbersome pikes. There is no record that any cannon shot had signalled the advance or that any other alarm had been given to the Royalists. The first Rupert knew that something untoward was happening was when he heard the sounds of firing and shouting. He leapt to his feet instantly, swung into the saddle and galloped towards the sound of the firing, collecting such of his bodyguard as he met.

What had happened was this, so far as can be sorted out from the confused accounts of a wide and confused battle: Hugh Fraser's dragoons, from their post on the extreme left of the allied line, had been sent to prise Rupert's musketeers out of the positions they held in the ditch. If that were done, the way could be cleared for the advance of Cromwell and his cavalry.

This task the dragoons – mounted infantry as they would be called in a later age – quickly performed. As it chanced, at that very moment, a tremendous thunderstorm broke. Rain fell in torrents on the Moor, putting out the musketeers' matches. Mounted or on foot, the dragoons worked their way along the ditch, flushing Rupert's snipers out of their cover and, incidentally, shepherding them in a direction where they were likely to be in the way of Byron's cavaliers when they rode forward to meet the Ironsides. The way was now open to Cromwell. He had come down the hill at a collected trot with five bodies of cavalry behind him, probably numbering, in all, about 1,500 men and horses. There was a second line numbering as many, and probably commanded by Commissary-General Vermuyden. After them came David Leslie's three regiments of Scottish cavalry, numbering fewer than a thousand. As Fraser's job had been to prepare the way for the attack of Cromwell's heavy cavalry, Leslie's would be to exploit the success of that attack. At this moment, the Royalists launched a riposte. Lord Byron, commanding the right wing, threw in his cavalry in an effort to prevent Cromwell from crossing the ditch. However, he was too late and he had under-estimated the grim power of these troopers from East Anglia. After a bitter clash, his cavalry broke in dismay. They were the fugitives whom Rupert met as he galloped forward to the battle.

On the other wing, matters wore a very different appearance, as Rupert would realise as he hurtled into the smoke and tumult of the fight. Looking anxiously over his left shoulder, he saw how matters were progressing there. Lord Goring was in command of a force of Royalist horse, numbering 2,000. He was not the man to wait the order to do what obviously had to be done. Immediately after Leven had given his soldiers the order to advance, Goring had launched an attack on the allied right wing where Sir Thomas Fairfax and Colonel Lambert commanded the cavalry, with Scottish horse behind them and Scottish infantry on their left. Goring's men, the troopers of the Northern horse, came forward with all the bravura associated with the word 'Cavalier'. There was Sir Philip Monckton, for instance, caracoling in front of his troop to show his contempt for danger and the enemy. The exhibition came to a sudden end. At a moment when Tom Fairfax's Parliamentary squadrons were almost upon him, Sir Philip's horse was shot from under him. Stumbling to his feet but having no time to get himself a new mount, he charged on foot, and helped to drive off the Roundhead regiment of Sir Hugh Bethell. After that, Sir Philip's groom arrived and gave up his own horse to his master. But by then the battle had moved on, so that he could see neither his companions nor the foe through the swirling clouds of gunpowder smoke which the wind was driving across the Moor.

The outcome was that Goring drove Sir Thomas Fairfax's cavalry from the field, although the allied cavalry reserve on that wing, the regiments of Balgonie, Eglinton and Dalhousie, stood firm. They were badly mauled. Lord Eglinton was severely wounded, whereupon his son took over the command from him. Goring's second line, led by Sir Charles Lucas and Sir Richard Dacre, swung in towards the centre where allied infantry were advancing. It seemed that Lucas was about to take the Scottish foot regiments in their flank, now left unprotected by the defeat of Fairfax's cavalry. Watching from the hill behind, and able through the shreds of smoke to judge of the course of the battle, Leven must have realised with anxiety that the struggle was entering a new and critical phase. The Scottish infantry who would meet the first impact of the Royalist assault were raw and, therefore, patchy in quality. And the onset of a charge of horse was a noisy and daunting thing to face.

Of all these happenings three-quarters of a mile to his left, Rupert riding forward, lips compressed, sword naked and ready to slash, had only a smattering of knowledge. Out of the corner of his eye he could see the standards, tossed in the violence of the action, snatched at by the wind. He could hear the shouted slogan 'God and the King' and, ominous but to him always exhilarating, the clash of steel on steel. On the left, then, as it seemed, the battle was going reasonably well. But in front of him, as he hurried towards the right wing, he had a graver problem. His cavalry, his own chosen men, had blenched before the massive onset of Cromwell's troopers. They had broken, and some of them were in flight. In this crisis, it was Rupert's task to rally as many of them as he could for a counter-charge. Meanwhile, although he did not know it, what seemed to be a serious misfortune had befallen the allied armies. Cromwell, riding into battle with the joy in his heart that always affected him on the eve of action, had been wounded. Not gravely; above the shoulder but serious enough to put him out of action for a time. Perhaps it was the outcome of a shot fired in mistake by a trooper behind him; perhaps as the result of a duel with Ensign Trevor, who was later rewarded for it by Charles II with a viscountcy.

At this time, it appeared that the infantry in the centre of the allied line was in danger of total collapse under the furious assaults of Goring, Lucas and Dacre. Some of the Scots infantry in the front line had stood firm. Lord Lindsay's Fife regiment who, being on the far right of the foot, had been the first target of Sir Charles Lucas' onslaught, was among those who held its ground. But other Scottish regiments had faltered and taken flight. Lord Loudoun's regiment and Buccleuch's were among those that took to their heels. Lord Leven, looking at the scene from his post on the hilltop, was appalled by what he saw. Thousands of men, most of them Scots, were running towards him up the slopes of Marston Hill, throwing away their arms as they ran and crying 'Wae's us! We're all undone.' They were 'so full of lamentation and mourning as if their day of doom had overtaken them'. So thought a young officer named Arthur Trevor who was an eye-witness of the scene. 'The runaways of both sides,' he reported, 'were so many, so breathless, so speechless and so full of fears that I would not have taken them for man but for their motion which still served them very well.' Such was the true face of war in the decisive battle of the Civil War. Trevor was, at that moment, looking for Rupert to whom he was bearing a message. But in the turmoil and the smoke he could not see the commander-in-chief nor could he get any sense out of the fugitives who rushed past. They looked at him uncomprehending, unanswering. And Rupert was somewhere in the thick of the wild cavalry mêlée on the Royalist right wing.

After thirty years' experience of war, Leven thought he knew disaster when he saw it. His staff entreated him to leave the field. He, therefore, made off with all due speed to Wetherby, a precipitate act which he later regretted. If he had waited a little longer, the hero of Stralsund would have seen Lumsden filling the gaps in the broken front with the Scots regiments from the second line, such as Cassillis, Coupar, Dunfermline and Clydesdale. He would also have observed that, farther along the line, Lord Manchester's foot regiments were resisting the infection of panic. However, it was a moment of desperate crisis. Lawrence Crawford, an impulsive young Scottish professional officer from Glasgow who commanded the front line of Manchester's infantry, saw to his indignation that Cromwell was sitting on his horse apparently idle at the head of his cavalry. He ran up to him, using such language as soldiers use in emergencies. What, he wanted to know, did Cromwell think he was doing? Cromwell answered by pointing to the wound in his neck. Immediately Crawford apologised and detailed a man to escort the stricken general to Tockwith, to have his wound dressed. The whole business cannot have taken long for it must have occurred no farther than a mile from the village. But it did not improve relations between the two men who were already at variance with one another on religious grounds, Crawford being a severe Presbyterian and, as such, odious to Cromwell. In the brief interval before Cromwell returned from the surgeon, who was to command his powerful cavalry brigade? It has been suggested that Crawford stepped into the breach. But this seems unlikely. The right to nominate would be Cromwell's. His obvious choice of a deputy would be David Leslie, commander of the reserve cavalry. In any case, Crawford had his hands full, holding his infantry in hand while he prepared to attack the Royalist centre. It should be assumed then that, for half an hour or maybe less, Leslie was in command of Cromwell's horse. For a little while, it seems, the battle was fought without four of the allied commanders. Leven was in flight; Cromwell was hurt, Manchester had withdrawn and Lord Fairfax was on his way home to bed.

Rupert, who had been taken by surprise by the sudden onset of the allied attack had no difficulty at all in deciding where the most imminent danger lay. It was directly in front of him, where Byron's charge had failed and his squadrons were in flight before the advance of Cromwell's cavalry. Among the infantry towards the centre of the Royalist line, Rupert's own regiment of foot, the Bluecoats, and Byron's infantry regiments were falling back under pressure. The Prince took his own Life Guards and a brigade of horse with him as he galloped off to deal with the crisis that had arisen on the Royalist right wing. He did so with a success that was real, if brief, breaking into the solid front of the Cromwellian horsemen in a ferocious counter-attack. It was a grim and noisy business of flashing, slashing swords and pistols fired at a few pace's distance into an enemy's face. It ended with Rupert, who is said to have accounted for five antagonists with his own blade, driving the Roundheads back for a time. By this time, Newcastle had put down his pipe and left his coach. He was, almost at once, engulfed by the fleeing horsemen of Byron's routed regiments and failed to stop them in their wild career. Instead, he hastily mobilised gentlemen volunteers and led them in a charge against some Scottish infantry in the centre. By this time, Cromwell, bandaged, had found his way back to the head of his cavalry. The second phase of the battle was about to open.

His troopers, after their first successful charge and the hard-fought, confused cavalry action that followed it, were once again a compact mass well controlled by their officers and ready to make another of those fast, close-knit attacks which were to become their, or, more exactly, Cromwell's, particular contribution to the science of war. All that they awaited was the general's signal and the call of the trumpets. When it came, the tide of horsemen struck Rupert's, with the savage, measured blow of a battering ram. Outnumbered, and not so coherently arrayed as the Ironsides, the Cavaliers fought back with desperate bravery. Then it seems – for absolute certainty on the sequence and timing of events in the turmoil of this battle is hard indeed to come by – that David Leslie's light horse of the reserve line were thrown in against the left flank of Rupert's regiments. All that is sure is that these Scots, seven hundred or, maybe, a thousand strong, riding on their hardy little nags, were vigorously engaged in the fighting. Immediately afterwards came the sudden collapse and flight of the Royalist right wing. The Prince, at one moment, in furious sword play with his comrades beside him, at the next found himself alone in the midst of a swirling torrent of steel-clad enemy horsemen. Engulfed in a disaster he could not control, he turned his horse's head out of the battle. The commander-in-chief of the Royalist army had for a moment become a solitary fugitive.

Cromwell, with superb mastery of the instrument he had created, prevented his men from pursuing the beaten enemy. The battle, as he could see and hear, was far from over. Far from won. It was a moment to collect his strength for a new blow. A minister who was chaplain to one of the Scots regiments, reported, 'God would not have a general in the army. He himself was general.' Leven had fled. Lord Fairfax had fled. Rupert was caught up in the disaster of his right wing. The commander-in-chief of the royal army, fighting like an ordinary trooper in the turmoil of the desperate clash of cavalry, had neither the time nor the opportunity – nor, maybe, the will – to direct the battle which was his proper task. Among the generals, Cromwell was an exception. And before long, Cromwell saw what had to be done.

On the far right of the allied infantry, two Scottish regiments, Lindsay's and Maitland's, were holding out as best they could against the furious attacks of the Royalist horse and foot. Some of the units of the second line who had not succumbed to the panic that had swept over their comrades were hurried forward by Baillie and Lumsden to reinforce Lindsay's and Maitland's. They fought off the Royalist cavalry by anchoring the butts of their pikes in the ground. It may be, too, that in this desperate defence they made use of 'Swedish feathers', five-foot staves, steel-tipped at each end, an anti-cavalry device developed by Gustavus Adolphus. It is certain that the Scottish army had brought with them into England 10,000 of those devices. The right centre of the allied front was thus holding precariously against attack when an incident occurred which transformed the scene. Sir Thomas Fairfax, whose cavalry had been scattered by Goring's first charge, was wounded and separated from his friends. In this situation, he tore from his cap the white badge which he and all the rest of the allied force wore.

Disguised like this, he rode, unharmed, behind the Royalist lines until he reached the allied left wing. There on the open moor he was rewarded by the sight of Cromwell at the head of his victorious cavalry. From Fairfax or possibly from a message passed along the allied infantry lines, Cromwell learnt of the dangerous situation existing on the distant right wing. At once he and David Leslie rode round Wilstrop Wood and struck Goring from the north. It was a brilliant tactical surprise which broke the spirit of Goring's squadrons. After that, the two generals turned to deal with the last and most heroic resistance made that day by the Royalist army. Newcastle's Whitecoats, 4,000 infantry, had been mutinous that morning in the streets of York and had come reluctantly and, in some cases, tipsily to the battlefield. Since then, they had reversed the initial success of the allied infantry and now, in an enclosed piece of land known as White Sike Close, they were holding out. Cromwell and Leslie closed the ring round them. But it needed dragoons to shoot a way with their muskets into the stubborn mass of white-clad pikemen so that the cavalry could drive in for the massacre. No quarter was asked. The harvest moon was high over Marston Moor before, at last, the clash of steel died away. At the end of the slaughter, there were only about forty Whitecoats taken unwounded.

So ended the battle of Marston Moor which decisively turned the tide of war against the King's cause. Four thousand dead; hundreds more wounded. York doomed. The North lost. A great new military reputation made. The encounter had lasted two and a half hours, perhaps a little more. Chief credit for the allied victory must be given to Oliver Cromwell's tactical flair – and the disciplined power of his cavalry. After that may be mentioned the work of a handful of Scottish regiments of horse and foot who, when the allied line buckled, stood staunchly to their duty and averted a total collapse. If that had come about, then Cromwell's spectacular victory would have withered on the bough as Goring's did. The Scottish regiments that broke and fled were bitterly upbraided by their ministers at morning service next day. The tragic glory of the day surely belongs to the Marquis of Newcastle's Whitecoats who would take no quarter and died in ranks where they stood.

In fact, not all of them died. Some slipped away in the darkness and the confusion of that dreadful night. And some of the fugitives found their way to the coast and to another occupation. Some time afterwards a traveller, crossing the North Sea, fell in with picaroons (pirates) who plundered the ship he was in. When they heard he was a friend of Lord Newcastle's they would take nothing from him. 'They desired him to remember their humble duty to the Lord General as they were some of his Whitecoats who had escaped death. If my lord had any service for them, they were ready.'

By that time, Newcastle was living in exile in the Low Countries.

XII

'Your Present Sad Opinion'

'Night is o'er England, and the winds are still.'

Walter de la Mare

It was eleven o'clock that night before Rupert reached York and found that the city had shut its gates to keep out the flood of defeated and, often, wounded men who poured in from the battle begging with pitiful cries to be admitted. But close on their heels came the Roundhead pursuers. To open the gates was a risk the Governor of York could not take. With Eythin to help him, Rupert gathered together outside the city walls as many men as he could find. The first news that reached the city was brought by one of the large gallery of spectators who had seen the opening stages of the battle. It told of a Royalist victory. Leven had been taken prisoner, said the report; Lord Fairfax killed. Bells were rung in the churches of the city; bonfires lit in the streets. Before their ashes were cold, the truth was known. The first bulletin to reach the King was equally misleading and was corrected by an express letter from Rupert.

The Royalist leaders consulted on their future plans. Newcastle said he would go overseas to escape the mockery of the court. Eythin would do the same. And Rupert? They asked him what he would do. His answer was what could have been expected. Gather as many of his army as he could find and march back across country to Lancaster! But he could persuade neither of the other two to follow his example. They left Scarborough for Hamburg along with forty other gentlemen who believed that the King had lost his war, and, probably, his kingdom.

In fact, the King's affairs were just then going better than could have been expected. The reason why Rupert had resolved to fight at Marston Moor without delay was that he believed his uncle's plight was desperate. But this was not so. Three days before the battle the King had won a handsome victory over Sir William Waller at Cropredy Bridge. The catastrophe at Marston Moor had, therefore, been a risk that there was no need to take. As for the blame for the loss of the battle, some of it could, no doubt, be attributed to Eythin and Newcastle, the one surly, the other apparently piqued by Rupert's assumption of the supreme command. If they had hurried to the battle that July morning, the royal army might have attacked the allies at a moment when they were strung out along the road to Tadcaster. On the other hand, Rupert had allowed himself to be duped by Leven's decision to attack that evening. He was not on the field at the moment when the allied army swept in a great wave down Marston Hill and swarmed across the ditch at the foot of it. Maybe he could not have prevented the disaster that followed. Certainly it would have required an extraordinary conjunction of good fortune and military skill to outweigh the numerical advantage of eight or ten thousand men possessed by the allies. But the truth remains that by being absent from the field during those first crucial minutes, Rupert lost control of the situation and could never recover it. The defeat was always something of a mystery to him: 'I am sure my men fought well, and therefore know no reason of our rout but this, Because the Devil did help his servants.'

Having arrived outside York on 1 July with 14,000 men, Rupert left it on 3 July with 6,000. He had lost half his army, all his baggage, his letters and the white poodle, Boy, who had gone everywhere with him since the days of his captivity in Linz. Boy had followed his master on to the battlefield and had been killed. Lost, too, was Rupert's legend of invincibility. A fortnight after the battle, the Venetian secretary in London passed on to the Doge an account of it which, mistakenly, gave credit for the allied victory to the Scots, who 'had charged with so much determination that after a long and bloody battle the prince [Rupert] was utterly overthrown'. A few days later the Dutch ambassadors had audiences of the two Houses of Parliament. Just before they entered, Parliament ordered an exhibition of all the flags and banners captured at Marston Moor. They numbered forty-four in all. Rupert's standard was the most conspicuous of the trophies displayed at the Bar of the House.

In the middle of September, Rupert's elder brother, the Elector Palatine, arrived in London; he was put up in a palace which Parliament placed at his disposal, along with a grant of £30 a day for his expenses. He went out of his way to treat Parliament with respect. Prince Rupert's brother was, in the opinion of the watchful diplomats from Venice, up to no good. He may even have been angling for the succession to the English crown, as eldest son of the King's sister. The Venetians, who were biased, reported that there was 'no limit to the Prince's hypocrisy'. For instance, on Sunday he attended the service in St Margaret's, Westminster, regarded as Parliament's own particular place of worship. However, said the Venetians, with some satisfaction, the Elector Palatine did not meet with the entire approval of the English public.

After Marston Moor, the allied army broke up. The Scots went north to reduce the town of Newcastle while, one after another, the Royalist strongholds in Yorkshire fell to the Parliament. It was perhaps as well that Scots and English, Presbyterians and Independents, were parted, because the one party was getting on the nerves of the other. The Scots were annoyed that so much of the credit for the victory was given to, and claimed by, Colonel Cromwell. The Scottish soldiers' pride was hurt; the Scottish ministers recognised with alarm that their hope of fastening the Presbyterian discipline on England had taken a sad blow from the prowess of the mainly Independent Ironsides whom Cromwell had led into battle and for whom Rupert had found the name.* Two days after the battle, before the three allied armies had parted company, Cromwell sent a joint letter to Parliament asking for an early decision about the kind of reformed church government that should be established in the two kingdoms. It was unlikely that the problem would be settled quickly and it was even more unlikely that it would give satisfaction to the Scots. When Cromwell seemed to claim an undue share of the victory for himself he was not acting from a personal sense of glory, however natural that might be. He had a theological motive, too. In addition, there was a political source of disunity among the allies.

Not long before the battle was fought, Sir Henry Vane, who had been one of the architects of the League with Scotland, had uttered the first faint whisper that the King might be deposed. And who was his candidate for the throne? Who but Rupert's elder brother, the Elector Palatine, still exiled from his capital at Heidelberg, still a refugee dependent on foreign contributions, and still letting it be known that whatever his wild young brothers, Rupert and Maurice, might be up to, he was on the Protestant, Parliamentary side. 'Neither can His Highness forbear, with unspeakable grief,' he wrote in the month that followed Marston

* 'Old Ironsides' was, in fact, the sobriquet he gave to Cromwell. The name spread from the leader to his troopers.

Elizabeth of Bohemia, Prince Rupert's mother, engraved by
W. J. Delft after Mierveld
    (*Radio Times Hulton Picture Library*)

Prince Rupert as a young man, by Honthorst
    (*Landes Gallerie, Hanover*)

Ruperta, daughter of Prince Rupert,
painted by Lely and engraved by
Sherwin

(*British Library*)

Elizabeth, Princess Palatine, sister of Prince Rupert,
painted by Honthorst

(*Radio Times Hulton Picture Library*)

Sophia, Princess Palatine, afterwards
Electress of Hanover, sister of Prince
Rupert, by Honthorst

(*Radio Times Hulton Picture Library*)

Prince Maurice, brother of Prince Rupert
(*By permission of the National Trust, from Ashdown House;*
photograph: Courtauld Institute of Art)

Mrs Margaret Hughes the actress, mistress of
Prince Rupert
(*Radio Times Hulton Picture Library*)

Mary, Duchess of Richmond, by Van
Dyck
(*Radio Times Hulton Picture Library*)

Colonel Will Legge
(*National Portrait Gallery*)

Prince Rupert in later life, by Lely
(*Radio Times Hulton Picture Library*)

Lord George Digby (*right*) and William Russell, Earl of Bedford, by Van Dyck
(*Radio Times Hulton Picture Library*)

William, First Earl of Craven, from the painting by
Honthorst

(*Radio Times Hulton Picture Library*)

Lord Goring

(The Earl of Clarendon)

'Head of an Old Man', signed by Prince Rupert

(British Library)

The Battle of the Texel, by Abraham Storck
(*National Maritime Museum*)

Moor, 'to observe that the public actions of some of his own blood have been such as have admitted too much cause of sorrow and jealousy ... But His Highness is confident that the justice of the Parliament, and of all honest men, will not impute to him such actions as are his afflictions and not his faults.' His Highness evidently believed that if he was going to be treacherous, he might as well do the job thoroughly. He probably thought, if things turned out in a certain way, Whitehall would do very well as a substitute for Heidelberg. Perhaps he could have both. Perhaps he could be a prince in Europe and a king in England. It was not impossible. After all, his nephew did eventually pull off the double. However, in that late summer of 1644, Leven, Fairfax and Manchester shrank with horror from the idea of deposition. The only outcome of the discussions was that Manchester, frightened by the spectre of republicanism, lost his enthusiasm for the Parliamentary cause and Cromwell, who was not frightened by it, began to quarrel with Manchester.

During those days when King Charles brooded despondently over his misfortunes, the lack of money, the shortages of supplies, the disunity of his followers, he consoled himself with the knowledge that greater troubles beset his enemies. Nor did the military situation appear to be as bad as we, with hindsight to help us, know that it was. A few days after Marston Moor, Rupert had met Montrose in an inn at Richmond. These two Calvinist Cavaliers found they had a good deal in common. Each was a soldier, born and bred. Rupert was the more experienced in war; the Scotsman, older by eight years, was a guerrilla fighter of genius. Each knew that the King's cause was in dire peril and neither was perturbed by the knowledge. For two days they talked while Montrose's troops, men from Cumberland and Westmorland, provided a rearguard for Rupert's depleted force in their retreat to Lancashire. Montrose told Rupert that if he were lent a thousand of the Prince's cavalry he could fight his way into the heart of Scotland. But when, at length, the two adventurers parted, it was Montrose who left his soldiers with the Prince while he and two companions turned their horses' heads towards Scotland. Rupert, on a less romantic errand, stayed and went to Shrewsbury to recruit and train a new army.

Strange to say, the defeat at Marston Moor seems to have done no damage to his standing with his uncle. And he had friends as well as enemies at court. His friend, the Duke of Richmond, could always be counted on to speak for him to the King. And the Queen, for ever jealous of Rupert's influence over her husband, had gone back to France.

The anti-Rupert party was divided. George Digby, the Secretary of State, who could usually be counted among the Prince's opponents at court, had quarrelled with Lord Percy and Henry Wilmot, both of whom were normally aligned against Rupert. For this reason, if for no other, Digby had temporarily become a partisan of Rupert's. There were further complications. Wilmot began an exchange of messages with the Earl of Essex of a near-treasonable tendency. Their purpose was this: If Essex would come over to the King's side, Wilmot would join him in removing Digby from office. After that, Essex and Wilmot would march on London with their joint forces and end the war. On 8 August, just five weeks after Marston Moor, the King struck against the conspirators. Wilmot was arrested and dismissed from his post as General, although he was allowed to cross to France.

All this time, Rupert had been rebuilding his shattered forces at Chester, finding new recruits in Wales and sending them to be trained at Shrewsbury, while seeking arms of which he was in desperate need. By the middle of August he was on his way south to join the King, assured by a letter Digby sent him that, as soon as old Lord Forth (now Earl of Brentford) could be decently put on the shelf, he, Rupert, would be appointed commander-in-chief. But one embarrassing fact stood in the way. Rupert's brother, the Elector Palatine, was in London. The idea spread that the Elector would be a claimant for the throne of England and Scotland. Although this notion had already been rejected by the leading English and Scottish generals, it persisted in Parliamentary circles and eventually reached the ears of His Majesty himself. The immediate effect was that the plan for making Rupert commander-in-chief was dropped. 'Concerning your particular fidelity and friendship to me, I have implicit faith in you,' wrote Charles. But one Palatine prince in supreme command, another a pretender to the throne – it would not do! So Rupert did not get the job of re-shaping the Royalist army so that it might be fit to meet the 'New Model' army which it was known that Parliament was training. Instead, he found himself taken up with the affairs of his Welsh viceroyalty. There, in the North, the farmers were grumbling because the cattle trade was suffering from the war. This part of Wales was particularly important to him because if it was in safe hands, it ensured the flow of reinforcements from Ireland through Chester. Lord Herbert of Cherbury caused him annoyance by refusing to allow a Royalist garrison to be installed in his Montgomery Castle and, then, by handing it over to the Parliamentary forces. The castle commanded the direct route between Chester and Shrewsbury. These local anxieties were, however, overshadowed by what seemed to be the splendid tidings that came from Cornwall in the last days of August.

The King's troops, by skilful manoeuvring, had driven Essex into a peninsula at Fowey. There he was trapped. Essex himself escaped by sea. His cavalry fought their way through the Royalist lines. But the infantry were forced to sue for terms. They were allowed to march out, leaving behind cannon, muskets and powder. The defeat brought gloom to the Parliamentary leaders sitting in the Committee of Both Kingdoms. But another consequence was more important. By discrediting Essex as a general, the defeat in Cornwall strengthened the influence of the energetic Cromwell who had urged in vain on his commander, Lord Manchester, that they should lose no time in marching to save Essex and his army. But by this time Manchester was more alarmed by the rise of Cromwell than concerned to bring Charles down. He went up to London to complain about Cromwell and the Independents to the Committee of Both Kingdoms. There he was sure of support from the Scots and their Presbyterian friends. But, as it chanced, Manchester had arrived at a bad time.

In the Highlands, Montrose had set the heather alight and scattered an army of Covenanters at Tippermuir. Now he was marching on Aberdeen, a Royalist town with a Covenanting town council. In London, the prestige of the Presbyterian Scots was at a low ebb among their Puritan allies. It recovered somewhat when Leven and his Scots army captured Newcastle-on-Tyne and by doing so ensured the winter's coal supplies for chilly London. But there was a complicating factor; the coal would be provided or cut off at Scottish pleasure. This was a card the Scots negotiators in London could use in the diplomatic game they were playing. All through the autumn of 1644, the King stood on the defensive in the neighbourhood of Banbury, while the Parliamentary army could not bring him to battle. In the last few days of October, the King and Rupert met at Bath and, together, went to Oxford. There Charles reviewed his army, a force of respectable size, 15,000 strong. There Prince Rupert was made lieutenant-general and, in addition, Master of the Horse in the Royal household, a prestigious, traditional office which had been held long before by the Earl of Essex who was Queen Elizabeth's favourite, and which this time the Earl of Southampton had hoped for. By that time there was no longer any danger of Rupert's brother, the Elector, reaching out for the English crown. Nor, if he had done so, would anyone of consequence have supported him. So that Rupert's family was no longer an embarrassment to him.

Meanwhile in the snowy Highland glens, Rupert's friend, Montrose, had struck another heavy blow at the Covenanters. He and his Scots-Irish troops marched westwards from Loch Tay and – to the glee of the Macdonalds, who were the strongest element in his army – laid waste Inveraray, the capital of the Campbells, who were the sworn enemies of the Macdonalds. The head of the Campbells was the Marquis of Argyll, the ablest Scottish nobleman in the Covenant's allegiance. News like this buoyed up the spirits of the Royalist leaders, but – which was more important – weakened the authority of the Presbyterian negotiators in London, and strengthened the hands of the Independents and, therefore, of Cromwell. By an adroit piece of political manoeuvring, Essex was prised out of his post as commander-in-chief of the Parliamentary army and Cromwell became Fairfax's second-in-command. It was plain that, when spring came and campaigning weather returned, the Parliamentary armies would be led with a new vigour. A series of savage executions in London, culminating in the beheading of Archbishop Laud, suggested that a degree of ruthlessness was entering the Civil War which it had not yet known. And, so far, the 'New Model' had not been blooded.

That autumn and during the winter that followed, Rupert found the task of reorganising the royal army a profoundly depressing one. Already he had been thrown into the deepest gloom by bad news from the Welsh borders and was much in need of the sympathy of his friend, Richmond, who wrote, 'I should be much more restless if I did believe your present sad opinion would be long continued, or that there was just cause for it.' All would be well when the King could speak 'with power'. But when Rupert went to Oxford he found new reasons for melancholy. He was plagued by defeatism, by stinging jealousies at court – Southampton annoyed over the Mastership of the Horse, Sir Arthur Aston sulky because he had not been made governor of Oxford, and he, himself, upset because Lord Bernard Stuart was made Colonel of the Life Guards, a post Rupert had coveted. From Paris, the Queen was always ready to contribute her quota of suspicion of Rupert and criticism of her husband, who was weak in dealing with the 'rebels', she said, and worse, was sceptical of the promises his loving spouse held out to him of help from the Continent – 10,000 troops from one quarter, 3,000 from another. Poor Charles! His situation was desperate enough – but to have, in addition, the bad advice of a beloved wife was too much.

In this atmosphere, Rupert made ready to renew the war when the bitter winter had passed and England, weary, impoverished, stripped of its forests by the urgent need for firewood, desperately short of fuel, prepared sullenly for a new round of fighting. He held Gloucester in check and planned to win Abingdon back from the Parliament. When he tried to do this by a surprise attack one night in January 1645, he was driven off by a vigorous counter-thrust. In Oxford, it was rumoured that the plan of attack had been betrayed to the Roundhead commander by an enemy of Rupert's.

Soon afterwards, when peace negotiations opened at Uxbridge, the Scots implored the King (through his representative, Edward Hyde) to become a Presbyterian; others among the Parliamentary negotiators gloomily predicted that, if there was no peace, the extremists in their party would use the New Model Army to set up a republic. But the King was unmoved. He would neither placate the Scots nor be frightened by the New Model. In Scotland, the star of Montrose was still rising. And from Ireland, Charles expected a stream of valiant recruits for his diminished army.

On 3 February, Montrose wrote to the King telling him of the destruction of Argyll's Campbells at Inverlochy: 'I doubt not that before the end of this summer I shall be able to come to your Majesty's assistance with a brave army.' With such hopes brought to him from such a source, what wonder that the King became less willing to compromise with the Parliament! He sent away the men who opposed his plan to bring in the Irish troops. He ordered Prince Maurice to relieve Chester, while his brother, Rupert, who was nominally the Royalist commander-in-chief, was sent back to Ludlow to prepare for a new campaign in the North. Rupert's strongest motive at this time was to avenge Marston Moor, a defeat which he was unwilling to accept as a just verdict on the military situation as it had then existed. He departed from Oxford, leaving his uncle to the counsels of a man whose character and ability he had reason to distrust, George Digby. Two months later the New Model, product of strenuous prayers and training, was ready to take the field. As happened before, when the Scots had arrived on the scene, the war was once more about to enter a new phase. Digby thought that the New Model, on which he lavished aristocratic sneers, would be knocked out before it was hardened in battle. Rupert still wanted to march to the North. He did not share the optimism of some of the King's advisers about the probable quality of the New Model. He had heard some rumours of those soldiers and he did not like what he had heard. Also, he had seen Cromwell in action.

Rupert's own project which he pressed on the King, was to win Yorkshire back for Charles. He was strengthened in his thought by the undeniable fact that the northern horse, commanded by Sir Marmaduke Langdale, were showing an inconvenient desire, amounting almost to mutiny, to return home. Langdale's Cavaliers went to Newark and were only brought back in time for the next – and, as it chanced, the last – set-piece in the military drama of the Civil War. Rupert had another worry. He had sent message after message to Lord Goring ordering him to come back from Somerset where, with a force of cavalry, he was investing Taunton: 'I shall expect by your lordship at least 3,500 effectual horse.' Goring paid no attention. The feud between him and Rupert had reached a point where Goring, on the grounds that Rupert invariably thwarted him, refused to take orders except from the King himself. All this he explained in a letter to the Prince, which was an adroit mixture of insolence and false subservience. The truth was that he liked having an independent command, as remote as possible from the interference of others, so that he could be left to fight as he wished or drink with his cronies. Fearing his influence over the King, Rupert was half-glad to have this rival far removed from the Court. A man with a stronger personality than the King's was needed to master the dangerous squabbles among his generals. Meanwhile, on the other side of the great dividing line, Parliament decided to give the highest priority to a scheme for the capture of Oxford, the Royalist capital of England. When this became clear to the Royalists, Rupert dropped his plan for an advance into the North. 'The Gentleman,' wrote O'Neill, anticipating the facts, was forced to quit Oxford at the approach of Essex and Waller with their prodigious number of Cockneys.' In the North, the Scots army of occupation was being drained to furnish battalions to defend the Lowlands against Montrose and his fearsome Highlanders. Parliament complained that the Scots were deserting them; Lord Leven retorted that his troops had been starved of pay and food for the benefit of the New Model.

The army that Parliament had raised was now at Newbury. Rupert decided that it should be met and countered with a force of equal power. He ordered Goring to march eastwards from Somerset and join the King's array at Market Harborough. As the month of May drew to an end, Digby, the Secretary of State, looked forward to a decisive battle in which Charles' reassembled troops would meet the New Model. There was only one defect in the plan. Goring, carousing at Bath, was in no hurry to join the other Royalist leaders. He was busy in the West Country. Very soon he would take Taunton; in the meantime, the time could be filled in agreeably with the bottle.

The King and Rupert moved on Leicester, a rich town in the Parliamentary allegiance, with decrepit fortifications and an absent governor. Rupert summoned it to surrender and put his siege guns in position. At this, the town protested, whereupon Rupert gave the inhabitants a quarter of an hour to consider the military situation in which they found themselves. After that, his guns opened up and fired for three hours, making a wide breach in the walls. Then the Royalist assault parties moved into the town against a brave resistance which was sustained until a last stand was made in the market-place. In the pillage that followed, the Leicester shopkeepers lost a good deal of property. The affair lost no element of horror in the inflammatory accounts of Parliamentary reporters. Ten days later, Oliver Cromwell was appointed second in command of the New Model, the commander of which was Fairfax. The results of the appointment were not slow to appear. Fairfax was ordered to find the King's army and follow it wherever it went. In the eyes of the new leaders the siege of Oxford was a matter of less importance.

This change of plans was not, however, grasped all at once by the King's advisers. Oxford must be saved, they said – Oxford and the ladies of the court who were living there! The only man who disagreed was Rupert. He did so with his customary vigour. Meanwhile, an odd task forced Rupert to stay for six days immobile at Daventry. Oxford being in danger of starving, a great procession of livestock had to be delivered there under the protection of his cavalry. The operation was not completed until 11 June by which time Fairfax was at Stony Stratford, a little more than twenty miles to the south-east. It was now hard for Rupert to avoid an encounter with the Parliamentary army, the leaders of which knew very well where he was. In Westminster that morning, the Commons prayed for an hour, beseeching Divine favour for their arms. On a day of heavy rain, Fairfax's soldiers trudged towards Northampton, cheered by the news that Cromwell was no farther off than a day's march. There, he was waiting to be joined by some reinforcements from East Anglia. Fairfax sent him orders to come at once, waiting on nobody. By nightfall, the Roundheads were a dozen miles from Rupert. But of that alarming fact he was ignorant, although he should not have been.

One of his cavalry patrols had seen the enemy and had captured some of his stragglers. But the patrol had failed to report this crucial information. Next day, the foremost riders of Fairfax's advance guard ran into Rupert's outposts near Daventry, where the Royalists had been preparing strong defences at Borough Hill. That night, Fairfax saw many fires burning on the hill and deduced, rightly, that the Royal army was in retreat. One of his scouts brought in an interesting find. A Royalist courier had been caught carrying a letter from Goring to Rupert, asking him not to fight until Goring could join him, which he would not be able to do for some time. At that moment, Fairfax knew more about Goring's intention than Rupert did. The deduction was clear. This was the moment when Fairfax should force Rupert to give battle. A few hours later, Cromwell arrived at Fairfax's headquarters.

By that time, the King and Rupert were in full retreat to the north, followed and harassed by Parliamentary cavalry. Late on 13 June the King, in bed at Lubenham, two miles west of Market Harborough, was dismayed by the news that the enemy had entered the village of Naseby, eight miles away. Fairfax and Cromwell were much closer than he had bargained for. The King hurried to Market Harborough where he roused Rupert with the news. A dawn council of the Royalist leaders, hastily summoned, came to the conclusion that the Parliamentary forces were now so close that there could be no shirking an action. Rupert alone was against fighting. The odds, he said, were too great. The retreat should go on to Melton Mowbray and Belvoir Castle. A chance to fight on better terms would be sure to come. And, in due course, Goring would arrive from the West. But Rupert's cautious advice was rejected.

Two miles north of Naseby there is a ridge of high ground running east and west. Here, the Royalist army would stand, facing south. And here, in fact, it was drawn up in the early hours of 14 June. Hours before that, Fairfax was on the move northwards from Naseby, cautiously, not knowing exactly where the Royalists were, how many they were or what they meant to do. With a small escort, Fairfax went ahead with Cromwell to reconnoitre. His first idea was to line his army up on low-lying ground south of Clipston. Cromwell argued against him. He pointed out that the Royalists were exceptionally strong in horse and this boggy dip in the surface of Leicestershire was not good cavalry country. In consequence, Rupert would either try to outflank the Parliamentary army or would stand on the defensive on the high ground farther to the north. Far better, then, said Cromwell, for Fairfax to occupy the ridge behind them in the hope that Rupert would commit his cavalry to an uphill attack. After a moment's thought, Fairfax agreed. The two generals, the impetuous Yorkshireman and the thoughtful squire from Huntingdon, his junior in rank, his senior by thirteen years, rode back to meet the main army.

At the same time, Rupert was out on a scouting expedition. He had asked his scoutmaster to report to him on the enemy's dispositions. He had been told that there was no sign of any enemy. Either the early morning light was still too weak or the scoutmaster had not ventured too near the Parliamentary outposts. In any case, Rupert did not put any faith in what he had been told. Calling a troop of horse to come along with him, he cantered off in the direction where he knew the enemy must be. So it came about that, when he approached Clipston, he caught sight of a small group of Roundhead horsemen riding with their backs to him up the slope that led to Naseby ridge. It was Fairfax, Cromwell and their escort. Studying the terrain, Rupert noticed the signs of boggy ground in front of Clipston – a death-trap for cavalry – and saw, moreover, that on the right was a slope which seemed to have a better riding surface. Perhaps, by a flanking manoeuvre in that direction he could bring his cavalry up to the level of Naseby ridge. Accordingly, Rupert rode off to the right and sent back a message to the army to follow him. Meanwhile, Fairfax, from his ridge, had been watching the movements of the young Royalist commander. His imagination followed Rupert's thinking; his orders conformed to those of his opponent. By nine o'clock, the Parliamentary army and the Royalists were marching to the west on parallel courses about half a mile apart.

Before ten o'clock the two armies had reached a point where the valley between the two ridges was shallow and the slopes were gentle. There they halted and were formed up for battle. Rupert took command of the cavalry on the right of the Royalist front; the horsemen on the other flank being commanded by Sir Marmaduke Langdale. Drawn up in the centre were the infantry under Lord Astley. It was the conventional order of battle again. All told, the royal army was about 9,000 strong; on the other side, the Parliamentary generals commanded 14,000 men. The odds against Rupert were, therefore, somewhat worse than they had been at Marston Moor.

He surveyed the scene from the neighbourhood of a farm behind his cavalry where the rise of the ground gave him a good general view, although he could not see what the Parliamentary general was doing

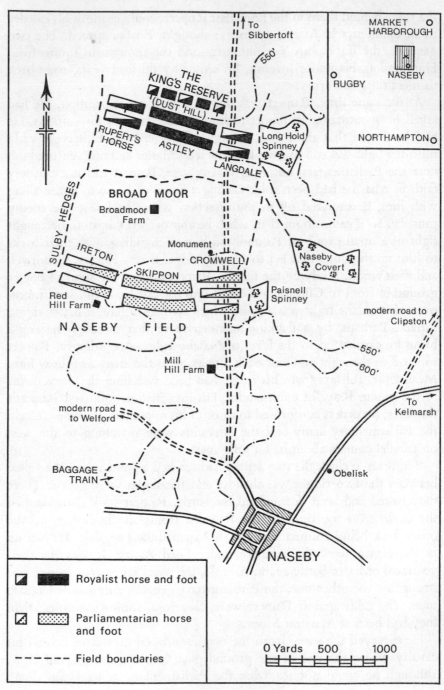

The Battle of Naseby

with men who were concealed by Fairfax's orders behind the crest of the hill. Immediately opposite him in the enemy line of battle, he was probably aware of a mass of cavalry under a commander he did not recognise. This was Ireton, whom Cromwell had picked as his number two. Cromwell himself was in command of 3,500 horse on the other wing. Between the two masses of cavalry, the Parliamentary foot were marshalled, under the veteran Skippon. They would be invisible to Rupert, although it is likely enough that he guessed where they were.

At the last minute Cromwell rode hurriedly across from the right wing where the buff-clad squadrons of the New Model cavalry were drawn up. He was perturbed by the possibility that Rupert, after disposing of Ireton's horsemen, would swing in and take the Parliamentary infantry on the flank. He had noticed, too, that a hedge ran across the valley at right angles to the army's front. The feature could be of vital importance in the battle that was about to break out. Cromwell sought out Colonel John Okey, who commanded a regiment of dragoons and was just then standing at some distance behind the front line handing out powder and shot to his dismounted men. Cromwell ordered Okey to take his dragoons forward and line the hedge so as to bring an enfilading fire of musketry to bear on Rupert's cavalry as it rode forward to the attack. Both Cromwell and Fairfax were confident that the Royalist general would be the first to move that morning. In this they were right. Hardly had Okey got his dragoons into position than the whole royal army surged forward, in good order and at a spanking pace, up the gentle slope that is called Broad Moor. They were wearing bean stalks in their hats and shouting 'Queen Mary', the identifying 'field word' of the day. 'Very stately,' said Okey, watching the advance from his observation post out on the extreme tip of the Parliamentary horse. It was not long after ten o'clock.

When the King had arrived on the field, Rupert's commission as commander-in-chief was at an end. Having obtained his uncle's permission, he rode off to the point on the ground where the cavalry were waiting. When the trumpets blew the charge, Rupert and his brother, Maurice, rode at the head of their squadrons on the right wing of the attack. Wearing a round Montero cap with ear flaps, he ignored the bullets of Okey's snipers taking pot-shots from the cover of the hedges as he flashed past. He paused only to dress the lines before the final clash. By this time, Ireton was in sight, having ordered his regiments to ride down the slope to meet the Cavaliers. 'God and our strength,' shouted the troopers of the New Model. Fighting fiercely, Ireton took his own

129

regiment clean through two Royalist regiments, one of them led by Maurice. In doing so he was cut off from his own troopers and turned to give a hand to the Parliamentary infantry in the centre who were just then being roughly handled by the more experienced Royalist pikemen. Instantly, Ireton ran into trouble. His horse was shot under him, a Royalist pike went through his thigh. A Royalist halberd ripped his face open. The commander of the Parliamentary left wing was out of the fight.

All this time the two Palatine princes and the hardened cavalrymen who followed them were hard at work breaking the resistance of the remaining New Model regiments in front of them. After some desperate swordplay, the Parliamentary left broke and fled, with Rupert and his wild horsemen in exultant pursuit. It was Edgehill all over again. Rupert did not pull up his horsemen until they had reached Fairfax's wagon lines, a thousand yards behind the battlefield. He had repeated the mistake – if it was a mistake and not simply the excitement of a warlike young man – that he had made years before. But this time, the mistake carried a heavier penalty.

In the centre of the battle, the two masses of infantry had come quickly to push of pike after exchanging a single volley of musket fire. Although heavily outnumbered – 4,000 to 7,000 – Astley's men had the better of the struggle. Fairfax's regiment stood firm but Skippon's regiment faltered and for a little it seemed that a collapse of the Parliamentary front was near. Had Rupert been there – riding in on the flank with his victorious horsemen – the setback might have been turned into a rout. But Rupert was far away. His horsemen were eagerly preparing to plunder Fairfax's baggage. And Cromwell was on the scene. His regiments, compact and far more numerous than their opponents, had poured down the slope to meet Langdale's squadrons. They had overcome the resistance of those Royalist horsemen and flowed round their flank so that the whole Royalist wing was soon in flight. The left wing of each army had, therefore, been routed. But Cromwell was not Rupert. The wine of success did not affect his judgment. Nor did it weaken the iron grip in which he held his squadrons.

At that moment of desperate crisis when something like a miracle was needed to save the Royalist fortunes, it looked as if the King himself was about to stake his life in the battle.

The King was about to attack at the head of his Life Guards – better if he had! – when the Earl of Carnwath, a Scotsman, intervened. Pulling

Charles' horse round by the bridle, he shouted, 'Will you go to your death?' The troopers behind who were serving as a screen for the beaten horsemen of the Royalist left wing, assumed that Carnwath's action was a hint to leave the scene. They did so at a full gallop.

It was at this moment, when all was still in the balance, that Cromwell revealed his stature as a fighting general. The infantry battle in the centre was still going on savagely with the New Model pikemen shaken, confused, but still in the fight, and the Royalists, winning but with an open flank. And no sign of Rupert and Maurice and their frenzied horsemen. Cromwell gathered his regiments. Fairfax rode alongside him, shorn of his helmet. Together, they led the Parliamentary squadrons of the New Model, the men who had just broken Langdale's cavalry, in a savage onset on the unguarded left flank of the Royalist foot. Soon they were joined by others. Colonel Okey, who had been watching the course of the battle, summoned his dragoons out of the hedge and ordered them to mount. Then he led them in a charge against the Royalist right centre. The King's foot were now assailed on three sides and began to throw down their pikes and ask for quarter. One brigade stood fast, Rupert's Bluecoats and the King's own regiment, defying the New Model swordsmen with their pikes, until Fairfax brought up his own foot and broke into the Royalist formation. Then the royal colours fell.

Meanwhile, Rupert had been able to pull his men off their prey in the baggage train, which was in any case being resolutely defended. Riding back at their head he saw at once that the battle was already lost. His weary riders and blown horses were in no state to take on the collected masses of cavalry under Cromwell's control. As for his infantry, it was no longer a coherent fighting force. The best he could do was to make a detour and join the King who, at that moment, was trying to bring some spirit back into Langdale's defeated regiments. But it was a long time and many miles before the Royalist rearguard made a stand against the pursuit of Fairfax's men. Rupert and the King tried to persuade the beaten Cavaliers to turn on their adversaries. The Royalists had had enough. Twenty miles farther on, the King reined in at Leicester in time for a few words with Rupert and Maurice. After that he rode on to Ashby-de-la-Zouch. His army had been swept away and, as it turned out, it was the last army he could raise capable of meeting the Parliamentary forces with any hope of victory.

Rupert lost his baggage in the débâcle. Far more serious was the loss of the King's correspondence, including the letters that had passed between him and the Queen. For these revealed that Charles had assiduously sought to bring an army of Irish Catholics into the country and that he had even been willing to abolish the penal laws against their co-religionists in England. 'The King's Cabinet Opened' made horrific reading to the Protestant English when it was published in London.

XIII

'Much Inclined to a Happy Peace'

'The treasury is exhausted; the country is wasted. A summer's victory has
proved but a winter's tale.'

John Rushworth, December 1644

After Naseby, Rupert realised that the war was as good as lost. Perhaps
he had glimpsed that disagreeable truth on the night after Marston Moor.
All the gallantry and devotion of the Cavalier armies could not prevail
against the massive resources which Parliament commanded, especially
now that these resources were directed by generals as able as Fairfax and
Cromwell. And now the Cavalier armies were melting away: Goring,
who had failed to turn up in Naseby, had been shattered at Langport a
month later, after trying and failing to outmanoeuvre Fairfax. The
Royalist army was forced out of a defensive position Goring had chosen
and was pulled back westwards. The Parliamentary army reached the
Bristol Channel from the south. There was no longer any hope that the
West of England could be held for the King. If the King hoped for help
from Ireland, Rupert was sure that he would be cheated. If the King
went to Scotland while he waited for those illusory Irish reinforcements
to reach him, he would make the situation in England worse while
gaining nothing in return. So Rupert, at that moment in Bristol, and
now cut off from any hope of joining Goring, saw the problem in all
its starkness. He told his uncle that the game was up. He urged Charles
in a letter which he addressed to the Duke of Richmond that he had no
way left to preserve his posterity, kingdom and nobility, but by
negotiating a treaty of peace. It was more prudent to retain something
than to lose all. The King's answer was firm: 'If I had any other quarrel
but the defence of my religion, crown and friends, you had full reason
for your advice. For I confess that, speaking either as a soldier or statesman, I must say there is no probability but of my ruin. But as a Christian,
I must tell you that God will not suffer rebels to prosper, or His cause

to be overthrown . . .' To an argument so exalted there could be no answer. The trouble was that the King's rhetoric and the mystical certitude that inspired it could not be matched by any practical strategy. While the King moved northwards along the Welsh border, encouraged by the unfaltering optimism of Digby, Rupert, shut up in Bristol, prepared to defend the town that once, in happier days for the King, he had stormed.

By this time it was clear that Fairfax and Cromwell had Bristol as their main objective. Rupert had a garrison of 1,500 men to command and a disgruntled city to hold. Bristol's perimeter stretched for five miles round the city – too long for his troops to hold against a heavily superior force of assailants. Two years earlier, he had taken the town against Parliamentary defenders more numerous by a few hundreds than the garrison he now commanded. Since that day the defences of the town had not been strengthened. The walls were no higher, the ditches no deeper. The Parliamentary besiegers who were beginning to gather outside had a far more powerful artillery than he had commanded in the first siege. Worst of all from Rupert's point of view, the citizens of Bristol were thoroughly sick of the war. They had been taxed too heavily to support the royal armies. There was also trouble in the countryside outside the city.

Crudely organised and badly armed, the peasants of Dorset and Somerset were in revolt against the war. They were known as the Clubmen. To them, the war was incomprehensible in its aims and intolerable in its effects. What had it brought them? Trampled crops, livestock taken for the armies, wagons commandeered and trade disrupted. The arms of these fighting pacifists were the scythes and forks that lay at every farmer's hand. They marched by night behind a banner consisting of a torn sheet. Their simple slogan ran

If you take our cattle
We will give you battle.

It was rumoured that they were gathering in the woods outside the town and that very soon they would raid Bristol. Rupert, having failed to persuade them to join the royal army – although they were no more eager to serve the Parliament – set about the grim police work of suppressing them. Parliament was busy at the same task.

In more ways than one, the war was making heavy inroads on Rupert's equanimity which, after all, was never very stable. A week after Naseby, he wrote to his friend, Will Legge, whom he had appointed Governor of Oxford, complaining bitterly of the ceaseless efforts of Digby to damage him with the King: 'Concerning our last defeat. Doubtless, the fault of it will be put upon [Rupert].' A little more of the calumnies of the court and he would march to join his young cousin, the Prince of Wales, in the West Country; from him he had always received more kindness. Digby, at the same time, was writing to Legge, deploring Rupert's distrust for him and defending Rupert against the accusation that he had fought at Naseby against advice. While doing this, he insinuated that Rupert would have done better at Naseby to await the enemy's attack; that he ought to have found a better position for his artillery, and that he should have formed a more accurate notion of Fairfax's strength before joining battle. Finally, he mentioned that Rupert had left the King inadequately protected from the onset of the Ironsides. In other words, Digby, while appearing to defend Rupert against his traducers, delivered a subtle attack on his conduct of the battle.

That Digby had done this was certainly the opinion of 'honest Will' Legge who told the Secretary of State in his reply that, while Digby had cleared Rupert of 'particular and general aspersions', he now brought charges against him that would 'to men ignorant of the Prince, make him incapable of commonsense in his profession'. If Rupert was to be criticised – and Digby criticised him for not holding a Council of War on the battlefield – then Digby, if he had thought a Council was needed, must be blamed for not insisting on one. As for the charge that the King had not been left with a sufficient bodyguard, that was surely not a matter for a commander-in-chief responsible for directing a battle. In short, Legge found evidence in Digby's letter of the complaints which Rupert had brought against him. Digby had said that his letter to Legge was written 'without reflection'. It did not read that way to Legge. 'Assure yourself,' he said at the end of his uncourtly reply, 'that you are not free from great blame towards Prince Rupert.' Very soon, Digby would be able to mount a more formidable attack on Rupert's reputation. In the meantime, the Prince prepared to defend Bristol, oppressed by the knowledge that his enemies in the King's entourage were busy and, a blacker and more ominous cloud, by his own deepening pessimism about the war. The siege began in the third week of August. Rupert was reasonably confident that with his active cavalry harrying the enemy, with as many defending cannon as he could handle and with ample supplies, he could hold the city for months, provided the circuit of Bristol's walls and forts was unbroken. Very soon he had a more exact

135

notion of his problems. Outside the line of forts at Bristol were Cromwell and Fairfax with a blockading army of 12,000 men, about eight times as strong as the garrison Rupert commanded and four times as strong as the force with which he himself captured the city.

On 3 September, Fairfax, a soldier who had fought for the Protestant cause in Europe, appealed to Rupert, a Prince who had suffered in that cause: 'I take into consideration your royal birth and relation to the Crown of England [which] is and will be where it ought to be ... in fight to maintain it there; but the King, misled by evil Counsellors ...' And so on. Rupert offered to negotiate: could he be allowed to send a messenger to ask the King's pleasure? Fairfax refused. Meanwhile, five Parliament warships anchored in the river forced the only naval craft on Rupert's side to run up the Severn to be safe. His Council of War next proposed terms of their own and sent them to the Parliamentary General. Fairfax refused them. Early in the morning of 10 September, Fairfax decided that Rupert was merely trying to spin out time. He launched his attack. Four siege guns opened fire on Prior's Hill Fort, the highest and strongest position on the north side of the outer defences. The fort commander bolted. Rupert's artillery replied, inflicting severe losses on the assaulting troops. But after an hour, two breaches were made in the defences on the Avon side of the town, while the garrison of Prior's Hill Fort, after heroically holding out against swarms of assailants, was captured after two hours of bitter fighting. Its defenders were massacred. Rupert now proposed to pull back his men to Bristol Castle. But Cromwell's cavalry were already in the streets of Bristol. They were between the men in the castle and those holding out in the forts.

Before opening negotiations, Rupert had obtained the consent, indeed, the insistence of his Council of War, ten veteran officers whose courage and loyalty could not be doubted.* By that time, the Council had to reckon not simply with enemy encroachments on Bristol's perimeter but with the fact that Fairfax had found means to appeal to the citizens and especially the trained bands of the town, promising them protection in their lives, liberties and estates if resistance ceased. In addition, Fairfax had written to Rupert direct, 'Let all England judge whether the burning of its towns, ruining its cities, and destroying its people, be a good requittal from a person of your family, which hath had the prayers, tears,

* The members of the Council were Rupert, Lord Hawley, Lord Lumley, Sir John Russell, Sir Matthew Appleyard, Colonel Tillier, Colonel Fox, Colonel Robert Slingsby, Colonel Walter Slingsby, Colonel Murray, Lt. Col. Osborne.

purses and blood of its Parliament and people.' It was an adroit appeal, made at a moment when the state of the defence had reached a crisis. Among Rupert's officers, Hawley, Appleyard and one of the Slingsbys, with all their troops, were now in danger of being cut off from the main body of the garrison. In a situation which was plainly hopeless, Rupert was pressed by his officers to treat for a ceasefire. Accordingly, he sent a trumpeter to Fairfax. By this time, houses were blazing in the town, lighted by Rupert in an attempt to halt the enemy's advance. The castle, citadel of the town's defence, was overlooked from Brandon Hill and its well water was scant and foul.

In all the time since the siege began, Rupert had received no letter from the King or the Prince of Wales. He knew that neither the one nor the other had moved a single soldier to take the weight off Bristol. The only message that had reached him from outside came from the Governor of Hereford who had asked for ammunition to meet an expected attack by the Scots! Between Goring's troops and Bristol was, he knew, a substantial Parliamentary force commanded by Colonel Massey whose defence of Gloucester had been a turning point in the war. In short, there was no hope of relief from the King or anyone else. These were the circumstances in which the Prince surrendered with the honours of war. The last scene did not lack dignity.

Impressive in scarlet and silver, mounted on a fine black Barbary horse, Rupert rode out of Bristol, at the rear of his troops with Fairfax at his side. He was greeted by the angry shouts of the townspeople, 'Give him no quarter.' This demonstration has been seized on as proof of Rupert's brutality to the citizens. It is more likely that the Bristol people were annoyed by the damage done to their town. They had suffered once through being on the losing side; it was infuriating to be caught again.

Leaving, the Prince exchanged grave salutes with Fairfax and Cromwell and rode towards Oxford with Colonel Butler, a Roundhead officer, on whom he made a deep impression. 'I am confident we have been much mistaken in our intelligence concerning him. I find him a man much inclined to a happy peace.' But Rupert rode out to disgrace.

The King disowned his nephew. Believing the accusations of treachery brought against Rupert by Digby and his partisans, he stripped his lieutenant-general of his offices and sent him a pass to leave the country. The pass had no value without the approval of Parliament which Rupert refused to seek without the King's licence. But the disgrace was a calculated blow at the Prince's reputation, all the more damaging because, just then, Rupert's brother, the Elector Palatine, made an agreement with the Parliament by which he received a large sum of money. The Queen was sure that the Palatine brothers were acting in concert. Rupert, she wrote, had sold Bristol to the enemy. This at a time when Rupert had not £50 in the world! The Queen was in Paris when she made the accusation, but there was no lack of voices to say much the same in Oxford. It was not a time when the King's judgment was at its most stable. His condemnation of Rupert, natural enough as it might be from a man in an hour of total ruin, was bitter and was bitterly resented. Rupert had his champions, men who argued that, by his surrender, he had saved the lives of soldiers who would otherwise have been slaughtered, as the garrison of Prior's Hill Fort had been and that he had saved the town from useless destruction. Officers who had fought on the Parliament's side, men like Colonel Butler, testified that he could have done no more to hold the town. The case for Rupert was strong. Yet, perhaps, there had been a time when he would have acted differently, when he would have seen Bristol disintegrate stone by stone, to form a tomb for its people, rather than give in. Now he thought differently. Now he was ready to count costs, weigh chances and mix a great deal of courage with a little prudence. And why? Because, for one thing, he was a man for a war of movement. Such men are not at their best fighting behind stone walls. Above all, because he did not believe any more that the cause could be won. The war was lost. This was something that the King could not face and forgive. He could not be persuaded that the fall of Bristol was a sound military decision. It must be treason. 'The House of Palatine do think themselves assured of the Crown.' So the King was told by evil tongues, and so, in his misery, he came to believe. It was freely believed in London that Fairfax and Rupert had agreed on terms which Rupert would compel the King to accept. His nephew's capitulation had brought home to him what Naseby should have proved, that his cause was lost, utterly, irretrievably lost. Bristol came as a deadly blow, destroying not only his hopes of victory, but his whole reason for existence as a king, the sort of king he believed that he was, the only sort of king he wanted to be. In dismissing Rupert, Charles was issuing a frantic protest against the God who had deserted him.

The dismissal was conveyed in a letter of icy reproach, 'This is the greatest trial of my constancy that hath yet befallen me. For what is to be done after one that is so near to me as you are, both in blood and friendship, submits to so mean an action? I have so much to say that I shall say no more . . . Seek your subsistence somewhere beyond the seas; to which end I send you herewith a pass. And I pray God to give you means to recover what you have lost.' And what had Rupert lost, in his uncle's opinion? His honour. It was not a charge that a man of Rupert's temper could possibly endure, especially since it was echoed faintly, irrationally, from some remote corner of his own conscience. Had the letter been written by anyone but a king and an uncle whom he loved, Rupert's challenge would have been sent by return. He could not believe that the King had, unprompted, reached that opinion of him. There must be evil tongues, whispering calumnies of him in the King's ear. As he wrote at the time, 'It hath been the constant endeavour of the English nation, who are prone to hate strangers, to blast and blemish my integrity to my uncle.' He rode to Oxford, black with anger and misery, to find that Charles had left the city and that Will Legge, his own loyal friend, had been dismissed from the governorship. But the matter between Charles and Rupert, so poignant, so fraught with tragedy, could not rest there.

The King's first intention had been to seek out Rupert's brother, Maurice, who had been ill at Worcester. At a time when he was in desperate need of moral support, one of his nephews had failed him; he sought the other. Digby, however, persuaded the King to escape from what would probably be an unpleasant meeting by going to Newark. After spending a fortnight in Oxford, jealously watched by Digby's spies, Rupert made a sudden dash to the North – with a guard of eighty horsemen, cavaliers who rode with him because they liked him, because they thought that he had been ill-used and because Rupert was now going on a journey on which he would need intrepid companions. Rupert's intention was to demand an audience with the King, and between the King and himself there stretched a belt of country a hundred miles wide, alive with Parliamentary patrols alerted to his coming and infesting every road. At Banbury, twelve miles to the north, Rupert met his brother, Maurice, who, by arrangement, had come over from Worcester with twenty armed riders. The two brothers meant to ride through Northampton to the Duke of Buckingham's house at Burghley near Stamford. This was a bold move, because Burghley was held for the Parliament by a garrison commanded by a renegade who had once served in Rupert's own troop of horse and would be sure to know him. The garrison came out to fight. Their chief, at the head of the main body, at once recognised Rupert and aimed his pistol at him. When it missed, he asked for quarter. The Prince shot him dead and made off.

By this time, the news had reached Parliamentary Intelligence in London that Rupert meant to break through to the King, and 1,500 Roundhead cavalry had been given the task of barring his way. Thirty miles north-west of Burghley, at a bridge near Belvoir Castle, Rupert's little cavalcade encountered an enemy force of 300 mounted men. Rupert squared up to them as if he meant to charge; then he turned abruptly away. At once, the enemy attacked. Rupert then reversed course once more and attacked at full gallop. The Parliamentary force broke after some fierce swordplay. When they re-formed, Rupert rode at them again and again and beat them back. After that, heavy reinforcements for the Parliamentary horse arrived on the scene. 'We have beaten them twice,' remarked the Prince to his friends, 'we must beat them once more. Then over the river and away!' And so it was. He was determined to reach Belvoir Castle, because there he meant to leave his baggage and his papers for safe keeping. On the way, the Parliamentary cavalry patrols caught up with him once more. But on this occasion, Rupert had an advantage over his pursuers. When he saw the Castle on its magnificent eminence above the river, he remembered something from his boyhood. This was a part of the country he knew.

During his first visit to England ten years before, he had several times stayed at Belvoir hunting and shooting rabbits. Remembering a hidden path that would take him to the castle, he divided his troop. He and a few others went one way while the rest of the party went another. However, forty Roundheads followed him and eventually overtook him. 'Will you have quarter?' they called, pausing on the crest of a hill. Rupert called his companions to close up and turn when he turned. The enemy came down the hill in some disorder and were an easy prey when, unexpectedly, Rupert and his companions set on them. Lord Molineux, who was riding with the Prince, killed a man who had been riding a good mare. This beast Rupert mounted in place of his own horse. After that, they arrived safely at the castle, where they found that the rest of the party, in a brush with the enemy, had been less fortunate. They had lost fourteen men and some of the baggage. Next day, Rupert arrived at Newark where the governor of the town, Sir Richard Willis, had ridden out to meet him. Rupert asked for an audience with the King. This was in direct opposition to Charles' wishes. 'You are no fit company for me,' the King had said. However, Rupert was in no mood to be denied and Willis was a friend of his. He and his brother, Maurice, broke in on the King, who was waiting for supper.

They were asked to join him at the meal which they did, standing respectfully behind the King's chair. He spoke to Maurice but did not address a word to Rupert. Sometime during that painful evening, Rupert asked for a court-martial to judge his conduct at Bristol. It was agreed that he would be given one. Next morning he stated his case and was unanimously acquitted. The King presided and signed the verdict that 'our right dear nephew' had not been guilty of any failure of courage or fidelity. However, Rupert was not content with this victory over the Digby faction. Although Digby himself had left the town on Rupert's approach, taking 2,000 men with him, his influence was still present and strong enough in the royal entourage to obtain the dismissal of Sir Richard Willis on the ground that he had no business to ride out and escort Rupert into the town. One evening while the King was about to dine, the two princes, accompanied by Willis and some other officers, came into the room. They were noisy and ill-mannered, Willis shouting that he had been unjustly treated, Rupert calling out, 'By God, this was done in malice to me. Digby is the cause of it all. He is a traitor.' The King retorted that those who said so were rogues and rascals.

At the end of this disgraceful scene, Rupert stamped out of the presence without bowing. That night he sent the King a request for a Council of War to consider his grievances. Instead, the King sent him his passport. However, the matter did not end there.

Will Legge, released by the King from his arrest, begged Rupert in repeated letters to make his peace with his uncle: 'I am of opinion you should write to your uncle. He is a king and, in effect, a parent to you. 'Tis your uncle you shall submit to, and a king not in the condition he merits ... I speak as a person that values you above all the world besides.' Lord Dorset added his appeal: 'Resolve, princely sir, to sink or swim with the King.' At that Rupert's anger dissolved. He would ask for forgiveness. The King sent him, for his signature, a formula which would have satisfied the honour of either party. Rupert tore it up and sent back a blank sheet with his signature at the bottom. The King could fill it as he pleased. To the fierce pride of the Palatines – or the Stuarts – had succeeded the human warmth of a young man who loved his uncle and belatedly realised the pathos of his present state. A marginal note occurs in the document known as Rupert's Diary which was, in fact, notes jotted down to his dictation by someone who was preparing his memoirs of the war. It suggests that the beauteous Duchess of Richmond had some part in this reconciliation. It is not impossible. She had reason to be fond of both men.

After the 'mutiny' at Newark, Rupert could not be restored to a command even if he had been pronounced free of blame for the Bristol disaster. His partisans, 'the Cumberlanders', as they were called after the Prince's English dukedom, were too numerous and too undisciplined to be given a leader. And besides, there was no significant armed force left to command. Digby, his enemy, was appointed commander-in-chief north of the Trent, which meant that he and Rupert were not likely to get in each other's way. Very soon, Digby lost his army in an abortive attempt to reach the Marquis of Montrose in Scotland. By that time, the Scots guerrilla leader had been decisively beaten at Philiphaugh. Digby fled to the Isle of Man on his way to the Continent. All over England, the branches of the Royalist tree were falling one after another to the axes wielded by Fairfax, Cromwell and lesser Parliamentary commanders. Here and there, Royalist raiding parties darted, having little influence on the general situation but doing a great deal of damage to property and to the popularity of their cause. The war was dying, but it was dying hard.

Towards the end of 1645, Rupert rejoined the King at Oxford. They embraced and Rupert was asked to raise, but not to command, a Life Guard regiment for Charles. After a bitter winter, spring returned – and campaigning awoke again. Charles confided to Rupert his plan to slip through the enemy cordon which was then forming round Oxford. He would go, he said, either to Scotland or Ireland. Rupert's opinion was that Scotland was the better bet; the King agreed. One night in April, while Fairfax's patrols were closing round Oxford, Charles called on Rupert at his lodgings and said that he meant to set off secretly with two companions, one of whom was a parson. Rupert volunteered at once to accompany the King. But Charles shook his head; Rupert was too tall, too broad, too easily recognised. The King stole off into the darkness and, by devious paths, rode towards the Scottish outposts at Newark.

Rupert stayed on at Oxford, skirmishing constantly with the Round-head besiegers, which if it did no more, may have disguised the King's departure. In one of these brushes, he was wounded in the shoulder, his first and last wound of the war. The blow jerked his pistol out of his hand. As it fell, it went off and killed the Roundhead's horse. A fortnight later Oxford surrendered to Fairfax, and by the terms of capitulation, Rupert and his brother, Maurice, were allowed to leave for the Continent. He and Maurice took ship from Dover to Calais on Sunday 5 July 1646. They sailed with a suite of seventy which included de Gomme and La Roche, the engineer and the 'fire worker' who had arrived at Tynemouth with Rupert four years earlier. Three days after landing on French soil, the brothers parted. Maurice, a sick man, went on by a ship of Van Tromp's to visit his mother at The Hague; Rupert waited for his servants and horses to come ashore; then he rode to St Germain, where the Queen of England was waiting to receive him. He had been at war in England for four years less forty-six days, almost without remission from 20 August 1642. During the intervening time he had travelled on horseback or foot several thousand miles. He had played his part in fourteen pitched battles and the storming of seven fortified towns. He had probably been a more active soldier in the English Civil War than any other on either side. Certainly, for a young man of twenty-six, it had been a crowded and maturing experience.

In the course of it, Rupert had made some bitter enemies and many loyal friends. He had never completely overcome the distrust that the English have for a foreigner of exceptional ability and abrasive self-confidence, especially when he has the advantages that belong to a prince of the royal house. And when outsiders meddle in a civil war, as so many of them did in the war between the King and his Parliament, they do so at some risk to themselves. Yet at the end of it all, after all the battles and the bitterness, the war had confirmed one truth in Rupert's heart: the strange, moody, sardonic young man had renewed his boyish love for England. For him, it seemed that the Civil War had come to an end when he landed at Calais on that day in July and took horse to Boulogne and the south. But, as it turned out, his part in the war was only interrupted.

XIV

A Beautiful Action

'Daily musters and preparations, and suchlike, which these tempestuous times afford, battles fought, so many men slain, monomachies, shipwrecks, piracies, and sea-fights. . . .'

Robert Burton, The Anatomy of Melancholy

It was a changed Rupert who returned to Europe after four years' absence, changed by time and experience. He had known triumph and disaster, adulation and hatred. He had rubbed shoulders with death many times. He was no longer a boy. He arrived on French soil at a time when a commander of established reputation was not likely to be long out of work. The French were on the look-out for experienced military talent to help them in a tiresome war with Spain in the Spanish Netherlands. And Rupert was not simply experienced, he was famous, with all the magnetism of a renowned leader. In short, he was just the man to attract into the French service the refugees from the English Civil War who were, by the score, being cast on the shores of Europe. The French authorities lost no time in snapping him up. He was made a maréschal de camp (a brigade commander) and given command of all the English troops in the service of Louis XIV. The only condition Rupert insisted on was that he must be free to serve the King of England if any chance of doing so should ever arise. He spent some months in recruiting English exiles – refusing however to accept the erratic Lord Goring, who, without undue delay, took service with the Spaniards. In the spring of 1647 Rupert set out with two French brigade commanders, Gassion and Rantzau, to relieve Armentières which was being besieged by 20,000 Spanish troops. The outcome was comic.

'You will see a beautiful action tomorrow,' Gassion promised. He led Rupert after dark to a small house on the bank of the Lys to observe the enemy positions; there they were surprised by a boatload of Spaniards who had rowed across from the other side. However, Gassion, pulling his hat over his eyes, ordered them sharply in Spanish to get back to their quarters. Then he took to his heels. 'This is always my luck,' he complained. 'I am not surprised,' said Rupert, 'if you often behave like that.' Next day, at Arras, Gassion ordered Rupert to stand firm against a vastly superior Spanish force. Rupert politely declined. At La Bassée, once more on reconnaissance with Gassion, he was ambushed and one of his friends, Captain Holmes, was badly wounded. Rupert lifted the wounded man on to his own horse and brought him to safety. A few days later, again in Gassion's company, the English party had another brush with the Spaniards and Rupert was slightly wounded. 'Monsieur,' said Gassion, 'je suis bien faché que vous êtes blessé.' 'Moi aussi,' said Rupert. By this time, he was becoming a little impatient with his French comrades. They disliked one another, Rantzau calling Gassion 'that madman'. But they were united in jealousy of Rupert. However, Rupert derived some small satisfaction from the campaign. He captured La Bassée after a three weeks' siege during which he defeated his old rival, Lord Goring, who commanded one of the Spanish cavalry units. During this action, Rupert was seriously wounded in the head. The remarkable good fortune which had accompanied him through the war in England had at last deserted him. He was treated by surgeons who, however, failed to realise the extent of the damage to his skull. Later in his life, the wound caused him persistent trouble. He left his command in Flanders and returned to St Germain. Now a new drama awaited him.

There arrived at court, after wild adventures on land and sea, his archenemy, George Digby. Already, on the way from Rouen to Paris, Digby had been given warning of trouble ahead. He and his party had seen a Mr Rainsford 'running past' with a long duelling sword at his side. 'On my life,' said one of the party, 'that gentleman is either posting from a duel or to one.' At Esquye, Digby and his friends were about to take horse when there arrived a coach in which were travelling a footman of Henry Wilmot's and a servant of Mr Rainsford's. Both denied that their masters were in the neighbourhood. This made some of Digby's party suspicious that some mischief was being prepared. But they laughed it off and went to bed in Digby's bedchamber in which there were four beds 'à la mode de France'. In the middle of the night, Digby's travelling companion, Daniel O'Neill, was roused: a gentleman had come from Paris to speak to him privately. It turned out that Henry Wilmot was challenging Digby to fight. O'Neill said that although there had been a quarrel between Wilmot and Digby, it had ended in a reconciliation a year before and that no new offence had been given. This Wilmot denied: he wanted to fight Digby before he reached the Queen's protection at St Germain and he insisted that O'Neill should carry the challenge to him. Digby sent Wilmot a letter next morning suggesting that they should allay suspicion by meeting at court in apparent friendship. They could fight thereafter. At St Germain, a time was duly fixed for the duel; Wilmot seemed to be satisfied and whispered to O'Neill that Digby should be on his guard, for Prince Rupert was planning some kind of foul play against him. However, at nine o'clock next morning a Frenchman, M. de la Chappelle, called on Digby to say that Rupert expected him, sword in hand, at the Cross of Poissy, three miles distant. Digby should bring three friends. Digby replied that he might be a little late, because he had a leg wound which had been made worse by a long wet spell in an open boat at sea, but if necessary he was ready to 'trainer sur le ventre' rather than miss the honour which the Prince proposed to do him. Soon afterwards, however, Lord Jermyn, the Queen's favourite, arrived with orders to prevent the duel.

'Be my second,' said Digby.

'If I am in the party, it will be against you,' Jermyn retorted. Both noblemen had lost their tempers. They rode off to the outskirts of the forest where the duel was to be fought. There the Queen's guards opportunely arrived and put them all under arrest. At the same time, the Prince of Wales, who happened to be hunting in the forest that morning, came on Rupert and his seconds. The quarrel between him and Digby was then examined by a court of honour composed of four gentlemen and was settled without much difficulty. Rupert said that he would not hold against Digby anything he might have written at the King's dictation. And Digby denied that he had said anything prejudicial to the Prince. So far as Rupert and Digby were concerned, the matter was now at an end; indeed, they became bosom friends. Wilmot, however, was far from satisfied with the way things had developed. Digby, he said, by accepting Rupert's challenge, had broken his promise to fight *him*, Wilmot. Accordingly, a four-a-side duel was arranged at a house belonging to the French King a few miles from Paris. Before they engaged, Digby said that the real reason he was fighting Wilmot was because he had said that Rupert was preparing some foul play against him. 'Whereupon,' says O'Neill, 'out flew bilboes and to work we went à la mode de

France.' It was, apparently, an undignified affair, O'Neill and one of Wilmot's friends, Lord Wentworth, having just told one another they would rather have met over a bottle, closed with one another and fell to the ground. One of the other fighters, a heavy man, fell on top of them. Digby wounded Wilmot in the sword hand. 'Take my life,' said Wilmot, 'but I won't part with my sword.' After that, Wilmot, annoyed at what he regarded as a merely temporary setback, refused to be reconciled to Digby. So the combatants parted, one party to Paris, the other to St Germain. But the long vendetta between Rupert and Digby was buried. After that, Rupert settled an old quarrel with Lord Percy who had been one of his most insidious enemies from a day when Rupert had accused him of military incompetence. One day, out hunting, Rupert laid a hand on Percy's bridle and demanded satisfaction. Both men sprang from their horses and drew. At the second pass, the Prince ran Percy through the side, whereupon one of the Prince of Wales' gentlemen stopped the fight. Rupert's next fight was of a different kind.

Soon afterwards life now took an unexpected turn for Rupert. Suddenly, he was involved in a kind of warfare of which he had no experience. In 1648, a year before the execution of the King, a mutiny broke out in the Parliament's Channel fleet which was at that time commanded by Thomas Rainborough. He, being a soldier, was unpopular with the seamen. The trouble in the ships coincided with a Royalist insurrection in the east part of Kent. On 26 May the officers and crews of six naval vessels revolted at a time when Rainborough was ashore inspecting the defences of Deal Castle. When he returned in haste to his flagship, the *Constant Reformation*, he was not allowed to go on board. The mutineers issued a statement explaining that they refused to serve under Rainborough who was 'a man not well-affected to the King, Parliament and Kingdom'. The government reacted with speed to this threat. The Earl of Warwick was appointed Lord High Admiral with power to negotiate with the mutineers. However, the negotiations failed. Indeed, there was some danger for a time that the rebellious sailors would seize the ship in which Warwick had arrived.

The Lord High Admiral retired from the scene of the rising and set about assembling a dependable fleet at Portsmouth. His task was made easier by the fact that, in the meantime, Fairfax had crushed the Kentish rising. The mutinous fleet, by the defection of some ships and the adherence of others, had now grown to nine ships, against which Warwick

147

could muster no more than seven on which he could rely. The insurgents sailed for Helvoetsluys in Holland where the Prince of Wales assumed command of the ships, having travelled from France to do so. About this time – in the middle of June – the 'revolted fleet' as it was called, was joined by Captain William Batten in the *Constant Warwick*. There was a certain amount of indecisive skirmishing between the two English navies at the mouth of the Thames. Then, in October, Prince Rupert was appointed admiral of the Royalist fleet, whereupon Batten withdrew in annoyance. While Rupert was on a visit to the Prince of Wales, Parliamentary agents went to work among the crews, as a result of which the *Constant Reformation*, the most formidable warship of the insurgent flotilla, went over temporarily to the Parliamentary forces. There followed a period during which Rupert and Warwick manoeuvred for control of the canal leading to Helvoetsluys. A Dutch squadron interposed itself for a time between the two English fleets and then withdrew. By that time, Rupert had posted cannon on the quay to discourage any of his captains who might be tempted to change sides. He had ill-disciplined crews, apt to complain about the quality of their victuals, liable to disobey orders. When one ship's company refused to help to rig another vessel, Rupert with a dozen 'resolute gentlemen' went aboard her. On this, the leader of the malcontents shouted, 'one and all', whereupon Rupert lifted him and held him over the ship's side. This threat, which was certainly no idle one, ended the strike. At the end of the troubles he could still depend on seven ships. But, plainly, the sooner he left Holland the better.

Rupert was short of men and money. To recruit the first, he needed the second. Seamen were paid – when they were paid! – 24s a month with food and clothes. This was quite a normal rate. The ships were old and in a bad state. Worst of all, he did not have a secure base for, now that Parliament was master in England, the Dutch could not be counted on to continue giving sanctuary to Royalist ships. As for money, although Rupert persuaded his mother to pawn some of her jewels, while he himself sold the brass guns of one of his ships, another source of cash was needed. He worked with such energy to keep the fleet in being that the Royalist leaders were amazed. And to energy was now added an equanimity of temper that was new to him. While he was preparing his ships for a voyage, he sent out some frigates into the North Sea on the hunt for prizes. One of the earliest prizes, a Hamburger, was so good a ship that Rupert made a man-o'-war of her. But he had decided that there was, in the political conditions then existing, a better hunting ground for him than Holland. He bluffed his way past the Parliamentary fleet in the Straits of Dover and reached Kinsale on the south coast of Ireland where he cast anchor on 31 January 1649, one day before his uncle was beheaded in Whitehall.

Revenge Our Guide

'I'll sing thy dirge with trumpet sounds
And write thine epitaph with blood and wounds.'
James Graham, Marquis of Montrose

The news of this appalling event reached Rupert twelve days later and threw him into a state of profound indignation. Of the Palatine family, only the Elector, preoccupied just then with his return to Heidelberg by the terms of the Peace of Westphalia, did not suffer from the shock of horror caused by the execution. But then, Charles Louis did not love his uncle, who had told him scornfully that he took the Parliament's money 'only to have one chicken more in my dish'. The Queen of Bohemia joined the Royalists – and lost her Parliamentary pension of £12,000 a year. Her daughter, Princess Elizabeth, sought consolation from the wisdom of Descartes, her friend. She failed to find it. Prince Edward, aged twenty, and married to a French heiress, insulted the ambassadors of the English Parliament at The Hague – 'their pretended ambassadors, whom Ned called by their true name', as the Queen put it. However, Ned was compelled to leave for The Hague for a time. Rupert's friend, Montrose, heard the news of the execution in Brussels where he was raising men for a new attempt on Scotland. Montrose fell in a faint and, when he had recovered, hurried off to see Charles II at The Hague and laid before him a project for an invasion of Scotland. Rupert's response to the news was of the same kind.

In a proclamation to his fleet, he announced his intention to make the Parliament pay for its crime. One of the men he had captured described his attitude: 'Provided he may ruin and destroy the English interest he cares not whether he gets a farthing more while he lives than what will maintain himself, his confederates and his fleet.' Rupert was embarking on a one-man campaign of reprisals. By this time, the Council of State in London had become aware of his activities and had sent ships to deal with him. It seems that they were not immediately successful, however, because, four years later, the merchants of Barnstaple were petitioning the Council about the losses they had suffered from the depredations of Prince Rupert, Irish picaroons and the like. Where once the North Devon ports had sent fifty or sixty ships a year to fish in New England waters, now they could only send ten. 'Clear and secure the Channel,' the merchants implored, 'so that the sad hearts and watery cheeks of the oppressed may bless you as the repairers of our English Israel.' By that time, Rupert had passed on to other prey.

While he still lay in Kinsale harbour in 1649, the main naval concern of the Commonwealth government had been to ship Cromwell's army over to Ireland. In that country, Rupert was tirelessly engaged in seeking recruits for his ships. He dreamt of meeting the Parliamentary fleet in a general action. But when the time came, the Council of War which he had established in his fleet to direct operations thought that the venture was too dangerous. Rupert did not press the matter. He was anxious to live down his old reputation for 'vanity'. Soon, too, he had troubles enough on his hands, troubles that were grave enough to compel him to seek another base for his operations. The garrison at Cork went over to the side of the Parliament, and the governor of the town plotted to seize the fort at Kinsale by treachery. Rupert decided then that the time had come for him to seek friendlier waters. By midsummer, he was eager to leave Ireland but he was persuaded by his officers to wait until the weather had grown worse so that visibility at sea would be reduced and their chance of evading the Parliamentary cruisers would be improved. At last, one day in September, he set off with seven ships, slipping through the blockade which the Parliament's 'general-at-sea', Blake, had established. He was on his way to Lisbon, having had a friendly message from the King of Portugal. He had with him his brother, Maurice, as second-in-command, and a group of devil-may-care Royalist officers.

On the way south, the Royalist fleet took several prizes for which they knew there would be a ready market in Lisbon, if Lisbon was really well-disposed. However, as it was not quite certain what kind of reception he would get from the Portuguese authorities, Rupert hung about outside the Tagus Bar until he knew that all would be well. While he was waiting, he had the luck to fall in with a large English merchant vessel, the *Roebuck*, bound for Brazil. Her cargo was Portuguese-owned, which led to trouble, but she could be armed and converted, without much difficulty, into a formidable fighting ship. In consequence, Rupert's little fleet of privateers was as strong at the end of 1649 as it had been when it left English waters. Meanwhile, there were political complications.

Rupert's presence in the Tagus was welcome to the King of Portugal, John IV, who sent members of the nobility to escort him to the palace, but it caused the Portuguese Secretary of State the most acute embarrassment. This increased with the arrival in Portuguese waters of a strong Parliamentary fleet with orders to 'pursue, seize, scatter, fight with or destroy all the ships of the revolted fleet'. Blake, its commander, said that he hoped the King of Portugal would not object if he attacked the Royalist ships in the river. But when Blake sailed in, the Tagus forts opened fire, and in consequence Blake dropped anchor between the Castle of St Julian and the 'wooden castle', a fort built on one of the shoals at the entrance to the river. He was two miles downstream from Rupert's flotilla. There followed a period of intense diplomacy in Lisbon. Rupert tried to persuade the King of Portugal that, if he left the Tagus, Blake should not be allowed to follow him for three days. Charles Vane, the envoy of the English government, prevailed on a group of English merchants in the city to petition the King to order both fleets out to sea. This the King declined to do. Further, he gave orders that no more English ships should be allowed to enter the river.

Rupert's mother, the Queen of Bohemia, when she heard of this incident, decided that the King was 'a young man of great hope and courage'. The Queen had been shocked by her brother's execution, and among those who frequented her court was one who shared her opinion, the intransigent Cavalier, Montrose, whose portrait she had ordered to be painted by Gerard Honthorst. While preparing his last, fatal military adventure, the Scottish hero found time, it was rumoured, to fall in love with Rupert's sister, the lively and artistic Princess Louise. But rumours of that kind about the princess were often to be heard.

In Lisbon, the King of Portugal persuaded the clergy to preach against the wickedness of any treaty between a king, that is, himself, and the rebellious subjects of another monarch. However, the Church's voice was not the only one raised in the city. Big business was on the side of Rupert's opponents, pointing out reasonably enough that it would be a mistake to quarrel with the English Parliament when the English Navy dominated the Atlantic and had at its mercy Portugal's trade with its great colony, Brazil.

During the first week of April, there was a new complication. Two French warships entered the Tagus and, perhaps by mistake, anchored amidst Blake's ships. The French captains were invited aboard the English flagship where they were asked to undertake that they would not join Rupert. When they declined to do so, they were arrested and were released only when the French ambassador had protested. The French ships then joined Rupert. Meanwhile, scuffles broke out ashore between seamen from the two English fleets. More serious, Blake planned an attempt to kidnap Rupert and his brother, Maurice, while the pair were returning from a hunting expedition. The Princes were to be ambushed and bundled aboard two pinnaces which were waiting at the water's edge. However, the attempt failed; the ambush party fled, and Rupert planned to take his revenge. This proved to be an ingenious project, typical of the Prince's interest in the technical side of warfare. He prepared an infernal machine, consisting of a bomb concealed in a barrel with a false bottom and fitted with a device which could light a quick match. One of his crew, disguised as a Portuguese, took the barrel over to the Parliamentary vice-admiral's flagship, the *Leopard*, in a boat rowed by two Negroes. He meant to pass it in at one of the stern ports of the vessel and, then, set the fuse mechanism in action. However, he found that these ports were shut and, before he had time to be rowed round to an open port, he was recognised and seized.

After this incident, Blake ordered his ships to be towed out of the river. There he was reinforced by a fleet of four powerful vessels and four merchantmen, the commanders of which brought instructions from the Council of State in London to the general-at-sea. These authorised Blake to attack Rupert wherever he might be found. The King of Portugal, however, remained firmly on the side of the Royalists; he arrested English merchants in the city who were known to have Parliamentary sympathies and he sent a fleet of thirteen ships to join Rupert. But the party of caution and prudence in Portugal had not exhausted its efforts. On its side was the Portuguese admiral, an elderly man who had no enthusiasm for war. For this failing, in due course, he was dismissed from the service. There was a renewal of desultory fighting in foggy weather, in the course of which a new Portuguese admiral, appointed to succeed the man the King had dismissed, dragged an anchor behind him so as to prevent his ship sailing too precipitately into danger. Rupert's ship lost its fore topmast, at the moment when he was about to board the enemy. He, then, decided that the time had come (12 October) to leave the Tagus. He had sold £40,000 of prizes and had victualled his ships for a cruise of four months. He realised that hostile intriguers, amply supplied with English money, were busy ashore. At any moment, there might be a change in the political situation in Lisbon, bringing to power a party anxious to please the English Parliament. This was headed by Conde de Miro. It was, simply, a question so far as Rupert was concerned of choosing the right moment to make a dash for the open sea. The moment was not long in coming.

While Blake was fully occupied looking for a rich fleet which he knew was due to arrive in Lisbon from Brazil, Rupert seized the opportunity. He sailed out of the Tagus with six ships and perhaps as many as 1,200 men aboard them. One man did not accompany him: Choqueux, the French surgeon, who had treated his wound in Flanders. Now he was sent back to King Charles with a letter in which recent events were narrated. As the anonymous chronicler* of the voyage says, 'Misfortunes being no novelty to us, we plough the sea for a subsistence and, being destitute of a port, we take the confines of the Mediterranean Sea for our harbour; poverty and despair being companions and revenge our guide.'

Passing the Straits of Gibraltar, they steered along the Andalusian coast, hunted by Blake all the way to Malaga and Cartagena, capturing some vessels on the way and attacking others with fireships. The Spanish authorities showed some willingness to co-operate with 'a royal fleet commanded by a Prince of the Blood', but there was a change when Blake appeared on the coast with a fleet vastly superior in gunpower and efficiency to Rupert's. He brought part of the Royalist fleet to battle at Cartagena, captured a frigate and forced three other vessels to run ashore. In the battle, Blake was assisted by the treachery of one of Rupert's captains. It was a crushing blow, but, as it chanced, it was one of which Rupert was unaware at the time. Storms had separated him and Maurice from the remainder of the fleet and a stroke of good luck had come his way. Off Cape Palos some miles to the east of Cartagena, he fell in with an English merchantman which refused his summons to heave to and with all sail spread made off to the south towards the Barbary coast. Rupert and Maurice went off in pursuit and, at eight o'clock that night, Maurice's ship came close enough to the merchantman to give her a

---

* It seems likely that he was Captain Valentine Pyne, who later became Master Gunner of England. Pyne served as a volunteer with Rupert for fifteen years and is known to have collected material for a Life of the Prince.

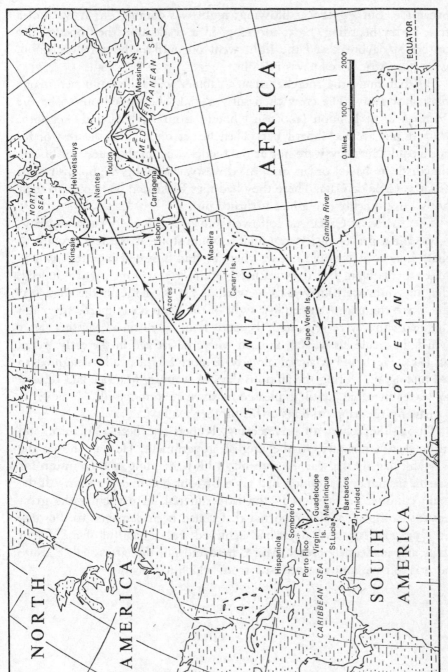

Prince Rupert's voyage, 1650–1653

broadside. But a gale was blowing; night was coming on; it was not a time to try boarding. Next morning, in a dead calm, they opened fire on her at daybreak and the fight went on until an hour before noon, when the African coast was in sight.

By that time, the merchantman's captain was killed and her main-mast shot away. The crew then surrendered. She turned out to be the *Marmaduke* of London (400 tons) bound from Archangel to Leghorn. Rupert put a crew aboard her. Then he set off to find the rest of his command. But they were not at the rendezvous. In the quest for booty, they had disobeyed orders and sailed westwards along the Spanish coast as far as Cape de Gata. There they had met Blake and had taken to their heels – not quickly enough as it turned out.

The disaster at Cartagena followed, but of this Rupert knew nothing, so he left a packet of letters under a white stone at the rendezvous, so that his associates would know where to find him. His intention was to make for Toulon. But the weather grew worse, so much worse indeed, that the ships were driven to leeward as far as Sicily. In the high seas that were running, Maurice lost sight of the lamp on Rupert's stern and the two ships were separated. Rupert went to re-fit at Messina, after which, he made his way to Toulon where he arrived in the early weeks of 1651. He found Maurice already in port and tearfully delighted to see him again. During the anxious days of waiting, Maurice had refused to leave his cabin 'until it pleased Heaven to remove all obstacles of sorrow by the happy tidings of his brother's safety'.

Throughout a year of privateering, Rupert had been a nuisance, and more than a nuisance, to the English government. He had shown the Royalist flag on the seas. As a result of his marauding, the premium for marine insurance in London had risen by four hundred per cent. All the main commercial interests in the land suffered, in particular the great Levant Company which reported that it had been damaged to the tune of £300,000. All this Rupert had achieved with a handful of indifferent ships and inadequate crews. More, he could not do; above all, because he was still without a secure base from which to operate.

The Design of this Grand Pirate

'Seamen are the forlorn hope of the world that bid defiance to terror and
are always posted within shot of the grave.'

Daniel Defoe

Rupert and his companions were in an unhappy plight. Most of his
ships had been lost by cowardice or treachery at Cartagena. The morale
of his officers was low, the material strength of his fleet far below that
of any Parliament force he was likely to meet. Rupert did what he
could to make up for his deficiencies, acquiring ships by one means or
another. He did so at a time when the political situation in France was
difficult. When Maurice arrived in Toulon, he had found himself involved
in a major political crisis, the uprising known as the Fronde of the
Princes. The town was on the side of the Prince de Condé; the flagship
of the French Navy was in the roads and was for the King. The captain
of this vessel warned Maurice that he might be attacked. The situation
continued to be difficult up to the day of Rupert's arrival and the two
brothers, 'who after so long time of hardship endured through the
malice of enemies, the raging of wind and seas, now found themselves
locked in each other's arms'. Now, they also found themselves faced
with complex commercial and political decisions. After considerable
haggling, the prizes they had taken were sold to Leghorn merchants.
Moreover, Rupert sent a gentleman to the Duc de Vendôme, Grand
Master of the Navigation of France, to obtain leave to refit and re-arm
his ships. Finally, he dealt with the question of the treachery which had
lost the battle at Cartagena to Blake. The case against one captain was
so strong that he fled. After that, the other captains involved in the
defeat were let off with a reproof. Rupert, who had at this juncture
only three ships and more seamen than he needed to man them, now
bought a ship which he named the *Honest Seaman*. Then, an English

Captain, named Craven, whose ship was at Marseilles, brought it to join the fleet. This ship was duly christened the *Loyal Subject*. In the first week of May, Rupert vanished from Toulon with five ships of his own and four Frenchmen, having spread a rumour that he was bound for the Greek islands, having made diligent enquiries, first, about the best way to get there. These enquiries were particularly energetic and indiscreet in quarters where the news of them would be carried to the English Parliament's spies. His hope was that the English admiral, Penn, who had taken over from Blake in the Mediterranean, would leave the Straits of Gibraltar open to him. Penn swallowed the bait. Rupert meant to slip out of the Mediterranean and try his luck in the West Indies, where he knew that Royalist sympathies were strong. He carried out his plan. By mid-June, he had reached Madeira, having captured a Spanish galleon bound from the Indies. Spain being friendly to the English Parliament at that time, Rupert ordered the Parliament flag to be run up. The Spanish officers, in their innocence, came aboard and were made prisoners. After that, the Spaniards were put ashore and Rupert sailed on to Madeira where he sold any of the galleon's cargo that he could not use. The Governor of the island entertained the officers, showed them the sights of Madeira and saluted their departure with a salvo of artillery.

At this point in the voyage, Rupert's council of war was rent by intrigue and disagreement. His flag-captain, Captain Fearnes, wanted to sail to the Caribbean by way of the Cape Verde Islands; most of the other officers were in favour of making for the Azores. Rupert would have preferred to take the Cape Verde route to the west, which would have given him a quicker crossing, but his flagship, the *Constant Reformation*, was leaking badly, so that he thought it wiser to make for the Azores, which were nearer. Meanwhile, the Council of State in London was alarmed at his disappearance and an urgent message to the generals-at-sea was sent. The Council had heard a report that Rupert was on his way to Newfoundland to disturb the fishing. It was quite a likely story, but it was not the case. Penn scoured the Mediterranean for him until, towards the end of September, he was told by a Lubeck vessel that Rupert was at the Azores.

At those islands, after an agreeable ceremonious reception by the Governor, including a guard of honour, Rupert had the good fortune to fall in with a galleon which had been the consort of the galleon he had captured on the way to Madeira. This vessel was bound for San

Lucar; she surrendered to a boarding party. After this incident, Rupert arranged for victualling the fleet with English merchants on the nearest island, St Michael. Then luck ran against the Prince's ships. A furious north-easterly gale drove them from their anchorage and the leak in the *Constant Reformation* grew so bad that in the emergency 120 pieces of raw beef were packed into the hole. In vain. 'The water increased so fast that the ship lay at the mercy of the sea.' In the storm, the ship's pinnace broke her tow rope and was lost. To make matters worse, a rebellious spirit appeared among some of the ship's company. 'So high was their insolence, that they infested [Rupert's] very domestics and so public was their improvidence that they concealed not their intentions in their cups, making private meetings in their cabins.' In this incipient mutiny, Rupert behaved with his customary resolution. He ordered some of the cabins to be pulled down; no meetings were allowed after the watch was set and no candle was to be lit between decks except when it was needed for the ship's use. Meanwhile, in the worsening weather, cannon were fired periodically to let the other ships know to keep near.

The chaplain, Watts, gave communion to any who would receive it. Rupert signalled Maurice to sail as close as possible to the ship's stern so that he could pass on to him all he ought to know as commander-in-chief. Maurice wanted to rescue his brother or die with him, but his officers refused to bring him alongside Rupert's ship. At this moment, the crew of the *Constant Reformation* showed themselves worthy of their admiral. They told the Prince to save himself in a little four-oared yawl on the deck. He refused, with thanks. Then they lowered out the boat and by main force put him in it. By this means, with luck, he would be able to reach the flagship's consort, the ship he had bought in Toulon with the last of the prize-money and had renamed the *Honest Seaman*. He took his page and seven others with him. The yawl made the dangerous crossing from ship to ship without mishap. Meanwhile, the crew of the *Constant Reformation* tried to keep their ship afloat by cutting away her main and mizzen masts and by throwing overboard the anchors and some of the cannon. It was not enough. Under Rupert's command, the *Honest Seaman* was brought close to the *Constant Reformation*'s poop ladder so as to enable the captain and four others to be saved. However, the third vessel, the *Swallow*, made no attempt to join in the work of rescue. Chester, her captain, walked his deck nonchalantly. 'Gentlemen,' he said, 'it is a great mischance. Who can help it?' By this time, the flagship's last pump was out of action. That night, about nine o'clock, two fire pikes were seen burning on the flagship's deck. It was farewell. The *Constant Reformation* went down and 333 men with her. The two Palatine brothers beat back to Fayal in the Azores. There they found more bad news. Another ship of the fleet, the *Loyal Subject*, had been driven from her anchorage by the storm and was breaking up on a rock.

At Fayal, Rupert kept himself hidden in Maurice's cabin, so the Portuguese authorities should not know how great had been the disaster to the fleet. In spite of that precaution, however, there was some difficulty with the local governor. He objected when the English ships opened fire, by mistake, on a Portuguese merchantman. As a reprisal, he arrested English officers ashore on victualling business. Only when Rupert had come out of his hiding place and threatened to use force, were the captives released. After that, the Prince went off to look for prizes in the neighbourhood of the Canaries and, finding none, sought a lonely harbour on the African coast where he could careen his battered ships. In the interval, he made up his mind to have no further public discussion of his intentions. From now on, he would rule the fleet by decree. He had had enough of the 'Council of War'. He first sighted Africa at Cape Barbas from which he worked his way south along the coast to Cape Blanc. At length, he found a suitable harbour. While the work of repair was being done, Rupert led a hundred men on a march into the interior, hoping to get in touch with the inhabitants, Moslems, tawny in colour and wearing vests like Turks. They were apparently rebels who refused to pay tribute to the local potentate. On the approach of the English, they fled, leaving their sheep and goats behind them. Having failed to persuade these people to talk, Rupert shot one of their camels. The rider dismounted and mounted another, leaving a small boy behind who clasped the Prince's legs, mistaking him for his father. The English party then withdrew to the ships, followed by the 'Moors' who wanted their baby back. Rupert, for his part, wanted to trade with them. After a truce, matters took an ugly turn. One Englishman went too far inland and was killed. There was a running fight, followed by a retreat to the ships. At this juncture, Rupert obtained provisions from a small Dutch vessel which he engaged to take a cargo of prize goods, sugar and ginger, to France for the account of King Charles II. At the same time he sent letters to the King and Sir Edward Hyde, who was told to sell any of the prize goods which Rupert had left at Toulon if either the King or the Duke of York was short of money.

After that, he was soon on his way with three ships to the Cape Verde Islands, 500 miles further south. At the island of Bonavista he found an abundance of good water, which was a commodity he badly needed. The local people were mulattoes, speaking Portuguese and living on goat flesh; they were clad in goat skins. While the crews were filling the ships' casks, Rupert went hunting goats. Eventually, he bought 1,000 dried goat carcasses to feed his crews. For Rupert, the West African coast had a powerful appeal. He remembered how one English trading voyage to Guinea in 1636 had brought back £30,000 worth of gold. So when the Portuguese governor of Cape Verde Islands proposed that they should make a joint expedition to the Gambia River to seize four ships which he had reason to believe were lurking there, Rupert fell in with the scheme. Fascinating accounts reached him of the wonders that were to be found in the river. Unicorns were there in abundance. No animal would drink until the unicorn had dipped a horn in the stream. Even more interesting to the impoverished adventurer was the news of 'a firm rock of gold of a great bigness'. As he made his way up the river for 150 miles, Rupert attacked various ships which he regarded as lawful prize. He was shocked, however, when the Africans slaughtered the crew of an English ketch, evidently hoping by this means to show their pleasure in his coming. 'His Highness, abhorring to countenance the shedding of Christian blood, signified his displeasure thereof through the Portuguese living among them.' He continued up-river, as far as Elephant Island, 150 miles from the sea. Here, Rupert was visited by the local king's son and brother, for whom he put out chairs. As a royal personage himself, alive to the problems of protocol, he was interested to find that they would not sit down, that being the privilege of their king alone. He observed, too, that the people had severe moral standards. For example, anyone who told a lie which damaged the community was sold as a slave to the first Christian trader who came alone. For a Moslem the punishment was, indeed, heavy. The Englishmen were impressed by the obsequious behaviour of the common people to their superiors. After a good deal of barter, the fleet had taken on board a great deal of ivory, wax, hides and ambergris. But now the tornado season was at hand. It was time to take their frail and leaky vessels out of such dangerous waters. Before leaving, Maurice changed his ship, deciding that the biggest of the prizes was a faster sailer. He renamed her the *Defiance*. As a result of his captures, Rupert, who had arrived in the river with three ships, left it with six ships and a ketch.

Farther along the coast, in the course of some confused trading with the local people, two of the crew were kidnapped. Rupert regarded himself as responsible for the lives of the two men, one of whom was an officer named Captain Holmes, who had fought beside him in the Civil War and in Flanders. This incident followed the kidnapping of a crew member who was a native of these parts and who had turned Christian; he had gone ashore to visit his parents on a promise that he would be allowed to return. The promise had not been kept. First of all, Rupert tried diplomacy to secure the return of the pair, using the services of an African interpreter known to the English as Captain Jacus. When after a day had elapsed, there was no result, Rupert manned the ships' pinnaces; from one of them he was able to speak to Jacus by word of mouth. He proposed to exchange a canoeful of Africans whom he had captured for the two Englishmen. Jacus believed at first that his people had accepted the arrangement and that they would carry it out. When he found that in this he was mistaken, he shouted to Rupert to re-capture the canoe. The outcome was a battle in the water immediately offshore. The Africans, assembled in large numbers on the beach, fought with determination. They waded into the sea up to their necks and ducked under water when the Europeans fired. Then they emerged and launched a volley of arrows, one of which hit Rupert in the chest. At once, he called for a knife and cut the missile out. In the end, Captain Jacus was able to accompany the two English prisoners to a distant beach and arrange for their rescue by one of the pinnaces: 'which act, being both an example of gratitude and fidelity, may teach us that heathen are not void of moral honesty'. Rupert offered to put Captain Jacus ashore at a part of the coast some distance away from the incident, but the African declined. He said he had done nothing to be afraid of.

And now it was time for the English to leave the coast. On the way back to the Cape Verde Islands, battling against strong headwinds, the Royalist flotilla took two English boats and lost two ships, one of them was the prize vessel, *Marmaduke*. On this vessel, there was a successful mutiny; the ship's master was overpowered by his crew and carried off to England. On arriving at St Iago, in the islands, Rupert and Maurice gave the governor, as his share of the proceeds of the Gambia expedition, eight or nine hundred hides. Early in May, they set sail with six ships from the Cape Verde Islands for the Caribbean Islands, intending to call first at Barbados. But when they were about fifty leagues east of the island they sighted a ship to the southward and gave chase. At this point, the flagship sprang a great leak, the pumps would not draw and they were compelled to give up the pursuit. They altered course, steering for St Lucia where they meant to stop the leak. By this time the crew were exhausted with baling. What was more, in the confusion they had passed Barbados without seeing it. At sunset they sighted Grenada and St Vincent to the westward and stood for St Lucia, where they dropped anchor and stopped the leak with sailcloth. As it turned out, it was as well that they had not gone to Barbados, for already the colony had been secured for the Commonwealth by the arrival of a fleet from England. Thus, the whole purpose of Rupert's Caribbean voyage had been chimerical. He had arrived too late to find friends in the Antilles. The ships now sailed north to Martinique where the governor gave Rupert a cordial welcome and told him the sad news that all the English islands in the Caribbean were now under Parliamentary control. The control was not, however, very firm. About Barbados, Governor Searle was reporting to London at this time that he was far from being confident about the loyalty of his people, some of whom, he said, had wanted to make the island a free state. Searle went on to speak of Rupert, whose presence in the neighbourhood plainly alarmed him. 'What the design of this grand pirate is we cannot imagine.' Rupert, in fact, was continuing his cruise along the chain of the Lesser Antilles, taking prizes where he could find them and trading with the local people – beads, looking-glasses, hatchets and gin for tortoiseshells, fine cotton yarn and green stones reputed to have many remarkable virtues, such as curing the falling sickness and easing labour pains. At Dominica they bought fruit from the islanders who, to protect themselves from mosquito bites, anointed their skin with red paint. The French reported that these people worshipped the devil who talked to them through a wooden image. And so, in due course, Rupert passed by way of Guadeloupe to Montserrat where he arrived on Whit Sunday 1652, passing on at once to Nevis where the shipping in the roads scattered in alarm at his arrival. He took two prizes after which he steered for St Kitts, where the Parliament flag was displayed and the fort showed fight. By this time, Rupert was on his way to a refuge he had heard about in the Virgin Islands. When he arrived there, he put into a harbour which at that time was called Dixon's Hole and was later known as Cavaliers' Harbour.* It was a

* Search of charts, ancient and modern, of the Virgin Islands has failed to turn up a harbour with either of these names. Warburton in a footnote in his *Memoirs of Correspondence of Prince Rupert and the Cavaliers* (vol. III, p. 378) says that this harbour is 'now called

spacious haven, with beautiful translucent water and an entrance so narrow that an incoming captain was advised to keep well to the port side where there were twelve fathoms of water. Carpenters were sent ashore to cut timber; some of them took the chance to seize a pinnace and make off to the Spanish island of Porto Rico. They were 'new men' recruited from one of the captured ships. After fortifying the bay, Rupert spent two months putting his fleet into a more manageable state. Three ships were burned and four were repaired. At the end of August, he sailed northwards with his quartet of vessels and then, when he was within twelve leagues of Anguilla to the south, he ran into disaster.

A hurricane blowing from the north struck the flotilla on 13 September, when the ships were seventy miles from Sombrero. Rupert was in the *Swallow* and, so bad was the weather, was unable to see more than a cable's length ahead. All sails were taken in except the main course which the storm in its fury tore from the yard. After that, the mizzen sail was blown away and the *Swallow* was helpless before the hurricane. At midnight, in thick fog, they were within half a league of Sombrero, as they reckoned, and feared that the end was near. But they were spared 'by the compassion of Divine Providence' from being driven on the rocks. They passed between Sombrero and Anguilita, 'where never ships were known to sail before'. When dawn came, the men watching from the *Swallow* could see no sign of the other ships. They tried to set the sprit sail to bring the ship's head about so that they could find some land before night fell. But the wind blew the sail out of its bolt-holes. At three o'clock in the morning, they were hard upon a ledge of rock ten leagues long between the Anagadas and the Virgin Islands, on which they would certainly have perished. Then, miraculously as it seemed, 'within half a league of our ruin, the wind veered two points to the east', so that they were able to weather the rocks and reach an anchorage in the Virgin Islands. They dropped anchor in a sound where the water was twelve fathoms deep.

By next morning, the hurricane had blown itself out and the *Swallow*, battered and stripped of sails, made her way back to Dixon's Hole, where

Rupert's Bay'. There is a bay of this name on the west side of Dominica which is favourably mentioned in a manuscript survey by Barth. Candler of HMS *Winchelsea* for the Admiralty in 1717–1719, with a river: 'good water and wood everywhere. Let not anybody anchor in the South part of the Bay . . . you can't land there for the sea runs high on the shores.' The likeliest candidate for Rupert's place of refuge is the landlocked St Thomas' Harbour in the Virgin Islands where there is a headland known as Rupert's Rock and there are two beaches noted in early charts as suitable for careening. (Current Admiralty Chart 2183.)

she spent three days refitting. Of the other three ships there was no sign. In one of them, the *Defiance*, Prince Maurice was sailing. But it was too soon – and the men in the *Swallow* were too busy – to think that the worst had befallen their comrades. In fact, one ship was safe. Unknown to Rupert, Captain Craven of the *Honest Seaman* had been driven ashore on the coast of Hispaniola, 400 miles to the west. There, he and his crew lived for a fortnight on turtles. When Rupert's ship, the *Swallow*, had been made ready for sea, she sailed first to Montserrat and then to Guadeloupe, seizing on her way a small New Englandman, and chasing a Spanish galleon which the *Swallow* sighted off Five Island Harbour. But the Spaniard proved too fast for the battered old *Swallow*, so they gave up the chase and made for Guadeloupe. The French opened their storehouses to the hungry English who, by that time, had been living for days on short rations. The Governor brought them interesting news. England – Cromwell's England – was now at war with Holland. The Dutch harbours in the West Indies would, therefore, be safe refuges for Rupert's ships. Immediately afterwards, a Dutch skipper sailed in with word that two English ships, from which he had received some bad treatment, were lying in Five Island Harbour, on Antigua, some miles farther north. No news could have been more welcome. Rupert sailed there at once, and found the ships lying under the protection of a heavy cannon mounted on shore. He landed fifty men under the command of Captain Holmes. They captured the gun, after which the two ships surrendered. A few days later, while lying in the roads at Guadeloupe, Rupert and his companions pounced on a homeward bound New Englandman and found her to be laden with provisions. These they carried off, 'like manna from heaven'.

Hearing from a passing French vessel that his brother, Maurice, was safe on the island of Tortuga, Rupert set off northwards once more, having at this point more prize vessels than he could find crews for. However, as it turned out, the report about Maurice was mistaken. The *Defiance* had vanished. The ship that had reached Tortuga was the *Honest Seaman*, which had lost most of her masts and sails in the hurricane. Her captain had the idea that he might find Rupert at Tortuga. Later, a strong wind blew the *Honest Seaman* on the rocks at Hispaniola where she broke up, without loss of life. Craven, her captain, eventually found his way to France. Rupert's manpower resources were now stretched to the uttermost. Failing to reach Tortuga, and finding that Nevis had been newly fortified, he fetched up at the Dutch island of St Eustatius, where he watered the ships. After that he headed northwards in the direction of Bermuda which, owing to fog, he was unable to sight. With the wind in the west, he sailed for the Azores where he was not allowed to go ashore. After that, through foul weather, he set his course for the Breton coast. Portugal had made its peace with the Commonwealth; he would go to France. He steered for Nantes. Rupert was ready to exchange shots with any likely prey but although he was ready to fight until he had reached the last stage in his voyage and he was off Finistère, he did not have the luck to take one.

One evening before darkness set in, he sighted Belle Isle off the Breton coast and tacked to avoid the rocks near the island. The following day, the ships entered the estuary of the Loire where, on 4 March 1653, Rupert dropped anchor at St Nazaire. 'Thus, having overcome all misfortune,' writes the diarist of the expedition, 'the Prince ended his voyage.' And what a voyage it had been, from Ireland to within a few degrees of the Equator, from Sicily to the Caribbean islands! Just over four years had passed (1502 days to be exact) since he had left Helvoetsluys with the modest intention of making sure of Guernsey for the King. He had been at sea for a year longer than Drake had needed to sail round the world although it may be admitted that, if the perils were as great, the proceeds of the expedition were not so rich. During those four years, Rupert had sailed 15,000 miles, had taken thirty-one prizes and lost twelve ships by enemy action, weather or mutiny. For Rupert, however, the most grievous stroke of fate was the loss of his brother, Maurice, his shadow in war, on land and sea, the nearest to his heart of all his family and, probably, in all the world.

The hurricane that had scattered the flotilla near the rock of Sombrero had engulfed *Defiance* and Maurice with her. 'In this fatal wreck,' says the diarist, moved to a burst of grandiloquence, 'besides a great many brave gentlemen and others, the sea to glut itself, swallowed the Prince Maurice, whose fame the mouth of detraction cannot blast, his very enemies bewailing his loss. Many had more power, few more merit: he was snatched from us in obscurity, lest beholding his loss would have prevented some from endeavouring their own safety; so much he lived beloved, and died bewailed.'

Years later, Rupert was still disturbed by rumours that his brother had been seen alive – for instance, as a slave in Algiers. On another occasion, it was reported that he had escaped from the wreck of his ship and was held a prisoner in the castle of Il Morro at Puerto Rico. On the first report,

166

his mother begged the French ambassador at The Hague to write to the Grand Turk and ordered Rupert, who was staying then at Heidelberg with his brother, the Elector, to go to Constantinople and arrange for Maurice's release. The Elector, who was sceptical about the story, thought that Marseilles was the right place to begin enquiries. It turned out, however, that the rumour was without foundation. It was only one of many tales of its kind. Ten years after the voyage to the Caribbean, Rupert was in England once more. Once more he sent out a ship to look for Maurice. All was in vain. The most convincing evidence of Maurice's death was provided twelve years afterwards when Captain Holmes fell in with a Spanish ship bound for Puerto Rico with a new Governor for the island aboard her. Holmes was assured by the Spaniards that nobody was kept prisoner at San Juan, Puerto Rico, and nobody was known to have been rescued from the *Defiance* but 'about that very time upon the southward side of the Island they found a ship cast away and several pieces of the wreck came ashore; among the rest was a golden lion which some of them saw and a great quantity of pipe staves marked MP. This was the mark that all Prince Maurice's casks had borne. This,' said Holmes, in conclusion, 'confirmed me that he was lost thereabouts.'

At St Nazaire, Rupert sold the *Swallow* and her fifty-four guns to Cardinal Mazarin. The prize vessels found the same buyer, and their cargoes were put up to auction at Nantes.

For three weeks after landing in France, Rupert lay seriously and even dangerously ill. It may be that he had picked up an infection of the kind that lies in wait for the unwary sailor visiting strange ports or, possibly, that his iron frame and gigantic strength were worn out by the hardships of that extraordinary voyage. Charles II sent his own surgeon, Choqueux, to look after him as well as a letter breathing solicitude. When he recovered, the King of France sent a coach and escort to bring him to Paris. He travelled in some state, as a prince should, accompanied by a retinue of devoted African servants wearing rich liveries, trimmed with gold lace. In addition, he brought with him a collection of brilliant tropical birds, evidence that all his time at sea had not been spent in taking prizes. Finally, he had acquired a reputation for having some insight into the secrets of Caribbean witchcraft. For a short time, Rupert was the talk of Paris.

One legal question relating to his voyage had become a matter of controversy in England. Were his naval operations to be regarded as acts of war, or were they piratical? To Rupert, the matter might be of small concern for he was sailing with King Charles' commission. But the question was debated by lawyers in England when it was raised by the owners of the *Marmaduke*, which had been captured by Rupert on her way to Archangel and, then, had been snatched from him by a mutiny of the crew. The owners asked the Commissioners of the Admiralty for compensation and for the return of their ship which, after the crew's abandonment of Rupert, had been retained in state service. The Admiralty Court ordained that, if Rupert was to be regarded as a pirate, then the owners were entitled to the return of their ship; if he was an enemy, then the *Marmaduke* belonged to the state, subject to the fact that the owners were entitled to compensation as the ship had been re-taken from Rupert without any hazard to the state. The matter went for decision to the Council of State, which declared that Rupert had been acting as an enemy and not as a pirate, and decided that the owners were entitled to £902 in compensation (a quarter of what they were asking), but that none of the money was to go to a certain member of the syndicate of owners, on the ground that he was a 'malignant', i.e. a Royalist. And so, it may be said, the most romantic naval adventure of the Civil War ended, as such adventures often do, in a wrangle among the lawyers.

Rupert, who had always been a dark-complexioned man, came back from his cruise blackened by the tropical sun and the Atlantic winds. It was not the only change in him. He had been a fierce, impulsive young man with an ungovernable temper. Now he was no longer a young man; his health was shaken, the head-wound he had got in Flanders troubled him at times. He was sardonic and rather melancholy.

The war was over, the war which had been for him an adventure more glorious than any young man could have hoped for, and in which he had won an enormous, if chequered, reputation. The men who had been his comrades were dead, in prison, living in poverty in some European town, serving some foreign prince, scattered by the winds of ill-fortune. Newcastle, who had deserted the cause after the disaster at Marston Moor, where he had behaved gallantly, was living in exile. It was said that he was in reduced circumstances, but this could be exaggerated; his children, who had made good marriages in England, sent him money. He was still able to own and train fine horses.* His wife calculated later on that he had lost £200,000 as a result of his devotion to the royal cause;

* Also, to write a manual which is still found useful, *La Méthode et Invention Nouvelle de dresser les Chevaux*, published in Antwerp, 1657.

some of it lost for ever, but not all; the pictures and the furniture might be dispersed among the sharper-eyed and more worldly of the victors, but the woods would grow again and, one day the rents would flow into the rightful coffers. Meanwhile the Marquis would depend on his brother and his children, while his equestrian feats amazed all the foreign observers to whom he gave exhibitions. Lord Eythin, that canny Scot who also had failed to stay to the end at Marston Moor, was hanging about the court of Charles II. The roll of victims of Parliamentary execution squads included Derby, whose wife had held out at Lathom House so long and who had crossed England with Rupert and fought at Marston Moor; Sir Charles Lucas, who had led a cavalry brigade on the left wing at Naseby, had been shot by a firing party at Colchester; and Sir George Lisle, who had met the same fate on the same day. Digby was in French service until he intrigued once too often against Mazarin – and found it prudent to cross the Pyrenees into Spain. Rupert's old enemies, Wilmot and Goring, were in exile, one in France, the other in Spain. And there was Montrose, whose last letter to Rupert had arrived at Lisbon while the Prince was held there with his ships and who, a few months later, had been barbarously executed at Edinburgh. One by one, the leaders of the King's party, Rupert's comrades in the lost war, had died or were refugees living in poverty abroad. Was everything changed then? Not quite. Rupert's old friend, Will Legge, who had championed him against Digby, and had prevented him from behaving badly to the King after the fall of Bristol – Will Legge, as usual, was in prison.

And where most things were changed, one remained the same. The new King Charles needed money. It was more disconcerting that he expected Rupert to provide it. There arose, accordingly, a dispute between the cousins, after Rupert's vessels dropped anchor in the Loire. Charles was dissatisfied with the share that Rupert proposed to allot to him from the sale of the ships, cannon and prize cargoes at Nantes. He was not a little irritated by Rupert's insistence on paying the debts he had incurred all those months ago when he was fitting out the ships at Toulon. Nor was the monarch any more pleased with Rupert's punctilio, unbecoming in a Prince of the Blood, in giving the pay that was due to the ratings priority over the King's clamant needs for ready cash. The business at Nantes was hard enough to wind up without these royal complications. When Rupert recovered from his grave illness, he left Captain Holmes to manage the problems of disposal. It was no easy task. The unpaid crews were on the verge of a mutinous outbreak. One of the captains had, it seemed, neglected to keep accounts during the voyage or, if he had kept them, was not prepared to produce them for inspection. Holmes had also to reckon with his absent chief, Rupert, who from Paris, sent a stream of demands: Would Holmes send the elephant's tusks; a bag of sugar; a little African boy of five who had attached himself to the fleet at Cape Bravo on the Guinea Coast? And so on. Eventually Holmes managed to finish the task and rode to join his exacting admiral in Paris. There he found Rupert in the midst of a vivid social life. The French court admired him; Mazarin, the all-powerful Minister, styled him 'one of the best and most generous princes I have ever known'. The Palais Royal, with all its enticements, was open to him. And he had the companionship of his rich and fashionable young brother, Prince Edward.

Rupert was at that time idle and famous, a man of thirty-two of striking physique, handsome in a severe way, a great dandy. And naturally there came perfumed letters from ladies who did not sign their names, and the consequences that sometimes follow such letters. Rupert was riding home from hunting one Sunday with Holmes, who had taken the fort at Nevis, and had sold the ships at Nantes. In the Cours la Reine, near the Louvre, two riders passed them who seemed in such a hurry to pass that Rupert pulled his horse aside. When they had passed, however, they turned and fired their pistols at the prince. They missed. After that, Rupert drew his own pistols and fired twice, killing one man and mortally wounding the other. His legendary skill as a marksman had not deserted him.

After that, a third rider, who was apparently the master of the other two, rode up, furious, and announced that he was the Comte de Mongiron. 'I don't believe you,' said Rupert, 'but as you say you are, I won't meddle with you.'

But all was not frivolity for the returned Ulysses. The dispute went on with King Charles over the division of the spoils Rupert had brought to Nantes. Not only did Charles demand all the prize-money but, in addition, he wanted half the value of the cannon in the *Swallow*. Edward Hyde carried on the controversy on the King's side. It complicated the political disputes in which Rupert found himself embroiled soon after his arrival in Paris. At that time the English Royalist exiles were divided into two factions. The Queen-Mother's party, to which Lord Jermyn and the Lord Keeper, Sir Edward Herbert, belonged, hoped to regain England with the aid of the Presbyterians. The King put his faith in the English Cavaliers who had lately banded themselves together in a secret society known as the Sealed Knot. These conspirators were planning an insurrection. Rupert, for once, sided with the Queen's party. In the spring of 1654, the Queen proposed that he should go to Scotland along with the Duke of York who was believed to be of tougher fibre than the King, a mistake which Charles' frivolous behaviour encouraged. However, nothing came of this Scottish project.

Meanwhile, Rupert's dispute about the proceeds of the sale of the ships at Nantes dragged on. Then, in the early weeks of 1654, Mazarin intervened on King Charles' side, realising that the sooner the King got his money, the sooner he would leave France and the Cardinal could then make his peace with Cromwell. At that time (1654), Rupert was caught up in the intrigues by which Queen Henrietta Maria was trying to destroy the influence of Sir Edward Hyde over her son, King Charles. Rupert was sought as an ally by the Queen's party but he would not lend himself to charges against Hyde in which he did not believe. Hyde was, he knew, an honourable man. Rupert was, therefore, not a reliable accomplice for the Queen. Eventually the intrigue against Hyde collapsed, as also did the scheme to invade Scotland. As the Queen and Rupert had been in agreement in thinking that the proposed expedition should be led by the Duke of York and not by the King, by the time the enterprise was abandoned the King was annoyed with his mother, his brother, the Duke, and his cousin, Rupert. It was soon after this that Rupert and Charles left France separately for Germany and Rupert went on to Vienna where he was involved in different attempts to find himself a suitable military command. The Emperor acknowledged that he owed the Prince 30,000 rix dollars, although he seems to have shown no haste to discharge the obligation. Nor was a command in the Imperial forces immediately forthcoming. In these circumstances, Rupert undertook to raise troops for the Duke of Modena, a scheme which had the support of Cardinal Mazarin. The Cardinal promised that France would put 2,000 of her best soldiers under Rupert's command, plus 1,000 Swiss and three other regiments. A difficulty arose at this point because Rupert was owed arrears of pay for his service in the French army seven years before, and there is no kind of debt a government is more reluctant to discharge than soldiers' pay for a campaign that is over. But the Palatines were not without influence in France. Rupert's sister-in-law, Prince Edward's wife, Anne de Gonzague, who was one of the ablest and most powerful intriguers at the French court, obtained a promise that the back pay would be provided at once. Rupert offered Lord Gerard the post of lieutenant-general in the force for Modena, while Lord Craven was to be general of the ordnance. At this moment, however, there was a change in the political scene. The French insisted that the leadership of the troops for Modena should go to an officer in their service, Count Broglio.* King Charles, probably under French influence, persuaded the Prince to drop all his engagements in order to serve Charles alone. To this Rupert agreed, provided he could make an honourable accommodation with Modena. In the meantime, he obtained a regiment in the Austrian army. About this time he was apparently aware of a Royalist plot to assassinate Cromwell, at least to the point where he brought the instigator into King Charles' presence. It need not be said that in the Palatine family scarcely any fate could be too bad for the man they regarded as a murderer. As Elizabeth of Bohemia had said, 'Cromwell is the Beast in the Revelations that Kings and nations do worship. I wish him the like end and speedily.' How active Rupert was in the business is not clear. All that can be said is that his surgeon, Choqueux, who was also King Charles', was embroiled in it, and that there is some evidence that Rupert was going on with it after King Charles had cooled off. The conspiracy was detected by the excellent Commonwealth secret service and those who were most closely involved in it were laid by the heels and executed. At this time, an undercover war was going on between Cromwell's agents on the Continent and Charles II's security service. One traitor in the King's camp, Colonel Bamfylde, was given by Cromwell the task of watching the Prince's movements and reporting on them to London. However, he was spotted. He had the imprudence to visit Germany on the pretext that he was looking for military service in that country and, in a wood near Cologne, he was killed. 'I have obeyed to the utmost your commands about Colonel Bamfylde,' reported Rupert to the King.

* François-Marie de Broglio, a Savoyard officer, naturalised French in 1654, had done Mazarin some service during the Fronde. He commanded the Army of Lombardy under the authority of the Duke of Modena and was killed in an ambush in 1656.

Family Business

'Although I have cause enough to be sad, yet I am still of my wild humour
to be as merry as I can.'

Elizabeth, Queen of Bohemia

While Rupert was still at sea, his brother, Charles Louis, the Elector,
had been restored to half of the former glory of the Palatine house. By
the Peace of Westphalia, concluded about the time Charles I was
executed, Charles Louis was given back the Lower Palatinate while the
Duke of Bavaria kept the Upper Palatinate. An eighth Electorship was
created for Charles Louis, and he was given the dignity of Arch-Treasurer
of the Empire. It sounded well enough but it was something of a come-
down for the former first Elector of the Empire. Instead of sitting on
the Emperor's right hand at the Imperial Diet, he was banished to the
foot of the table. However, it was better than exile and dependence on
others. His mother was not so fortunate. Since her brother's death on
the scaffold at Whitehall, she had received no money from the English
government. The Elector, too, was notably stingy about the remittances
he sent her; in particular, he refused to hand over her dower house at
Frankenthal. It was a poor return for all the affection she had given him.
Meanwhile, the long-suffering tradesmen of The Hague pressed harder
than ever for the money she owed them. It was a difficult life for a woman
with a hereditary talent for extravagance. In the circumstances, the
Queen kept remarkably cheerful and the faithful Lord Craven, although
he was no longer as rich as once he had been, did what he could to help.
His heart still beat true. The Queen, however, had family troubles in
addition to the perpetual worry about money. Of some of them Rupert
was already aware while the Civil War was still raging.

Thus, in the month of May 1645, not long before the fight at Naseby,
he had received a letter from Paris, which contained an item of family

news. His younger brother, Edward, who had just come of age and had been spending his time studying at Paris, not too energetically, had married Anne de Gonzague, daughter of the Duc de Nevers. The girl was thought to be beautiful and was certainly very rich, reputedly with an income of £7,000 a year. Her sister, Marie, was the Queen of Poland, after a spectacular career which had cost one of her lovers, Cinq Mars, his life. On the other hand, Anne was a Catholic and, apparently, on marrying her, Prince Edward had, without too heavy a strain on his conscience, adopted his new wife's religion. This was a bitter pill for a dedicated Protestant like Elizabeth, Queen of Bohemia, to swallow.

However, the religious and financial considerations were not the only matters that had to be taken into account. Anne de Gonzague claimed that she had been secretly married one day in 1638 to Henri de Lorraine who later, and unexpectedly, became the Duc de Guise. Lorraine had even obtained a dispensation from the Pope to enable the marriage to take place, for the two were within the forbidden degrees of consanguinity. When Henri became a duke, however, his views about marriage underwent a sudden change, and in 1641 Anne learnt that Guise had married the young widow of Comte de Bossu. Anne continued to call herself Duchesse de Guise and, in the meantime, put her claim before the ecclesiastical courts. She lost her case, however, owing to certain alleged technical defects in her marriage to Guise. Looking around, as a young woman might who had been shamefully treated, she found what she wanted – a student at M. de Benjamin's Royal Academy in Paris, Prince Edward, a Bavarian duke, a prince, impoverished, eight years younger than herself, and although handsome, of notably weak character. He was just the husband for a determined young woman like Anne. The two were married secretly and then, openly, in St Sulpice. Anne de Gonzague, generally known as La Palatine, became a leading actress in the feverish politics of the Fronde. She was an intriguer able to cross swords with Mazarin himself.

As for Prince Edward, he looked on the situation with an unruffled composure; he became a naturalised Frenchman; he drove about from one social event to another in a splendid carriage; his position might not be glorious, but it was undeniably comfortable. In due course, his mother reconciled herself to the marriage.

Edward was not, however, the only one of the Palatine brood that gave Elizabeth reason for worry. Among her horses, her dogs and her monkeys, with adoring old friends to amuse her, in her audience chamber, which was kept hung with black since the death of her husband, the Queen of Bohemia had always looked on her children with some measure of detachment. Unruly sons, undowered daughters – what could she be expected to do with them? All her hopes had been pinned on her eldest son, Charles Louis. Now, somewhat to her surprise, the wild boy of the family, Robert the Devil, had become a famous general and an heroic admiral. At this moment an event at once irritating, embarrassing and even shocking, ruffled the Queen's serenity. It happened a few days before Rupert landed at Calais. The news was that his brother, Prince Philip, had committed murder!

The circumstances were these: Jacques de l'Epinay, a Frenchman attached to the hunt of Gaston d'Orléans, brother of Louis XIII, known to the French court as Monsieur, had been expelled from France because he had supplanted his master with Louise Roger, daughter of a criminal lieutenant. Living in Holland, this enterprising young man was believed by the scandalmongers to have seduced Princess Louise, an accomplished and lively member of the Palatine family. Even worse, he had been heard to boast that he had enjoyed the favours of the Queen of Bohemia herself. This story was calculated to cause the greatest possible offence to all the Palatine family. The most indignant of them all was Princess Elizabeth, Rupert's eldest sister, the one who was fondest of him. She incited her brother, Philip (aged nineteen), against the traducer. Philip killed l'Epinay in a chance encounter in the street at The Hague one June evening in 1646. The crime was one which no royal privilege could cover, at least, not in Holland, especially as fifty Frenchmen had vowed, drinking wine mixed with blood, to be avenged on the murderer.

Accordingly, Philip fled to the frontier and, in due course, was reported to be raising a regiment in Hamburg for the Venetian service. The Queen was furious at the scandal, especially over the behaviour of her daughter, Elizabeth, in provoking it. But from her family she received no comfort. They were all firmly on the side of Philip's act in vindicating the Palatine honour.

When the Elector, Charles Louis, won back his castle at Heidelberg, his three sisters, Elizabeth, the intellectual of the family, Louise, and Sophie, the youngest and most satirical of the girls, left The Hague to live with their brother. Prince Philip was nominated chairman of the Regency Council which ruled the Lower Palatinate until the Elector himself returned. The fourth Palatine daughter, a delicate blonde girl, named Henrietta Maria, had, in the meantime, found a husband in

Sigismund Rakoksky, brother of the Prince of Transylvania. Considering her Protestantism, it was an excellent match. But, unhappily, the princess, frailer than most of the Queen's brood, died five months later.

Matters moved swiftly for the Palatines during Rupert's absence at sea.

About his brothers, the news that greeted him on his homecoming was varied. Philip, killer of M. de l'Epinay, had been killed in the battle of Rethel (1650), fighting in Turenne's army against the Spaniards. Edward had settled down as the husband of one of the most active political women in Paris. The Elector had matrimonial troubles. The youngest of the Palatine girls, Sophie, was the first of the family to discover that all was not well between the Elector and the wife he had married after his restoration to the Palatinate. When Sophie met her sister-in-law at Mannheim, she found her tall, with a good complexion and an exceptionally handsome bust. Her manner, however, was haughty and reserved until a chance remark of Sophie's opened a flood of bitter resentment. Sophie had chanced to say something in praise of the carriage in which at that moment they were bowling along to Heidelberg. Sophie quickly realised that she had chosen the wrong object for her praise. A torrent of words showed that the Electress considered the vehicle was vastly less luxurious than the one possessed by her married sister. After church, next morning, the new Electress, who had been Princess Charlotte of Hesse-Cassell, told Sophie that she had been forced by her mother to marry a 'jealous old man' although any number of eligible dukes and counts had been eager to obtain her hand. Her behaviour to her husband made it quite clear that the Electress was disappointed in her marriage. But it appeared that, at that time, the Elector was sufficiently in love with his wife to take a tolerant view of her fits of temper. However, matters went rapidly from bad to worse. There were stories of unpleasant scenes at the Electoral court – a dish thrown across the dinner table by the Electress, an ear boxed by the Elector. The Queen of Bohemia heard the news with sorrow and remembered that 'the dear late King' had always prayed to be delivered from the House of Hesse.

However, when it was clear that the Elector had fallen in love with Luise von Degenfeld, one of his wife's maids of honour, and that he might even make her his morganatic wife, the Queen's inherent puritanism asserted itself. 'If everybody could quit their husbands and wives because of their ill humours,' she wrote to Charles Louis, 'there would be no small disorder in the world. It is against both God's law and man's law, for though you be a sovereign, yet God is above you.' It was just at this time that Rupert arrived at Heidelberg, hoping to obtain a respectable appanage. He was attracted at once by the quiet, studious Luise, so much so that he wrote her a letter in which he complained of her coldness to him. This, by a mischance, fell into the hands of the Electress, Charlotte, who read it and thought that it was meant for her. She was all the more inclined to do so since she had formed a warm admiration for her brother-in-law. She chided Rupert for his imprudent, although flattering letter, whereupon the Prince, profoundly embarrassed, blurted out the truth. The Electress was naturally upset by this muddle and, immediately, had a search made of Luise's room. There she found, in a casket, a packet of love-letters to Luise from her husband, the Elector. She flew at her supplanter and almost bit off Luise's little finger. After that, there could be no reconciliation between husband and wife. The Elector assembled a council of divines and lawyers who duly declared the marriage null and void owing to the wife's conduct. Charles Louis, thereafter, made a morganatic marriage with Luise to whom he gave the title of Raugrafin. Thereafter, she bore him fourteen children. In Paris, Prince Edward heard with stupefaction the news of the second marriage. Surely, he said, one wife was enough to annoy any man! Princess Elizabeth, on whom her mother laid the blame for the whole sordid business, made a great display of grief, 'taking vanity in her suffering, as usual', as the Queen uncharitably put it. She advised Charles Louis to ignore his sister but not on any account to send her to Holland: 'I will not have her with me for many reasons.'

For Rupert, the affair could not have come at a more inconvenient time. After negotiations with his brother, he had been granted a piece of land by the Elector and had given his old shipmate, Valentine Pyne, the task of measuring it. Pyne found that, in circumference, it was ten English miles and ninety paces. It was, in short, a substantial little property suitable to the dignity of a prince of the Empire. However, the business of transfer dragged on. The house needed repair. The paddock was enlarged to meet Rupert's wishes. And then came the scandalous revelations at Heidelberg. One brother writing a love letter to another brother's inamorata! A wife discovering her husband's infidelity because she was too fond of her brother-in-law! The Elector was, understandably, furious and withdrew his grant of an appanage to Rupert. He went to live in a house where there was no room for his brother. After a violent quarrel, Rupert found that the city gates of Heidelberg were closed to him by order of the Elector. He asked to see the order. There it was, written in his brother's own hand. Rupert took off his hat and swore that never again would he set foot in the Palatinate. He kept his promise.

The Queen of Bohemia thought that her daughter, Sophie, who was unmarried at the time, should, for the sake of her own reputation, leave Heidelberg without delay. There was a question of propriety involved. When Charles Louis protested to his mother that in his union with Luise he was only following the example of his illustrious ancestor, John of Gaunt, the Queen replied that the only stain on John of Gaunt's character was his association with 'a low woman. We should seek to follow our ancestors' virtues and not their vices.' She referred to Luise as 'that wench'.

The rift in the Palatinate family was not quickly healed. Years later, Sophie, although she treated the children of her brother's morganatic marriage kindly enough, was annoyed when one of the Raugrafin's daughters remarked that she was supposed to resemble the Queen of Bohemia. 'Good gracious, Annelise,' said Sophie, 'you must not flatter yourself that you resemble your grandmother. Not only had she quite a different countenance, but you have sandy hair, a broad face and high colour. The Queen of Bohemia had black hair,* a long oval face and a high nose.'

Rupert was not the only member of the Palatine family who was driven from Heidelberg by the unpleasant atmosphere that prevailed there. There was also Princess Elizabeth. She had grown up to be a grave and thoughtful young woman known in the family as 'La Grecque'. Having been rather angular in youth, she was now beginning to put on weight. And she had all the middle-aged spinster's aptness to interfere in the lives of her relatives. Elizabeth was considered 'the most learned woman in Europe', not only in the judgment of those who had no particular authority in the matter, but also in that of the most illustrious philosopher of the age, René Descartes. He dedicated his masterpiece, *The Principles of Philosophy*, to 'The Most Serene Princess Elizabeth'.

The friendship between the two had begun after Descartes had left France for Holland anxious lest his opinions brought down on him the condemnation of the Catholic Church.

In Elizabeth, the melancholy side of the Palatine temperament was

* But earlier, the Queen had been a blonde. Apparently, as her hair lost the gold of youth, she dyed it.

fully developed. The misfortunes of her family, her uncle's death, her brother Edward's desertion of the Protestant cause, all inclined her to pessimism. Life was a mystery to which she sought in vain for the key. How, she wondered, could one have free will and yet be attached to the decrees of Providence? How could the Divine Power be both infinite and limited? She put the questions to Descartes and was, not surprisingly, unconvinced by his answers. Other members of her family did not share her taste for the Cartesian dialectic. Her sister, Sophie, for example, dismissed the philosopher's writings as 'an excellent cure for insomnia'.

In 1649, the long correspondence between Elizabeth and her philosopher had reached something of a crisis. He was by that time a bachelor of fifty-three, immensely distinguished and very lonely. She was thirty – unmarried, with looks that were beginning to fade. At that moment, a princess more famous, powerful and demanding than Elizabeth, Christina, Queen of Sweden, invited Descartes to Stockholm so that they could discuss philosophical matters. It was a temptation which the philosopher could not be expected to resist. Descartes, however, assured Elizabeth that he would remain hers all his life. It might even be his good fortune, he suggested, to bring the two princesses together in a union of minds and souls and shared affection. However, as it turned out, what might have become a long, sad story, had a sad and early ending. One bitterly cold winter's morning, Queen Christina summoned Descartes to an audience. The great philosopher caught a chill and died.

At the end of 1657, another of Rupert's sisters caused some concern in the family. This time the subject of the scandal was Princess Louise, the last of the Queen of Bohemia's children to remain with her, and the last whom anybody would have suspected of a purpose of rebellion. She was pretty, good-natured and had a certain talent for painting, which like her sisters, she had cultivated under Gerard Honthorst, an artist who frequently visited the house at The Hague to paint that celebrated beauty, the Queen of Bohemia. One December morning, Louise vanished from her mother's house without taking any of her clothes or jewels with her. Nor was she accompanied by a maid of honour. She had, it seemed, gone out on foot. The house was at once in an uproar. The princess' room was searched and there a letter addressed to her mother was found which explained the mystery. Louise had become a convert to Catholicism and had fled so as to avoid the injury to her conscience involved in receiving the sacrament on Christmas Day according to the Protestant rite.

At once the Queen wrote to the Dutch States-General asking them to help her to find her daughter, after which their High Mightinesses sent orders to the governors of towns where the princess might be hiding, to arrest her and send her back to her mother. In the meantime, the Queen carried out a more thorough search of the princess' rooms and found two letters from Elizabeth, Princess of Hohenzollern. These made it clear that the flight of Princess Louise had been carefully planned. A boat would be waiting to take her to Bergen op Zoom, where the Princess of Hohenzollern lived, and from there to Antwerp where she would enter a Carmelite convent. The Queen was furious with the Hohenzollern princess whom she had regarded as a friend; she used her influence with the States-General to deprive the princess of the right to appoint the magistrates of Bergen op Zoom. The princess retorted with a volley of accusations against the reputation of Louise. She said that Louise's real reason for seeking the shelter of a convent was because she was about to have a child. And who was supposed to be the father of Louise's child? To those ready to believe the worst, the answer was not in doubt. Louise had been escorted from The Hague by a French officer, Captain La Roque, formerly of the Prince de Condé's Guards. It was remembered that, when Prince Philip had murdered M. de l'Epinay twelve years before, it had been widely believed that the victim was boasting of an amour with Princess Louise – and perhaps with her mother as well! Writing from Frankfort, Rupert added his plea to his mother's. He thanked the States-General for all that they had done for his family, and implored them to protect the Palatines against the slanders that were being cast on the family's good name. The States-General were willing enough to help but perplexed to know what to do.

The Elector, when appealed to by his mother, took a cooler view. Publicity would probably do more harm than good, he thought. It is possible that he did not entirely trust his sister, Louise. Gradually the wind of slander died down, Louise's servants denied that she was about to have a child. The Queen of Bohemia spoke contemptuously of her daughter's supposed lover, M. La Roque: 'He is no Adonis, for he is lean like a skeleton, and hath but one eye that is good, a red face and goes very weak upon his pasterns.' Of all the Palatines, Louise was the least affected by the turmoil. Before long, it was reported that she had taken the veil in a fashionable convent at Maubuisson outside Paris, of which, in due course, she became abbess. The event should not have come as a complete surprise to her family. Not long before, Louise had sought to enter an aristocratic Protestant order to which her sister, Elizabeth, had sent assurances that she possessed the requisite sixteen quarterings of nobility. However, the Lutherans rejected what the Catholics later accepted. At Maubuisson, Louise lived cheerfully until her death at the age of eighty-eight, ruling her little community of nuns and painting industriously. In due course, too, her mother forgave her, 'although you don't deserve it', but she had been asked to do so by the King and Queen-Mother of England and could not refuse.

By 1660, Elizabeth, Rupert's eldest sister, was living in Berlin as an impoverished dependent on the Elector of Brandenburg. Her future could hardly be regarded with much optimism. Just then, however, things took a turn for the better. Through the influence of the Brandenburg family, Elizabeth became abbess of the Lutheran nunnery of Herford, a richly endowed refuge for aristocratic Protestant spinsters which had retained, among other anomalous privileges from the days before the Reformation, the right to nominate a delegate to the Imperial Diet. Rupert heard the news with relief and pleasure. Elizabeth had always been the nearest to him of all his sisters. At the same time, the Elector Palatine received a letter from Elizabeth in which she hoped that now he need no longer be wearied by her company, he would stop being surly to her. The Elector replied coldly, as might have been expected. Sophie, the youngest of the family, remarked tartly that it was the first thing Elizabeth had ever succeeded in doing. She spoke of Elizabeth's abbatial rank as her 'canonisation'.

Sophie had, herself, made a marriage by this time which her mother did not think was good enough for a girl of her exalted station. Indeed, the Queen of Bohemia blamed her son, the Elector, head of the family, for consenting to it. The circumstances of the marriage were certainly bizarre enough to disturb a mother. Sophie had been, first of all, betrothed to Duke George William of Brunswick-Luneberg. But, at the last minute, the prospective bridegroom felt that the burdens of matrimony were more than he could endure. He backed out and sponsored Sophie's marriage to his brother, Duke Ernest Augustus. Most girls might have been put out by such behaviour, but Sophie was, by nature, a realist. After twenty years of gilded poverty, she did not expect much from life. When her cousin, Charles II, during his term of exile, courted her, she had no doubt at all that Charles was making up to her not for her beauty, which she did not rate too highly, but in the hope that through her influence, he could get some money from Lord Craven, the very rich and faithful friend of the Palatine family. But, if remarkably clear-headed,

Sophie was also of an optimistic frame of mind. 'Thank God,' she said on one occasion, 'I trust in God's goodness. It has never entered my head that He created me to do me harm. I have complete confidence in Him.'

The marriage, which was solemnised at Heidelberg in September 1658, seemed to require from the bride an exceptionally hopeful nature. The ceremony went off agreeably enough, the path having been smoothed by George William's promise to remain unmarried during the lifetime of Sophie and her husband. When Charles Louis, the Elector, doubted whether George William would have the strength of mind to keep his promise, he was reassured: George William's excesses with a Greek prostitute had left him in no condition either to marry or to father children. It was six years before George William married morganatically. Meanwhile, Charles II conferred the Garter on Sophie's bridegroom; the two brothers spent much of their time enjoying themselves in Venice, as they were accustomed to do. If Sophie wearied of her solitude, she bore it stoically: 'When one cannot have what one wants,' she remarked, quoting a song, 'one must want what one has.' Her husband to whom the remark was repeated thought that it referred to his brother, and sulked for a day or two. In 1661, Duke Ernest Augustus, a married man and a Protestant, became titular Bishop of Osnabruck, thanks to one of the most complicated provisions of the Peace of Westphalia. Sophie was not allowed to take part in her husband's solemn entry to his new – and well-endowed – see: 'It was thought that I should be out of place in this ecclesiastical ceremony.' As usual, she did not mind.

When the Brunswick brothers went travelling together in Italy, as they often did, Sophie wrote: 'I weary during their absence, for I am the miracle of this age, I love my husband.' Whether George William ever regretted his failure to go through with the marriage is not certain. Probably not, although on one occasion when he was ill, he told her he did not want to be anywhere but with her. Sophie was a lively and intelligent companion with some of the sunny disposition of the Queen of Bohemia. Like her sister, Elizabeth, she, in due course, acquired her own pet philosopher, Liebnitz, the inventor of the calculus, on whose invincibly cheerful convictions Voltaire, in due course, founded the great Doctor Pangloss. Rupert paid a visit to his sister after her marriage and, to her relief, got on famously with both of her Dukes. The three men shared a passion for hunting. It might have fallen out quite differently: as Sophie well knew, Rupert was not the easiest of guests or of brothers.

*   *   *

Rupert made his way to Vienna in the style suitable to a Prince of the Empire but the black servants, the fine liveries and the glistening horses were a façade behind which was a less glamorous reality, dwindling resources and no occupation. It was the last that was hardest to bear for a man of boundless energy and a restless mind. The Civil War was over. The hopes of a new campaign in Scotland had come to nothing. King Charles, who had already had his fill of Scotland, had been willing for Rupert to go there. Rupert himself was tempted by the notion. But when the idea was floated in Scotland, the answer that came back was a discouraging one. It was reported that Rupert was regarded 'with dread' by the Scots. So ended a scheme, the rumour of which reached the ears of attentive Commonwealth agents in Paris and Cologne, for a descent on the Scottish coast by Rupert at the head of 6,000 Spanish troops.

In Vienna, Rupert's affairs prospered no better. As he told Will Legge, he was on the most excellent terms with the Hapsburg family. He was constantly bidden to hunting parties by the Emperor. But behind all this pleasant social façade there was a singular lack of practical substance. It was all very Austrian. The frequent rumours that Rupert was going to be given an important command in the field, for instance, under the King of Hungary against the Turks, or to lead a Dutch fleet against the Commonwealth Navy, or in the Swedish service – all these came to nothing. So far as the Imperial service was concerned, there was invariably some Austrian general whose military pride would be wounded were the appointment to go to Rupert, a foreigner; German no doubt, but English rather than German. Moreover, the Prince's obstinate attachment to the Protestant, nay Calvinist, religion was a factor that must be considered in the Hapsburg capital. So the Emperor's ministers were economical in their cordiality and adroit in evading the questions of policy in which Rupert was mainly interested. As for money, the often promised 30,000 rix dollars* of the Peace of Westphalia, it appeared that nothing would give the Imperial government greater pleasure than to hand the money over but somehow there was always a reason, hard to define, harder to grasp, but inexpressibly cogent, why the moment of payment had not yet arrived. Months passed in those agreeable Viennese surroundings, in the field sports for which he shared an enthusiasm with the Emperor himself, in the other diversions which the city could afford. After a time, he went to call on his cousin, King Charles of Britain, at Frankfurt, to

* About £10,000 in money of the time.

report that in Vienna the rumour ran that the Spaniards were about to make a peace with Cromwell and that, accordingly, Charles would be well-advised not to press Spain for an alliance.

Much of the time, Rupert was in the territory of the Archbishop-Elector of Mainz, who had become his friend. There he lived obscurely enough and probably in straitened circumstances. He was not idle, however. He had taken up once more two of the hobbies of his boyhood, art and metal-working. By chance, they interlocked. One day when he was in Vienna, Rupert had met a colonel in the Landgrave of Hesse's service, Ludwig von Siegen, who had perfected, not long before, a novel system of engraving with metal. The process was simple enough. The surface of a copper plate was roughened uniformly all over and then was worked on so as to remove more or less of the roughness. Prints were then made from it, the deepest shadow occurred where the rough surface had been least scraped away. The effect was that a copy of a painting could be made in monochrome of a remarkable luminosity. It was just the thing to interest the technician and the artist who lay not far below the surface of Rupert's mind. He tried his skill on mezzotint, as it was called, and very soon he was able to produce engravings of fine quality. He and Ludwig von Siegen agreed that the secret of the process should be imparted to only a few chosen pupils. With one of these, a professional artist named Le Vaillant, Rupert worked hard at the art of the mezzotint. Later on, in London, John Evelyn, the diarist, was impressed by the Prince's contribution 'to the dignity of that art, performing things in graving comparable to the greatest masters'. However, Evelyn also noted that Rupert would not give away the secret of the process, saying only that he would explain it to anyone who did not find his account in the archives of the Royal Society sufficiently instructive.

Art was not, however, Rupert's sole occupation during the years of his frustration. He had an enquiring and inventive mind, in particular where mechanical and metallurgical innovations were concerned. He set up a workshop in Mainz where he carried out a series of experiments of which more was to be heard later on when, once more, the world had changed for him.

The restless young horseman of the Civil War had a reflective strain in his complex character which would have surprised the Parliamentary pamphleteers as much as it was to surprise the courtiers of Charles II. In truth, Rupert, like his sisters Elizabeth and Sophie – and, for that matter, his grandfather, James I – was an intellectual. It was one of the things that distinguished him from many of the Cavaliers, who had been his comrades in the war. Another distinction was, of course, his religion. He was a Puritan, which did not mean that he was strait-laced. A sportsman, an athlete, one of the most elegant men of his time, Rupert had the interest in women normal to a healthy young man of his kind. With it, however, went an unusual caution to balance the exceptional opportunities that came his way. He had, it may be surmised, an addiction to personal independence which even the most affectionate marriage might injure. With one exception, the women who are known to have appeared in his life are not women he would be likely to marry. The exception is the Duchess of Richmond, but she was the wife of one of his closest friends, and, therefore, for the most honourable of reasons, was forbidden to him. Richmond died in 1655, two years after Rupert's return from his wanderings. But, by that time, the friendship between the Duchess and Rupert had cooled. However, there comes a time in a man's life when aimlessness and loneliness work together, with ill-health and an uncertain future to assist them, to think sympathetically of a comfortable marriage with a rich and amiable woman. Such a time seems to have come to Rupert when his long voyage was over and Maurice, his beloved Maurice, was lost. There were rumours that he was about to marry a lady of the French royal family, or his cousin, Mary, widow of the Prince of Orange. Nothing came of either project if, indeed, they had ever been more than imaginings.

Rupert continued his vagrant life in Germany, hunting with the Emperor, carrying out alarming experiments with gunpowder in his laboratory at Mainz, visiting his sisters, Elizabeth and Sophie, and making notes for the autobiography which he meant to write one day to refute all his detractors, open and anonymous.

His mother, deserted by sons and daughters, desperately hard-up, kept alive in her palace at The Hague the spirit which makes her, with all her faults, the most attractive princess of her time. What was the secret of the spell which she exerted over a staid diplomat like Sir Thomas Roe, and which could make a warlike prince like Christian of Brunswick subscribe himself 'your humblest, most constant, most faithful, most affectionate and most obedient slave'? She herself attributed it to her sense of humour.

One day in 1660, the Queen took up her pen with unusual relish. Cromwell, 'the old rascal', was dead. 'He lived with the curse of all good people and is dead to their great joy.' Her Majesty began to plan her return to London. She was particularly indignant when her son, Charles

Louis, declined to help her to get her jewellery out of pawn. But such things were no more than trifling irritations. The Queen was conscious that suddenly the world had changed. Said the Duque de Feria shortly before the death of Philip II, 'When he goes, we shall find ourselves on another stage and all the characters in the play will be different.'

XVIII

The King Comes Home in Peace

'The final phase of a period in history lies in comedy. Why? So that
mankind can bid farewell to the past in a spirit of gaiety.'

Karl Marx

Cousin Charles was already in London, crowned on the very day that
his cousin Sophie, after three days of labour, produced her first-born son,
George Louis. Rupert was present in Westminster Abbey for the
coronation. Now Charles was seated firmly on his throne, with every
intention of staying there. The Royalists, dazed by the revolution in their
fortunes, were not so dazed that they failed to tot up what they were
owed if justice were done and to make the sum greater than they were
ever likely to be paid. The Marchioness – now Duchess – of Newcastle,
for example, calculated her husband's loss, eighteen years' rent of £22,000
a year at six per cent interest, making £733,000 on top of which were
damage to woods and parks, lands that had been lost under the Commonwealth and would never be restored, lands sold after the return to
England to pay His Grace's debts. She arrived, generously, at a total of
£941,000. The Newcastles were enormously rich but not alone in their
sense of loss. Lesser sufferers in the cause worked out similarly optimistic
claims on royal gratitude. However, the man who now sat on the throne
of England was intelligent, unscrupulous, self-indulgent, and disillusioned.
He was well fitted by nature to defend what was left of the royal
patrimony against the looters, unless of course they were pretty women.
One visitor came over to London on a private visit in September 1660,
and was seen by Samuel Pepys. 'Prince Rupert,' he confided in his diary,
'is come to court, welcome to nobody.' Apparently, the anti-Rupert
faction at court had survived the transit to England. In due course, Pepys
would join it. In the meantime, he echoed its views.

Rupert was too haughty (read independent), rough (read plain-spoken), to be any more popular with the second Charles' entourage than he had been with that of the first. Thus, he sailed against the prevailing wind in the corridors of Whitehall when it was proposed to marry the King's sister, Henrietta – Minette – to Philippe, Duke of Orléans, 'Monsieur', brother of Louis XIV. Rupert's opposition was based on the ground that the bridegroom was an avowed and fanatical pederast. Rupert's advice was, however, rejected and one of the most deplorable of royal marriages was celebrated. When Minette died ten years later, Rupert was one of those who swore that her husband had poisoned her. In this, he was mistaken, although the mistake was shared by others. The French ambassador, Colbert de Croissy, in reporting to Paris, attributed Rupert's attitude to his readiness to think evil of others. Rupert's family had not finished with Monsieur. When a new wife was sought for Monsieur, one was found in the Elector Charles Louis' daughter, Elizabeth Charlotte – Liselotte – who was Rupert's niece.* The marriage negotiations were opened by Prince Edward's wife, Anne de Gonzague. She may have underestimated the obstacles to marital happiness in the marriage since she was believed to have seduced Monsieur in his youth. As it turned out, Liselotte's buoyant temperament enabled her to surmount the difficulties of the marriage. 'How am I supposed to sleep with that?' asked Monsieur when he saw his strapping new wife. However, with the help of holy medals, he did.

Rather to his surprise, Rupert found that the popular hatred of him which the Civil War propagandists had whipped up was now dead. He was apparently in favour with the people of England. There would be no need, after all, for him to write the defensive autobiography he had been planning. The King himself was anxious that Rupert should stay; he had work for his cousin to do. But Rupert, who had suffered from a recurrence of the fever that laid him low after his return from the tropics, was a professional soldier in the Emperor's service and it seemed that war with the Turks was imminent. If he were to stay in England, he would require the Emperor's consent. So after spending New Year in London, he set off in the spring of 1661 for Vienna, calling on the way at The Hague where he found his mother preparing to cross to London in spite

* According to Liselotte, whose sources of information were not very reliable, Minette was poisoned by order of Monsieur's mignon, the Chevalier de Lorraine, although the actual deed was done by the Marquis d'Effiat. Saint-Simon tells much the same story. According to these accounts, Monsieur had no knowledge of the conspiracy against his wife. The official explanation was that Minette died of cholera.

of the fact that her nephew, King Charles, had not invited her. After all, that was a trifle which a woman of her imperturbable, all-conquering charm could afford to ignore. The good Craven would find her a London house and she would take with her the Palatine furniture however much her son, the Elector, might protest. After all, was he not keeping her out of her dower house at Frankenthal? The tradespeople at The Hague prepared for the Queen the friendliest of farewells. Probably they were genuinely sorry to see the delightful creature go and, probably too, they thought that, with the Queen in London, they had a better chance of ensuring that the English Parliament should pay her debts.

Rupert travelled across Germany finding time on his way to send letters to his old friend and factotum, Will Legge, reporting on a variety of matters that had interested him: he had met a German engineer of exceptional skill who would be useful to King Charles in fortifying Portsmouth; he had seen a pure distilled rainwater which dissolved gold; he mentioned a book which he had come across in Vienna, it spoke of his part in the Civil War 'in most base language'; a tun of Rhine wine was on its way to London from the Elector of Mainz – Legge was to make use of it; 'I hear our cousin hath got the small-pox, pray God she may not fall into the Frenchified physician's hands, let blood and die'; 'the Hungarian wine is marching off the river towards Ratisbon, eight pipes, which I hope will serve our court this winter'; Legge was to give Lord Lindsay 'the doleful news that poor Rayall is dying after being the death of many a stag. By Heaven, I had rather lose the best horse in my stable!' However, the main business that had taken him to Vienna ended in frustration.

The Emperor was friendly and invited Rupert to bring his greyhounds to a hunt. But, as before, the ministers barred a Protestant from holding a high command. The matter was made worse by rumours from London that King Charles was going to marry the Portuguese Infanta, which annoyed the Spaniards and their Hapsburg relatives in Vienna. In consequence of all these matters, the military command that Rupert sought was given to Count Montecuculi, who led an army into Transylvania on an expedition which called for forty hours of prayer in Vienna, but which for one reason or another did not have much military success. Rupert, watching events with a sardonic eye, reported very soon that in the Imperial high command only Montecuculi was in good health. Meanwhile, the commander of the troops on the frontier had made a raid on Turkish-held territory, 'took some oxen, a few prisoners, showed his teeth and came back. If this draw not the Turks into these parts, the devil is in them.'

Rupert arrived in London early in 1662 not many days before his mother died in Leicester House, which she had rented from its owner, the Earl of Leicester. Before dying, she had summoned the King, the Duke of York and Clarendon, the Lord Chancellor, asking them to continue her pension after her death so that her creditors in The Hague could be paid in full. In the darkness of a February night Rupert, as chief mourner, followed his mother's coffin from Somerset House, where it had lain in state, to a barge on the Thames which bore it to Westminster Bridge. And so to the Abbey gates where the Queen's funeral torches met the tapers of the Dean and Chapter who led the way to Henry VII's chapel. By her will, she left her famous pearls and diamonds to her son, Rupert. Needless to say, her other son, the Elector, bitterly disputed Rupert's right to the jewels which, he said, were heirlooms. But Rupert was in no mood to fall in with his brother's wishes or, unless under the most severe constraint, recognise his brother's rights. While he was in Vienna, the Elector had caused him a great deal of embarrassment by telling the Austrian court that Charles II was negotiating with the Turk and that Rupert, if he wished, could tell the Emperor more about the business! This at a time when Rupert was hoping to be given a high command against the Turks! 'A brotherly trick,' as Rupert commented in a letter to Will Legge. 'By heaven, I am in such a humour that I dare not write to anybody; therefore excuse me to all.' Rupert clung tenaciously to the Queen's jewels.

In coming to England, he had finally abandoned all notion of making a career in Austria. He was now a stately, hawk-nosed gentleman of forty with a pension from King Charles of £1,500 a year and apartments in Whitehall, looking out on the Privy Garden. Later, he moved to a house in Spring Gardens, at Charing Cross. His health had suffered from tropical climates and the hardships of war. He had a head wound which had not been properly treated by the surgeons and would eventually need to be trephined. In the meantime, it was probably responsible for the sardonic outbursts which alarmed men of quieter temper, like Samuel Pepys, for example, who sat with Rupert on the Navy Board. Pepys noticed the hole cut in Rupert's periwig to prevent it from irritating the wound and concluded that the Prince had the pox.* This was no doubt the common belief at court. Given the times and the social circles in

* But see Appendix, 'The Hole in Rupert's Periwig'.

which Rupert moved, it would not have been an unlikely misfortune, although Pepys for reasons of his own was not a reliable witness where Rupert was concerned.

It was true, however, that bad health was the reason why Rupert was not given one command which he coveted. The Royal African Company had been founded with a capital of £30,000 and with Rupert as one of its patentees. To the annoyance of Pepys, who was alarmed by his distrustful attitude to Admiralty accountancy, he was chosen to command its first expedition. After a farewell banquet, he sailed out of the Thames with the King and the Duke of York who came down to bid him godspeed. Stormy weather drove the ships to seek refuge in Portsmouth and there Rupert, by his angry demands that the victualling of the fleet should be drastically improved, had his first brush with Pepys. Weeks passed before the fleet resumed its voyage and, in the interval, Rupert's health broke down. His old head wound suffered a new damage from some accident on shipboard. The Duke of York sent the French surgeon, Choqueux, to see him as soon as he heard the news: 'I conjure you, if you have any kindness for me, have a care of your health ... I am very glad to hear your ship sails so well.' Choqueux operated and Rupert remained in his cabin on the surgeon's promise that he would be well in a few days. Instead of that, the illness grew worse and Rupert went up to London. 'He is mightily worn away, and, in their opinion that are about him, is not long lived.' He longed to sail to Guinea, confident that the warm climate out there would help to restore him. But the illness went on too long, the ships were due to sail, and finally his old shipmate Holmes was given the command of the expedition in his place. Rupert stayed at home 'much chagrined' at the idea he might die and, when assured that he was going to recover, 'is as merry, and swears and laughs and curses and does all the things of a man in health'. So Pepys noted in his diary in January 1665. Holmes came home with vivid impressions of the extreme heat of the Gambia. He had also brought a huge baboon which Pepys believed could understand English. 'And I am of the mind it might be taught to speak or make signs.' But of gold, not an ounce. However, other expeditions were to follow. Forts and warehouses were built on the Guinea coast and the first steps were taken towards the commercial war with the Dutch. Before that war broke out, Holmes was already a rich man.

XIX

Such Judgments and Calamities

'And now brave Rupert from afar appears,
Whose waving streamers the glad general knows;
With full-spread sails his eager navy steers,
And every ship in swift proportion grows.'

Dryden

The King, who had a shrewd idea of the ways in which Rupert's energy could be harnessed to the business of government, had appointed him to the Privy Council soon after his arrival in England. He was also made one of the committee for the government of Tangier where that unfriendly witness, Pepys, was shocked by his behaviour at the meetings. 'Prince Rupert do nothing but laugh a little, with an oath or two.' The Prince, it is certain, was never a good committee man, too impatient to endure the prolonged debate, too openly contemptuous of the opinion of others and too abrupt, if not actually inarticulate, in presenting his own. The King was intelligent enough to see that in government there is room for such a man, if only to attract to himself annoyance that might otherwise fall on the King's friends. In addition to these appointments, Rupert was made a member of the Board of Admiralty on which his interest and experience alike were more engaged. Finally, he was elected a Fellow of the Royal Society, a newly founded institution in which another, and unexpected, facet of his nature came into view. Rupert was not Newton or Harvey or Locke, but as the first royal scientist, he was, as will be seen, a key figure in these dawn years of the Enlightenment. From this list of his administrative tasks it is plain that his time would be fully taken up, if he was to be anything more than a figurehead in each of them. And Prince Rupert was not cut out by nature to be a figurehead. His private life was busy, too.

In the year 1664 he paid a visit to France to which belongs the only amorous correspondence in which he is known to have been involved.

Characteristically, the letters of which a record is preserved are to Rupert and not from him. An unknown lady, writing in French, makes a passionate avowal: 'You are infinitely dear to me . . . I should be in despair if I lost you for ever. I love in the world only you . . . Have the kindness not to refuse to come as you promised me.' There is also a note of the same year, written in the same hand, in which the writer complains that she has 'none of your dear news, not the least remembrance of you although I have sent about a hundred messages'. These outpourings show that a woman was deeply in love with Rupert, and suggest that Rupert was cool towards her. Another letter, bearing a date two months after the last one, comes apparently from a woman who has been acting as an intermediary between Rupert and a lady whom he had some design of marrying. This lady has learned that Rupert has for a long time been 'fort engagé près une duchesse', presumably the Duchess of Richmond. The writer has denied this allegation 'à tout hazard' but asks to be told what Rupert wishes her to say. Who was the lady he sought after?

It is evident that she was French and very rich. No more can be said except that one phrase in the intermediary's letter suggests that Rupert was not deeply involved. He should listen, she tells him, to the sentiments of his heart – and reply to the same address at Nantes as before. After that, silence. The affair seems to have petered out. There was nothing in it such as might discourage his sister, Elizabeth, from writing to him as she did on the subject of marriage. Elizabeth was mainly concerned with the political and religious consequences of her brother's bachelor status. The Elector, Charles Louis, had one son who, although married, was delicate and in an advanced state of religious mania; at any rate, not likely to produce an heir. The Elector's children by his union to Luise von Degenfeld could not inherit the electorship because of the dubious legality of their parents' marriage. The electorship would, in these circumstances, be likely to pass to the Neuberg branch of the family, who were Catholics. This prospect Princess Elizabeth, the devoutly Protestant abbess of Herford, regarded with something like horror. She urged Rupert, her favourite brother, to marry out of his duty to religion and the family. She had in readiness a list of Protestant ladies of suitable rank, such as a Princess of Courland and a Princesse de la Tremoille. Two Quakers, William Penn and Barclay of Ury, who visited Elizabeth in her convent, were entrusted by her with a mission to win Rupert over to his dynastic duty. All was without avail. Rupert was by that time firmly settled as part of the English establishment. His health was bad. He had enough to occupy him as a man in whom the fires of ambition were dying down. In short, he was not inclined to marry and certainly would not do so merely for dynastic reasons. His detested brother could dig himself out of the hole he was in as well as he could. Later on, when Luise von Degenfeld had died, Rupert suggested that the Elector should once more approach his wife to seek her agreement to a divorce, so that he could make a new marriage. The suggestion had no chance of succeeding against the hatred that divided the Elector and his wife.

The youngest of the Palatine sisters, Sophie, was drawn into the game and wrote to Lord Craven, begging him to use his influence with Rupert. Further to smooth the path of negotiations, she sent a consignment of Hanoverian deer to help to re-stock Windsor Great Park. But this move was no more successful than the others. Craven told Sophie that if she could provide some rich woman who would be ready to marry the Prince he was prepared to act as a go-between; otherwise, not. And it seemed that Sophie had no candidate in mind able to support a husband in the state becoming a married prince. 'So there,' she admitted, 'I am stranded!' In the last phase of the comedy, the Elector himself wrote to his brother, being depressed by the thought that he was leaving his children by Luise to the care of his Neuberg cousin; nor would they be any better off, he feared, were they looked after by his legitimate son, whose wife had shown only too plainly her dislike for them. He wrote to Rupert promising to give him all that he wished if only he would come back to the Palatinate, marry and raise a Protestant family. It was too late. Rupert remembered the gates of Heidelberg that had been shut in his face at his brother's command. He wrote to the Elector: 'Thanks to you, I have taken an oath that I will never again set foot in the Palatinate. This oath may be regrettable, but I will keep it.' Now, he might be willing to forgive but he had sworn an oath, and he was a man of his word. He was very comfortably installed at Windsor Castle. Moreover, he had children of his own, English children.

At the time that Charles II came back to Whitehall, Rupert made the acquaintance of Francesca Bard, elder daughter of Sir Henry Bard, a harum-scarum Royalist who had lost an arm at Cheriton Down in battle with the Roundheads. Sir Henry, when he was made Governor of Campden House, had allowed it to be burnt down, apparently through carelessness. He went into exile with Charles II who raised him to the Irish peerage as Viscount Bellomont. As Bard, in his youth, had travelled extensively in the East and acquired a knowledge of Oriental languages, Charles sent him on an improbable mission to see if he could raise money for the exiled King from the Shah and the Great Mogul. While he was in India on his way to Delhi, Viscount Bellomont died in 1655, leaving a family which was impoverished even by the standards of that threadbare court-in-exile. His daughter Francesca became mistress of Prince Rupert. A son was born who was called Dudley Bard, sometimes Dudley Rupert. Rupert sent the boy to Eton, his grandfather's school, and, in due course, to Sir Jonas Moore, a distinguished mathematician of the time, who was Surveyor-General of the Ordnance and had a house in the Tower of London. It was hoped that, coached by Sir Jonas, Dudley would learn enough mathematics to fit him for a career in the army. A soldier, in due course, he became. Francesca was a devout Catholic. Later on, stories were spread to show that Rupert had married her in secret or even that he had duped her into a false marriage. When Rupert lay on his deathbed, the rumour ran that he had acknowledged his marriage to Francesca whose son would, in that case, be the Elector Palatine. No such claim was ever made for the boy.

Later, an alleged marriage certificate was in existence according to which the marriage had been celebrated on 30 July 1664, at Petersham in Surrey 'by me Henry Bignell, Minister'. But no great credence has ever been given to this document. Francesca lived to become a friend of Rupert's sister, Sophie, Electress of Hanover, at whose court she lived. Sophie wrote of her, 'She says she was married to my brother, but it will be very difficult to prove.' There is no word from Rupert about her. Francesca remains a shadowy figure on the margin of his life. She outlived him by a quarter of a century. It appears, though, that 1664 was a year in which many strands of fortune crossed for Rupert. In that year his affair with Francesca probably began, his marriage project in France took place, if the dating of the letters from his mysterious correspondent is correct; the Guinea expedition sailed and came to nothing, and he had a serious breakdown in health; finally, in that year, the Duchess of Richmond, for nine years widowed, married for the third time. Twice, she had married to please the court, she said: this time she was marrying for love. The important fact was that she did not marry Rupert but Colonel Thomas Howard. It is tempting, but it would be futile, to try to make a pattern out of these events. But all that is certain is that Rupert and Francesca soon parted and that, when he parted from her, Rupert had not finished with women.

Before the new amorous episode in his life occurred, a great deal was going to happen to the most versatile member of King Charles' court.

Not many months after Rupert had recovered from his serious illness in 1664, England went to war with the Dutch. It was a commercial war, a colonial war, a war springing from foolish mercantile jealousies but popular, for the moment at least, in a nation where shipping interests were strong and rivalry was sharp between two tough seafaring peoples. 'What we want,' explained the Duke of Albemarle, who as General George Monck had done more than anyone else to put Charles II on the throne, 'is more of the trade which the Dutch now have.' The trade was, it seemed, to be had for the taking. It is unlikely that one member of the Navy Board thought it would be as easy as all that. Rupert, who had lived longer in Holland than he had in England, whose mother had shared in the profits of Piet Heyn's famous capture of the Spanish treasure fleet in Matanzas Bay all those years ago, was not as likely to under-rate the fighting qualities of the Dutch navy as, say, was the Duke of Albemarle.

When the war broke out in February 1665, Rupert, as a member of the royal family with a redoubtable reputation as a fighting sailor, would have been the natural choice as commander-in-chief of the English fleet. He was, however, still desperately ill, so ill that at one time he was given up by the doctors, and assuredly, it was no time for a man to be ill. Already plague had appeared in St Giles parish and the first red crosses were to be seen, chalked on doors in Drury Lane. The well-to-do were very soon making off to the country. When fighting began that summer, the first sea command went to the Duke of York, who, as Lord High Admiral, was Admiral of the Red, while Rupert, by that time hardly more than convalescent, led the White squadron and Lord Sandwich was Admiral of the Blue.

After weeks of inconclusive manoeuvring in the North Sea, the two fleets, English and Dutch, met in battle in Southwold Bay, the English being marginally the stronger. It was a seafight on a scale bigger than anything seen in these waters since the clash with the Spanish Armada. Two hundred and seventy ships were engaged and the English fireships were particularly effective. Frail though he was after his illness, Rupert led the attack on the Dutch who had very much the worse of the ensuing battle. After their flagship had blown up, during a furious exchange of fire with the Duke of York's ship, other units of their fleet pulled out of the engagement. Thereupon the Dutch in some haste and all in a huddle made for the coast of Holland. The Duke of York made the signal for a general chase, after which he retired to his bunk. Sir William Penn, sailing with the Duke as first captain of the fleet, followed his example soon after. Darkness had fallen. The wind was blowing hard towards the Dutch islands. The situation was one calling for cautious seamanship. During that night, Mr Brouncker, the Duke's Gentleman of the Bedchamber, urged Harman, the captain of the flagship, to slacken sail. This Harman did, reluctantly, believing that the order came from the Duke. Thus, when daylight came, the enemy was out of sight and the Duke was furious. Rupert blamed Penn, whom, as a former Commonwealth officer, he did not trust, believing that Penn had brought his old colleagues, 'the roguish fanatic captains', into the fleet. But Penn proved that he had been asleep at the time the order was given. Eventually Brouncker confessed to Parliament that he had acted on his own responsibility because he was alarmed about the growing danger to the Duke. After the battle was over, Rupert fell ill again – 'laid by the leg, by a small mistake of the surgeon . . . This is writ abed as you may see by the ill character.' In the years that followed more would be heard about Rupert's trouble with his leg. After the fleets had re-fitted, the adversaries got to grips once more. But this time the Duke of York did not hold a command, having been forbidden to go to sea. The Queen Mother had plagued the King to keep the Duke out of danger and, at length, the King had given in to her entreaties. The Duke of York was, after all, heir to the throne. Rupert, to his disgust, was persuaded to share the naval command with Lord Sandwich, whom he distrusted. But at a moment when Rupert's personal staff had already gone aboard, Sir William Coventry, who was no friend of Rupert's, persuaded Charles to change his mind and recall the Prince. The dual command would not succeed, he said. Rupert, 'wonderfully surprised, perplexed and even broken-hearted', returned to court.

By the end of the sailing season, Sandwich had done nothing and was deeply suspected of dishonesty. In his troubles, Rupert treated him with great consideration, as even Pepys admits. But Parliament made its view of the matter insultingly clear by proposing to vote Rupert a grant of £10,000 and half a crown to Sandwich. When the war was renewed in the following year, Rupert shared command of the fleet with the Duke of Albemarle. In this new phase of the war the English faced a combination of Dutch and French navies and the news reached Whitehall that a French fleet under the Duc de Beaufort had left Belle Isle and was sailing towards

197

the western approaches of the Channel. The Council thereupon decided to divide the fleet, sending Rupert with twenty ships to meet the French before they could link up with the Dutch, while Albemarle, with sixty ships, was left to deal with the Dutch. When the Dutch, under Admiral de Ruyter were sighted, eighty ships strong, Albemarle rashly went out to attack them and emerged from a furious battle lasting two days with his fleet badly mauled. Rupert, meanwhile, was looking in vain for the French in the Channel farther west. In fact, the English government had been wrongly informed and had now discovered their error. Orders were sent to bring the Prince back to help Albemarle but through negligence in Whitehall – a secretary who was too frightened to disturb a sleeping Minister – they did not reach the Prince in time. Thus, when the counter-manding order reached Rupert, he had already heard the rumble of cannon and was hurrying on his way to join Albemarle. In consequence of this delay, the main English fleet was compelled to fight it out with de Ruyter until the afternoon of the third day, and once again was heavily punished.

Albemarle had taken his ships – those of them that were fit to sail and fight – into the shelter of the shoals and sandbanks at the mouth of the Thames. There they lay when, in the afternoon, Albemarle's look-out men in the crow's nest sighted the sails of Rupert's leading ships and a cheer went up from the hard-pressed crews. The battle was not yet ended. In trying to link up with the Prince, Albemarle's ships sailed into trouble on the Galloper Sand and the *Royal Prince*, flagship of one squadron, ran aground and struck her flag. The Dutch made prisoners of her Admiral and his crew and set the ship on fire. Next morning, after a conference of the two Admirals, Rupert's squadron led the fleet on a mission of revenge. The renewed battle was long and savage but at the end of four days of almost continuous fighting, the Dutch had plainly come off best. Touchy as usual, Rupert was annoyed on this occasion, because, while a Dutch dispatch had spoken disparagingly of his conduct, the English official account of the battle did not give him adequate credit for his part. After Rupert's secretary, James Haynes, had protested, a note was added to the communiqué from Whitehall: 'Never any Prince or, it may be truly said, any private person, was in an action of war, exposed to more danger.' Haynes replied, 'You have done right to a brave Prince.' At this time, Rupert was carrying on a bitter campaign against the Com-missioners of the Navy, in particular the victualler, Samuel Pepys. As soon as he stepped ashore, he hurried to the King to make his protest with all the force of language of which he was a master. Pepys shook in his shoes: 'I . . . do fear he may in violence break out upon this office some time or other.' But duty called the furious Prince to sea once more with his wrath against the Navy Office unassuaged. In fighting off the North Foreland, Tromp, the Dutch second-in-command, was heavily defeated by the English rear squadron which he had engaged without orders from his chief, de Ruyter. In a general English attack, Rupert almost lost his life and was saved by a gunner, George Hillson, whom he later promoted.

On 28 July, at a meeting of admirals in the English flagship, it was resolved to carry a new attack into the Dutch harbours. The Prince ordered his little yacht, newly built and named *Fanfan*, to carry out a reconnaissance along the Dutch coast, taking with her a distinguished Dutch renegade, Lauris van Heemskerk,* who was a recognised expert on the mysteries of the inshore waters in his country. Heemskerk brought back important news. The islands of Vlie and Schelling were insufficiently guarded and on them were well-stocked warehouses of the East India fleet. On hearing this, Rupert and Albemarle ordered Sir Robert Holmes to land 500 men on Vlie, burn and loot as much as he could, keep the seamen from drinking too much and then re-embark them. A similar operation was to be carried out on Schelling. The assault parties were to be two-thirds soldiers, one-third pikemen. Three days' rations were to be carried. When Holmes entered the Vlie-Schelling channel flying his flag in the little *Fanfan* it was early of a thick dark morning. But the sky cleared magically about eleven and Holmes to his joy saw before him 170 sail crowded together at anchor. They were merchantmen with two small warships in attendance. Holmes did what was clearly the right thing. With him he had five fireships. He sent them in.

In a few minutes, flames burst out from one of the vessels and soon afterwards the whole mass of shipping was ablaze. Holmes then sent in his shore parties. Out at sea, Rupert and Albemarle saw a vast cloud of smoke on the horizon and thought that it came from burning warehouses. They sent Holmes a signal to return without delay lest the Dutch surprise him with overwhelming force. But the seamen and soldiers, put ashore among abundant loot, were not easily persuaded to leave. In the end they were brought off with twelve casualties. The Dutch had sustained a loss of 150 ships or thereabouts and cargoes worth a million

* When van Heemskerk fell on evil times five years later, Rupert kept his wife and children from starving.

199

pounds. It was their biggest single calamity of the war. However, the revenge was not long in coming.

A few days after Holmes' exploit the fleet moved back to Southwold Bay,* short of beer, water and ammunition. While they waited for the Dutch to come and take their revenge – Rupert laid Albemarle a bet of five pounds they would not do so; he won – the two admirals complained testily and often to London, about the failure of supplies. Rupert in particular was by no means willing to accept Pepys' counter-charge that the pursers had falsely declared the beer was stinking. 'Let us have plenty of water,' said Rupert and Albemarle, 'and if we take a prize of wine and brandy, we shall be able to make a wholesome beverage.' They had recently taken just such a prize and had sent it to the Prize Commissioners; now they asked for it to be returned. Pepys particularly enraged them by sending accounts of supplies which had already been sent them but which had inexplicably failed to arrive. However, a new crisis swept these minor troubles aside. A message from the King recalled Albemarle to London to grapple with a terrible emergency – the Great Fire. When Rupert heard the news, he exclaimed, 'Now Mother Shipton's prophecy is out: Ah, what a goodly city this was and now there is scarcely a house can let us have drink for our money.'

However, Rupert had not forgotten his grievance against the Navy Commissioners. While London was still stinking from the fire, he went up to Whitehall to have it out with the men who, in his view, had robbed the fleet, starved the seamen and swindled the State. They had falsified the accounts and lined their own pockets. Above all, his attack was directed against Pepys. It was delivered in the presence of the highest in the land. Rupert was an impressive spokesman for cheated sailors and unvictualled ships. He was tall, with an aquiline nose and blazing eyes. His normally passionate temperament was heated to rage by what he had seen and, with others, had suffered. He was a Prince and a famous warrior. But it would have been a mistake to under-rate the skill in controversy of a man of Pepys's calibre. His defence consisted of a diversion of the attack. He has described the encounter. 'Anon we were called into the Green Room where were the King, Duke of York, Prince Rupert, Lord Chancellor, Lord Treasurer, Duke of Albemarle, and Sir G. Carteret, W. Coventry, Morrice. Nobody beginning, I did and made, as I thought, a good speech, laying open the ill state of the Navy by the greatness of the debts; greatness of the work to do against next year, the time and

* Then known as Sole Bay.

materials it would take and our own incapacity through a total want of money.' It was incautious of Pepys to suggest that under Rupert the fleet was in a poor condition. This, in the King's presence, was more than the Prince could endure. Rising to his feet and speaking 'in a great heat', he told the King that no fleet had ever come back to port in a better state than his. It was short of no more than twenty boats; while all the cables and anchors lost in the storm could be recovered. 'I was not a little troubled at this passage,' Pepys confided to his diary, 'and the more, when speaking to Jack Fenn about it, he told me that the Prince will now be asking who this Pepys is – and will find him to be a creature of my Lord Sandwich', who was notoriously an enemy of Rupert's. Rupert would, therefore, assume that Pepys' speech was part of a plot against him by a man who hated him.

All through the ages there has been a simmering quarrel between the fighting men and their suppliers. This was one of the occasions when it broke out into flames and fury. Pepys, waspishly, professed to believe that Rupert's bad temper was due to the coolness of his reception in Whitehall at a moment when he had expected to be welcomed as one who had won a great victory. Captain Batten, whom Rupert had suspected of treachery when the 'revolted' fleet lay in Helvoetsluys in 1649, was now sent to report on the state of the fleet. He brought back a report hostile to Rupert which he intended to present to the Duke of York. But Rupert was present in the audience chamber with the Duke when Batten entered. Says Pepys, 'It was pretty to see how, when he found the Prince there, he did not speak out one word . . . when I asked him, he told me that he knew the Prince too well to anger him and that he was afraid to do it.' But – to Pepys' relief – 'the Fire deaded everything'. However, the administration of the navy in 1666 was incompetent and corrupt and Pepys was likely to bear the brunt of the Parliamentary criticism that was sure to come. Through his sleepless nights of worry over his danger, he was relieved to notice that those who might have united against him, Rupert and Albemarle, were now not on good terms. On the friendship of the Duke of York he thought he could count, but unhappily, the Duke 'is wholly given over to this bitch of Denham.'*

The Great Fire was not, however, the last or worst of England's calamities during those months. There was – most bitter humiliation of all – the brilliant Dutch naval raid on the English fleet base in the Medway. The ships lay there disarmed, immobilised by a Parliament which, since

* Lady Denham, the Duke's mistress of the moment.

it could not control the King's policy, would not vote him enough money to pay his seamen and supply his ships. So Jan Danielszoon van de Rijn broke the chain across the Medway and the *Royal Charles*, which had been Rupert's flagship only a few weeks before, was towed off to Amsterdam by the gleeful Hollanders. The Thames was blockaded. The price of coal in London rose from 15s a ton to 140s and Pepys, who had an exact sense of priorities, hurried his private hoard of gold (£1,300) off to Brampton. He was able to get another £500 from the bank before the run began. He was furious when he found out that his father had buried the bullion in broad daylight – and furious again because his father had forgotten where he had put it. John Evelyn went to the play one evening, troubled in conscience that he should be doing anything so frivolous 'in a season of such judgments and calamities'. What made it all the more disturbing was that for the first time he saw women appearing on the stage.

Rupert, like Albemarle, rushed to the danger area to improvise means of preventing the Dutch from sailing up-river and destroying the shipping at London. He could not be blamed for the calamity, which had occurred after he had laid down his command. And he had warned the King that a Dutch raid on the English coast must be expected. The King for his part did what he could with the resources that Parliament allowed him. He strengthened the defences of Harwich, a port where Rupert thought the first blow might fall. But the King had neither money nor munitions to do more. Peace came six weeks after the Dutch attack, and lasted for five years. During that time, Charles concluded the secret Treaty of Dover (1670) which made him the pensioner of Louis XIV and made the British Navy an instrument of French policy. It also provided for French military support when Charles should decide to announce his conversion to Catholicism. Only two men knew of the existence of this clause although others may have suspected it. But as it happened the Treaty of Dover was not the only reason for anxiety at this time: the Duke of York, heir-presumptive to the throne, became a Roman Catholic. Protestant alarm bells, never silent for long in seventeenth-century England, began to clamour, the London mob began to demonstrate, and the Test Act was passed in 1673. This barred Catholics from office under the Crown and – the main purpose of the Act – barred the Duke of York from the post of Lord High Admiral. From that moment onwards, Rupert was the obvious choice as head of the Admiralty. Already, he had made himself the leader of those who were dissatisfied with the state of the Navy. After his return from sea in 1666, he had been asked by the House of Commons to report on the causes of the recent naval disasters. He criticised the separation of the fleet into two flotillas, referred to the 'intolerable neglect in supplying provisions, notwithstanding the extraordinary and frequent importunity of our letters'. Wood-bound casks were found to be staved; the gauge of the beer barrels was twenty gallons short; bills of credit came instead of provisions; 'the want of seamen was too great to be forgotten' – they took jobs in merchant ships where the pay was better than in the Navy. However, the King took a tolerant view of the rumpus: 'If you intend to man the fleet without being cheated by the captains and pursers, you may never have it manned at all.'

Having discharged his broadside against the naval administration, Rupert had retired from the fray, with the thanks of Parliament. He found diversion of a different kind when the court went to Tunbridge Wells and the King's Company of Players were in attendance. After that, he went to live in Windsor Castle, of which he had been made Governor. There, he occupied himself by repairing and decorating his residence, the Round Tower which, according to his taste, he made suitable as the home of a fighting Prince. The passing of the Test Act and the approach of a new war with the Dutch changed everything. While the London apprentices cheered the appointment of a Protestant prince, some people, especially high naval officers who thought that they had been passed over, sourly pointed out that a German (Rupert) was in command of the Fleet and a Frenchman (Marshal Schomberg)* was appointed to lead the expeditionary force which, all going well, was to be landed on the Dutch coast.

All did not go well in the new and unpopular war in which, as a first fruit of the Treaty of Dover, the English found themselves in alliance with Louis XIV against the Dutch. It is likely enough that Rupert had some suspicion of the secret bonds that tied his cousin, Charles, to the French. In that case, it is unlikely that he approved of them. He was a Protestant prince, not only according to the slogans of the London crowd, but by conviction. But he was loyal to the King, as he had been loyal to the King's father. He was a serving officer. The situation in which he found himself was, therefore, an irksome one and circumstances conspired to make it still more disagreeable. In the Admiralty and at court he had to contend with a host of ill-wishers, victims of his tongue who

* He was a nobleman of the Rhine, a Huguenot, French by naturalisation and a Marshal of France.

203

sought their revenge. Thus, when he wanted his old friend, Sir Robert Holmes, an admiral, to be his second-in-command, the government would not have it. Rupert had to be content with Sir Richard Spragge, whom he was known to dislike. For various reasons, then, some good and some petty, Rupert was an ill-tempered man when the new war began. By prompt and daring action, he frustrated a Dutch plan to block the exits from the Thames with hulks filled with stones. But the English fleet was, as usual, undermanned, and ill-provisioned. Rupert raged to the King, to the Navy Office, to anybody who would listen. In vain. He was forced to fight as best he could with a fleet that had been 'merely huddled out' as he complained. When it came to battle, which it did off Schoonveldt on 10 August 1673, he soon had another grievance. His French ally, Admiral d'Estrées, not only refrained from giving him what he regarded as an adequate salute but showed some reluctance to get to grips with the enemy. All this might not have mattered so much if the Dutch fleet had been led by some run-of-the-mill commander. It was led by de Ruyter. All day long, the battle raged off the Texel. At midday, Rupert found himself in a desperate mêlée, with de Ruyter to leeward of him and the Zeeland squadron to windward. His rear-admiral's ship, badly damaged, had fallen away and was only saved from a pack of worrying Dutch ships when Rupert bore down with the wind behind him and forced the Dutch to sheer off. One crisis followed swiftly on another. Rupert, discerning through his spyglass another British squadron some leagues away, went to join it. De Ruyter went after him. When Rupert reached the squadron he found it without a commander. Its admiral, Sir Richard Spragge, who had thought that he should be in Rupert's place and had ignored Rupert's signals, had been forced to abandon two flagships. Trying to reach a third, he had been drowned. Spragge's squadron had been terribly battered and now its disabled ships came under attack both by Cornelis van Tromp and de Ruyter. Rupert, having tried, and failed, to induce some ships lying idle to windward to follow him to the rescue, drove his ships between de Ruyter and his prey. At the same time, he signalled to the French to join in the fight. They did not do so and, in consequence, the Dutch squadron opposed to them was free to join in the attack on Rupert's ships. When darkness fell over the North Sea, the fleets sagged apart to lick their wounds.

That night Rupert exploded in anger against d'Estrées. 'I must have routed them,' he wrote in his dispatch, which has the eloquence of total conviction. 'It was the greatest and plainest opportunity ever lost at sea.'

Hearing the news from sea, the King was afraid to call Parliament because he knew that Rupert meant to denounce the French admiral in public. The French second-in-command, De Martel, agreed with Rupert. He called his admiral a coward and was sent to the Bastille to teach him a proper respect for his superior officer. Not that Rupert's annoyance was reserved solely for his ally. Schomberg enraged him by ordering a frigate to carry a flag on her main-top which she had no right to do. The impudence amused the fleet but did not amuse Rupert. He ordered the flag to be hauled down and, when this order was ignored, he fired on the frigate. After this, Schomberg sent Rupert a challenge and the King was forced to forbid the duel between his two commanding officers. That was not all. Rupert could, and did, name officers in the fleet who had failed in their duty and, perhaps, in their loyalty.

The outcome of this fighting was doubtful but on the whole the battle had gone in favour of the Dutch. The loss of ships had been light on both sides; the casualties among officers and men had been heavy. Rupert kept his ships in station off the Dutch coast until, in a day or two, the weather broke and drove him back to seek shelter in English waters. Schomberg's expeditionary corps, in its camp at Yarmouth, all agog to attack, was dispersed. Rupert returned to London in such a fury with the Navy Commissioners that it looked as if he would use his cane on their backs. He told the French Ambassador what he thought of Admiral d'Estrées' behaviour. D'Estrées answered by accusing Rupert of failing to push home the attack owing to his general disapproval of the war. However, to charge Rupert with cowardice was not likely to carry conviction with the English public. At that moment, he was at the height of his popularity. It was true, however, that he had no particular animosity against the Dutch and from that time onward called Cornelis van Tromp his spitzbroeder – comrade in arms. The result of the Texel battle was that Holland was saved from invasion. What is more, she had, as it turned out, won the war.

The British were sick of fighting expensive naval battles against an adversary who was, as most Englishmen were, Protestant, and who was threatened at this moment by the power of the French army which, in a matter of days, had stretched out its paw over the southern Netherlands as far north as the mouth of the Scheldt. Only a few years ahead and, already visible to Protestant forebodings, were the Revocation of the Edict of Nantes and the great Huguenot Diaspora. France, its policy deeply influenced by Jesuits, was the master of Europe and only a miracle, it seemed, could save Holland. It was no moment for Protestant England to make Holland's danger greater. In February 1674, the war was hurriedly brought to an end by a treaty of peace signed in London.

As for Rupert, the final broadside off the Texel was the last time he heard a shot fired in anger. It was thirty-one years almost to the day since he had seen King Charles' standard raised at Nottingham. With only the briefest intervals of tranquillity, they had been for him years of continuous conflict. Now 'Robert the Devil' was going to spend the remainder of his days in peace. As he slammed his telescope shut on his way into the Admiral's cabin of the *Royal Charles*,* on a night of freshening wind and rising sea, it may have seemed an unlikely future to the grim-lipped Vice-Admiral of England. But that was how it fell out.

---

* This ship had been built to replace the vessel of the same name captured by the Dutch in the Medway.

Inventions and Discoveries

'Perceiving thee advanc'd in feats of Arms so far,
At once the Mars and Vulcan of the War . . .'
Anon. An Elegy on that Illustrious and High-Born Prince Rupert
Who Dyed on Wednesday, 29 Novenber 1682

War was over, but politics went on, the savage, bigoted politics of the age which reached their climax in the infamous 'Popish Plot' and the stream of lies poured out by Titus Oates. The Earl of Shaftesbury, who as Anthony Ashley had once been a member of Cromwell's Council of State and later was one of the ruling Cabal, organised the 'brisk boys' of the London streets to maltreat Catholics as, long before, Pym had mobilised them against Charles I. The lead was followed only too readily by others. On the day of Queen Elizabeth's accession, which had been seized on as a day suitable for Protestant celebrations, a torchlight procession carrying anti-Popish images marched to Temple Bar where there was a statue of the Queen. There, in the King's Head Tavern at the corner of Chancery Lane, the leading Whigs of the Green Ribbon Club were gathered, singing

> Your Popish plot and Smithfield threat
> We do not fear at all
> For lo! beneath Queen Bess's feet
> You fall, you fall, you fall!

Behind all this hooliganism there was not only the vicious propaganda of a ruffian like Oates, there was also the fact that the secretary of the Heir to the Throne, Edward Coleman, had written to the confessor of Louis XIV, 'We have a mighty work upon our hands, no less than the conversion of three Kingdoms . . . There was never such hope of success since the death of Queen Mary.' It can scarcely be wondered if the publication of such a letter caused a shiver to run down the spines of

English Protestants or that the City Chamberlain, Sir Thomas Player, exclaimed, 'I don't know but tomorrow morning we may all arise with our throats cut!' Sir Thomas' language was confused but his meaning was clear enough.

In such a controversy, there could hardly be any doubt about the views of an obstinate Protestant, the son of that arch-victim of Popish oppression, the late King of Bohemia. Rupert was, by nature and upbringing, in sympathy with the Country Party; in other words, a Whig, a name which was just on the point of being invented. He was a friend and business associate of Shaftesbury's, whom the King had identified as his chief political antagonist. Rupert and Shaftesbury worked together against the King's pro-Catholic policy. 'His Highness' coach was often seen at Shaftesbury's door.' When Shaftesbury was ill, Rupert called on him; more significant, when Shaftesbury was disgraced, Rupert visited him. On the other hand, Rupert was a loyal Stuart, the plain-spoken but devoted cousin of the King, who it seems was much less shocked than most of his courtiers by Rupert's excesses of candour and who treated his tantrums with a philosophic calm. When Rupert came raging back from his leaky, ill-provided ships after the battle with de Ruyter, swearing he would never thrive at sea till some were hanged on land, the King went to see him, smilingly prepared to be scolded, although 'he had sweetened him by letter all he could'. He knew that he could handle his fiery cousin. At the time that the Popish crisis was blowing up, Rupert was the idol of the crowd, a naval hero, conspicuously anti-French, a Protestant. The possibility of playing a political role might have tempted him if he had been younger and a different man. He was aware of the growing danger to the throne, distrustful of the course that Charles, the King, was steering, despondent when he thought whither James, the Duke, might venture. But he was firm in his allegiance to the family with which he had made his life. Rupert was, in any case, a soldier not a politician. He was also a 'foreigner' in the eyes of the crowd; for the moment popular, but well aware of the xenophobia that was never far below the surface in England. He knew from experience that foreigners were wise to walk warily in British internal quarrels.

As a high officer of the Crown, he could not, however, completely avoid being involved in the events that followed Oates' accusations against Roman Catholics. In the absence of the King, who had gone racing at Newmarket, he presided at the Privy Council in 1678 which first heard Titus Oates give a spoken account of the alarming story he had told in writing. This meeting sent an urgent message to the King urging him to return to London. The Council that followed, with the King in The chair, gave orders for Edward Coleman's letters to be seized. The letter to the confessor of Louis XIV was thereupon discovered. Charles went back to Newmarket, leaving the investigation of the Plot to a secret committee of the Council, headed by Rupert. Shortly afterwards the question passed out of the hands of the Council; the House of Commons and the judiciary took over.*

At the height of the crisis, in December 1679, Rupert led a deputation of seventeen Whig peers who petitioned the King to summon an elected Parliament . . . something that Charles was determined not to do. It was the nearest Rupert came to a political initiative, an open disavowal of the King. By that time he was out of sympathy with the trend of policy. In the following year, when the Council moved to commit Shaftesbury to the Tower, Rupert was one of three members who withdrew to avoid signing the warrant for committal. This, inevitably, annoyed the King. So, as a writer said, when Rupert died, 'He had of late years proved a faithful counsellor to the King but a greater patriot to English liberty and therefore was, towards his latter end, neglected by the Court.' He had other things to do. He was the Governor of Windsor Castle, responsible for its forests and game, charged with the duty of ensuring that nobody except those whom he selected should enter its bounds. There, he went on his rounds, followed by his big black dog, which was reputed in the neighbourhood to be a wizard, as he told his sister, Elizabeth. When the King gave warning that he was about to go down to hunt at Windsor, Rupert travelled ahead of him to the Castle to prepare the red deer for the chase. For a journey of that kind, he was allotted a carriage and two carts from the royal mews and for his table six bottles of claret a day. He was also the commander of the company of footguards at

* An old acquaintance of Rupert's was involved in the confused probings and counter-probings that followed Oates' original depositions. Antoine Choqueux, a French Papist who practised as a surgeon in the Savoy, where he had a wine cellar, was prominent among those Catholics who worked actively to expose Oates as a liar. He had already suffered from Protestant prejudice when the myth was spread that he kept a 'fireball' in his rooms in the Savoy. After the Great Fire, London was very sensitive to any threat of incendiarism so a file of soldiers was sent to guard Choqueux's house and the alley between it and the Strand. Later, Choqueux and a Tory pamphleteer, Sir Roger L'Estrange, were apparently collaborating to draw a minor conspirator, named Simpson Tonge, out of the Oates camp. Choqueux swore on oath that L'Estrange came to see him about certain memoirs relating to Rupert's actions in the Civil War and in Flanders. All that seems certain is that Choqueux was an active politician as well as a surgeon.

Windsor Castle, which might be a military office less onerous than he was accustomed to – he, who had commanded armies and fleets – but he took its duties as gravely as he did other tasks. However, he also had his own regiment of dragoons, the Barbados Regiment. He was Lord Lieutenant of Surrey. For an elderly man with impaired health he had plenty to occupy him. The Round Tower at Windsor he began to restore, redecorating the stairway with a 'furniture of arms', pikes, muskets, pistols, drums and so forth, 'and thus those huge steep stairs had the walls invested with this martial furniture, all new and bright and set out with such study as to represent the pilasters, cornices, etc.' In contrast were the 'tapestry and effeminate pictures' in his bedchamber, 'very surprising and divertissant' as John Evelyn thought. It would all have been quite usual in the sunset phase of one who had been a strenuous and busy man of action and was now worn out by the hardships of campaigning and glad to rest. Except that Rupert was not at all an ordinary man of action. He was, as we have seen, an artist. Not a great artist, no doubt, but the development of the mezzotint had not merely been a technical exercise; it had called for some degree of sensibility. Rupert had made for himself a modest niche in the history of European art. And there was science, in which his accomplishment was more impressive and more various.

At Windsor, as in London, he had a workshop where he continued the experiments which he had carried on at Mainz during the years of exile. He was one of the most active Fellows of the Royal Society. The Society, founded on the initiative of Sir Robert Moray, son of a Perthshire laird, was a Royalist foundation which enjoyed the special favour of the King. Intelligent young noblemen were encouraged to show an interest in scientific investigations and for them the path to a Fellowship was made smooth. However, for Rupert, science was not simply a modish pastime. He was, as he had already demonstrated on the Continent, a serious experimenter, a prolific inventor, a man of the most diverse technical interests. Through Moray, whom he had probably met in Europe in the days before the Restoration, he sent to the Society a stream of reports during the six years after he became a Fellow. In a company which included men of the calibre of Isaac Newton and Christopher Wren, Rupert was looked on with a profound respect. It was justified by his work. For instance, he found a method of making a quality of gunpowder which had eleven times the explosive power of the best English powder. A long and detailed description of the manufacturing procedure was given: it included the insistence that the charcoal used should be made from *spina corvina*, a tree bearing a kind of blackberry. The Society made its own tests of Rupert's method and found that the claims made for it were fully justified.

This was only one of several technical improvements which emerged from Rupert's laboratory. He devised a method of making small shot which he described to John Locke, the philosopher, whom he met regularly at the Council of Trade and Plantations. Locke made a full record of the method in his notebook, without which posterity would not know about it. Rupert discovered a method of toughening steel so that it could not be pierced by bullets fired from a pistol. He contrived a gun which could, without difficulty, discharge a succession of bullets, evidently a forerunner of the machine gun. He reported that in his employment was an artificer who had made an airgun which could shoot a needle through a plank and another gun which, he claimed, was both smokeless and noiseless. In another branch of enquiry, he sent to the Society plans, based on a principle already known abroad, for a machine to raise water to a higher level. He constructed a quadrant enabling altitudes to be taken at sea even in rough weather. When he came ashore in 1675, after his last spell of duty against the Dutch, he brought with him an embossed chart of the English Channel which he presented to the Society. When he visited Germany in 1663 he brought back fossilised horses' teeth. The instrument for drawing in perspective which, as a boy captive in Linz, he had worked on long ago, was now constructed by the Royal Society's workmen and ideas for improving it were suggested. In these early years of the Society, Prince Rupert was its most prolific contributor. Yet, in the 1670s, he was often a sick man and usually a busy one. The cavalry commander who had faced Cromwell in battle, the self-taught admiral, who had exchanged broadsides with Blake and de Ruyter, the man of fashion, the penniless adventurer, the artist – to these images must now be added another, that of the scientific pioneer, the practical inventor, his face black with the smoke of the furnace, his reputation as a savant spreading across Europe.

He was an exceptionally versatile man. For, while he was busy in the laboratory and the workshop, he was also a man of affairs. Thus, he was attuned to the spirit of Restoration England which, as in the days of Elizabeth, was throbbing with commercial interest and enterprise. One May day in 1667, Rupert's private secretary, James Haynes, opened a letter from Lord Arlington who, at that time, was in Paris and had reported that a disaffected Frenchman, named Médard Chouart, Sieur des Groseilliers, asserted that in the country round Hudson's Bay there was a great wealth of fur-bearing animals, especially beaver. Rupert was, at the time, getting over his serious trephining operation but, when he recovered, he saw the Frenchman several times in his chambers in Whitehall and at Windsor. Soon afterwards, the Secretary of the Royal Society wrote to Robert Boyle, the physicist, and told him that the North-West Passage had been discovered by two Englishmen, and a Frenchman, who had been received in audience by the King at Oxford. The story was not quite correct: there was only one Englishman in the party, and two Frenchmen, Groseilliers and Pierre Esprit Radisson and, of course, the North-West Passage had not been discovered.

The Frenchmen, adventurers – and, perhaps, knaves – familiar with the American wilds, declared that the best route to the abounding wealth of America in furs was by sea into Hudson's Bay. The King, like Rupert, was interested. James Haynes, the Prince's secretary, saw in it the possibility of a career, possibly a fortune, for himself. On 3 June of the following year, Rupert, along with his friend, Lord Craven, and Haynes went down to Wapping Old Stairs and were rowed out to a fifty-ton ketch anchored in the Thames. She was called the *Nonsuch*. Later that day she weighed anchor, and, with a consort, set sail for Hudson's Bay. The voyage was, in fact, completed by only one of the two vessels, that in which Groseilliers sailed, but the news it brought back was highly encouraging and so, too, was its sample cargo of beaver skins. From that time, matters progressed rapidly, with James Haynes as the active organiser of the enterprise and Rupert as its Chairman. It was a project in which his royal prestige and practical energy could alike be usefully harnessed. Long ago, when he was a boy in his teens on his first visit to England, he had been dazzled by a plan to conquer Madagascar and make him its king. His mother had scoffed at the project, likening it very sensibly to some fantasy of Don Quixote's; fortunately, nothing had come of it. And now here, in sober reality, was something vaster than even Madagascar could have been, appealing to a man of action, one who was curious about nature, excited by the hope of discovery, and equipped with the boldness of mind suited to vast and ambitious designs. Between one desperate seafight and another off the Dutch coast, Rupert found in the dream of the Bay something that had a lingering magic of its own.

The first necessity was to persuade the King to grant a charter of monopoly conferring on Rupert and seventeen noblemen and gentlemen sole rights of ownership and trade in the regions watered by the rivers which flowed into the Bay. Rupert's approach to the King was successful, which was hardly surprising since he could tactfully remind his cousin that he had recently granted the proprietorship of New York and Delaware to the Duke of York. After all that Rupert had done and suffered in the Royalist cause, he had hardly been generously rewarded. Hudson's Bay – it would be a magnificent gift, and one that need not subtract a penny from one of his Majesty's ladies! So a chartered company was founded in May 1670 and styled 'The Governor and Company of Adventurers trading into Hudson's Bay'. Rupert was the Governor. The territory lying round the Bay was named Rupert's Land. And the company's first ship to sail from the Thames was named the *Prince Rupert*. Never, it seemed, was he so completely identified with any enterprise as with this one. When the ship returned with 3,000 weight of beaver skins, the Company's first auction was held in Garraway's Coffee House in the City on 5 December 1671. Rupert went along from Whitehall to be present as also did his cousin, the Duke of York. It seems, too, that John Dryden was in the crowd that day. At any rate, he wrote:

> Friend, once 'twas Fame that led thee forth,
> To brave the Tropick Heat, the Frozen North,
> Late it was Gold, then Beauty was the Spur
> But now our Gallants venture but for Fur.

The sale was highly successful. London had taken an important step towards challenging Amsterdam, Paris and Vienna as the leading fur market of the world. Rupert put up £200 of the capital of the new company. Craven did the same. James Haynes, who probably had access to City finance, invested £300 and later built it up to a dominant holding of 1,500 shares when he drove Lord Shaftesbury and his associates out of the Company.* The expulsion was not carried out without provoking some resentment. Shaftesbury, himself no angel, denounced Haynes as a despicable profligate and a pander. However, while he was still a member of the company, Shaftesbury did Rupert one useful service. At one of the early meetings of the board of directors, in the course of 1671, Rupert, who had been in the chair, excused himself and left. When the door was closed behind him, Shaftesbury raised the question of some definite payment being made to Rupert in recognition of his special services in obtaining the Charter from the King. An unknown, but substantial, sum

---

* Shaftesbury had 1,100 shares, about one-ninth of the total share capital.

was agreed.* But, even apart from that, Rupert did pretty well from the beginning. The usual annual profit to the Adventurers was 200 per cent. The Hudson's Bay Company was Rupert's most important commercial venture. But it was not the only one.

In that acquisitive Restoration world, when court and City, the old landed families and the new wealth of those who had done well out of the wars, were all alike stretching out for profit, Rupert had some qualities suitable to the age. He had the social position and the driving force. As a prince without a principality, he needed money. While one of his private secretaries, James Haynes, was the promoter of the Hudson's Bay Company, another, Thomas Holder, became Treasurer of the Royal African Company, dedicated to furthering Britain's trade with that west African coast on which, in the days of his vagabondage, Rupert had once careened his ships.

He was appointed, in 1663, Governor of the Mines Royall and was, therefore, linked by yet another strand to the development of industry in Britain. Later, he was one of a syndicate that was granted a monopoly of any metal found in Scotland which was the King's property. He was, too, involved in the commercial exploitation of some of his own inventions. He had devised a secret method of casting cannon from an alloy to which he gave his name. Apparently, however, the English did not show sufficient interest in the invention because we find Rupert, in 1681, asking the Privy Council for leave to sell to Louis XIV guns made to his formula. He contended that, as his invention was undervalued in England, he could not be blamed for seeking a market elsewhere. After this, capitalists were brought in who built a water-mill on Hackney Marsh to provide power for the manufacture of the guns, which the Ordnance Commissioners undertook to buy. Unfortunately, Rupert died just at the time when the project was getting under way and the secret died with him. In consequence, the capitalists lost their money. So, at least, says Daniel Defoe who claims to have seen the cannon, 'of a reddish brown colour', on the gundeck of the *Royal Charles*. Characteristically, Rupert, between two of the hottest actions of the Dutch war, reported to the King about a new 'petard' he had perfected. It was calculated, he said, to destroy any enemy vessel that it hit.

By this time, the Prince had achieved an international reputation as a metallurgist. When the Venetian Secretary in London received an enquiry from the Chamber of Artificers at Venice about the use of fuses for

* It took the form of an allotment of free shares in the company to Rupert.

cannon to avoid damage to the touchholes, he called on Prince Rupert, 'unique in such matters'. Rupert said the idea was new to him but was not impossible. In writing to Venice, the Secretary, who had obviously been greatly impressed by his interview with the Prince, reported that his Highness had perfected a novel method of casting cannon of fifty pounds and upwards which gave the gun a colour like brass. But it was lighter in weight and cheaper than ordinary cannon. The Prince, however, was keeping secret the process of manufacture which probably involved some change in the proportions of the metals from which the gun was cast. This was the secret that 'died with him'. It was not the only direction in which his ingenuity was working.

There was a machine worked by horses for towing large ships against wind and tide. There was, too, a 'diving engine', although it seems that this had not advanced beyond the prototype stage. It was said* to have been used in 1687 when Captain William Phipps salvaged the wreck of the Spanish treasure ship *Nuestra Señora de la Concepcion* off Hispaniola and made £300,000 for himself and his backers. The ubiquitous James Haynes, who may have heard about the diving engine from Rupert, was a member of the syndicate that financed this treasure hunt, one of the most successful ever undertaken. 'A lottery of a hundred thousand to one odds,' exclaimed Defoe. 'Bless us, what folks should go three thousand miles to angle in the open sea for pieces of eight with an engine that, when the Prince died, had hardly a hand to own it until the wreck voyage so happily performed by Captain Phipps.' It is certain that Phipps took a diving bell to help in his search for the treasure but how far this was an invention of Rupert's remains conjectural. After all, an instrument called the 'Catalan Bell' had been known for some time. This, however, can be said: although the final chapter in Rupert's life is much more tranquil than its predecessors, it is full of incident and surprise.

* By Defoe.

215

XXI

A Night at the Theatre

'The bad end unhappily, the good unluckily. That is what tragedy means.'
Rosencrantz and Guildenstern are Dead, Tom Stoppard

One February night in 1667, Samuel Pepys went to the play. In a piece called *The Virgin Martyr*, he saw and, later, he kissed a young actress newly arrived on the London stage called Peg Hughes. She was the mistress of Sir Charles Sedley, 'a mighty pretty woman and seems, but is not, modest. Took up Knepp into our coach and all of us to her lodging.' A lively young woman, obviously, with talent and looks and high spirits. Just the kind to appeal to a lonely man like Rupert when he first set eyes on her at Tunbridge Wells in 1668. In this semi-rural resort, the Court and the fashionable set of London were assembled, strolling on the lawns, drinking the waters and, at the appointed hour, starting on the serious business of the day, flirtation. The Queen had ordered the King's Company of Players down from London, hoping, as the malicious said, to divert her husband's mind from the allurements of his current mistress. Among the actresses was Peg Hughes, who was the first woman to appear on the London stage in the role of Desdemona.* Very soon, King Charles' court was amused by the news that the warrior had succumbed to the charm of the young actress. It was exactly the sort of situation that strait-laced John Evelyn had feared would follow the revolution in the theatre which had led to the appearance of women on the stage: 'Inflaming young noblemen and gallants [they] become their whores, witness the Earl of Oxford, Sir R. Howden, Prince Rupert.' Very soon, it was known that Prince Rupert had bought Mistress Hughes a splendid house at Hammersmith which had been the property of the Brandenburg envoy.

* It is not unreasonable to think that she may have belonged to the same family as Will Hughes, a well-known actor of the Elizabethan age who was, at one time, believed to have been the mysterious Mr W. H. to whom Shakespeare's sonnets were dedicated.

216

Very soon, too, a dispute arose of the kind that occasionally troubled King Charles' court: which of the two sirens was the more beautiful, Peg Hughes or Nell Gwynn? The question was brought to trial by battle when one of Peg's brothers, who was in Rupert's service, was killed in a fight by one of the King's men. The Prince's sister, Duchess Sophie, who was well-informed about the goings-on in London, wrote that the Danish ambassador thought Mrs Hughes very modest, adding in her caustic way, 'I was going to say the most modest of the court, but that would be no great praise.' Sophie's chief fear was that Peg, through Rupert's infatuation, would get her hands on the Queen of Bohemia's famous jewels, which had presided over many an ill-furnished dinner table at The Hague and gleamed softly out of many a royal portrait by Honthorst. 'We each have our weakness,' said Sophie dryly. Years before, the Elector had tried to filch them from his brother. The States-General of the United Provinces claimed that the jewels were theirs by right as the late Queen's creditors. All of them under-rated the tenacity of Rupert's grip on his mother's jewellery.

One day in 1673, the year of the Test Act, the year before Rupert's hardest fight at sea, Peg Hughes gave birth to a daughter, a little girl with glowing dark eyes, who was named Ruperta. Three years later, Peg had resumed her career on the stage. Rupert was by then spending less time in Whitehall and more in the Round Tower of Windsor Castle. His health was failing. The trephining operation had been bungled and the wound in his head had broken out again. But, when he was well enough, he still hunted with the old hereditary enthusiasm. Writing to the King, with the sardonic humour which he shared with his mother the Queen, and his sister Sophie, he broke off discussion of some knotty point of military protocol to say, 'I am now going to hunt the most tyrannical deer, on which the whole county has declared war.' By that time, one question had been settled.

If Rupert had ever seriously intended to marry, it was, by this time, too late. Elizabeth and Sophie might plead, his brother, that cold fish the Elector Charles Louis, might implore him to forget the past, return to the Palatinate, settle down, marry and raise a Protestant heir to spite the Neubergs. But Rupert was comfortably housed at Windsor with his dogs and the horses he stabled across the river at Eton. He loved to roam the woods with his dog, that wizard dog, at his heels and a hawk on his wrist. He was affable to the local people whom, a generation before, he would have terrified. He had an honourable, even a splendid, position and enough to occupy his mind and the body that, once so powerful, was more and more betraying him. Besides, he had loved England from the first moment he had set foot in it as a boy.

Rupert had not, however, finished with his family. Nor had his family finished with Britain. When Sophie thought about London, she was not only concerned lest her mother's gems found their way into unworthy hands. She had anxieties on an altogether higher plane and she had a family to provide for. George, for instance, her eldest boy, might not have the looks or the stature of the Palatine male at his best. He was not, she confessed, another Rupert, that handsome giant. For that sort of thing, it was necessary to go to her second son, Friedrich – called 'Gustien' by his mother – who was, Sophie assured herself and others, the very image of Rupert in his youth. Sophie had the idea that George might make a suitable husband for the second daughter of the Duke of York, Catholic heir to the British throne. Without peering too far or too speculatively into the future, but being an intelligent woman who knew something about politics, Sophie sent young George over to London at the end of 1680. The King responded with characteristic affability. Hearing that George had rented rooms in London, he sent a barge to bring the young man by river to Whitehall, and there, with Rupert present, he received the bashful young Hanoverian. More than that, he lent 'his cousin' a suitable lodging in the Cockpit in Whitehall, while George's Uncle Rupert, tortured by the malady in his leg which forced him to spend a great deal of time in bed, visited the young man almost every day. However, the marriage negotiations did not go smoothly. George did not care for Princess Anne, then aged eighteen. And, perhaps more important, he did not fancy what he saw of English politics. His arrival in London had coincided with the 'Popish Plot' and the barbarous executions that accompanied it. He was staggered by the bloodthirsty manner in which the English went about their public business. He departed, far from enamoured of his mother's marriage project.

Rupert, however, continued the negotiations by letter, realising no doubt that a matter of this weight could not be decided by the whims of a callow youth. English religious quarrels might in the end exclude – or drive – the Duke of York from the throne. He was well aware – who better? – of the strength of feeling against the Duke among the Whig aristocrats. And, then, who could tell what would happen? The game was still an open one. So, helped by that amiable Frenchwoman, the Duchess of Portsmouth, he pressed on with the business side of the proposed marriage contract, writing to tell Sophie, not many weeks before his death, that a capital sum of £40,000 was offered, plus £10,000 a year during the lifetime of Sophie's husband, the Duke Ernest Augustus, in the hope that young George would be able to spend some time in England, learn the language and become acquainted with the people. However, it was clear before long that George was going to marry his cousin, Sophie Dorothea of Celle, a young woman of wayward morals – as time was to prove. Rupert heard the news without enthusiasm: 'All I can say is, Now thou art chosen thou art well chosen. However,' he told Sophie, 'I can never regret any pains I have taken in your service.' Before the betrothal was announced officially, Rupert was beyond caring about family concerns.

In November 1682, when Rupert was spending a few days in his town house in Spring Gardens, he went out one evening to the theatre. There, he was suddenly taken ill and grew rapidly worse. The wound in his leg which had been troubling him for years now broke out again and so did the old wound in his head which, after a quarter of a century, the surgeons had failed to cure. He grew rapidly worse, developed pleurisy and a fever. On 29 November, after suffering a great deal of pain, he died. The funeral was conducted at Westminster Abbey, with all due pomp, although neither the King nor the Duke of York was present. Lord Craven was the chief mourner, supported by eight peers and seven gentlemen. They were followed by the dead man's huntsman, tennis-player, turner, gunsmith and coachman. No member of the family was present, although a Mr Hughes, who was there, may have been a relation of Peg's. The King ordered the court into mourning – three weeks in purple, and three weeks in black. Shaftesbury, now an exile in Amsterdam, heard with sorrow of the death of his old friend.

By his will, Rupert left the bulk of his property on trust to staunch old Lord Craven who had the duty of seeing that it was divided equally between Peg Hughes and her nine-year-old daughter, Ruperta. Dudley Bard,* Rupert's son by Francesca Bard, was left the house at Rhenen, which Rupert's father had built as a summer residence half a century earlier. The total of Rupert's possessions was valued at £10,415 of which the most important single item was the Queen of Bohemia's famous pearl necklace. This Craven sold for £4,520 to Nell Gwynn. Sophie

* Sometimes called Dudley Rupert.

cannot have approved. The States-General put in a claim for possession of the jewels; their High Mightinesses were too late. James Haynes paid £350 for Rupert's shares in the Hudson's Bay Company. Craven bought his yacht.

Rupert von Wittelsbach – to give him here his proper patronymic – is certainly not one of those men whom fame has passed by. If he has a grievance against history, it is that he has been remembered too well for one phase of his life, a single aspect of his talents. But what is remarkable about him is the range of his interests and the diversity of his gifts. He has been called the most brilliant of the Stuarts which is, perhaps, not to say much. For the family, remarkable for charm and misfortune, are hardly outstanding for mental attainments. True, James VI and I was an intellectual, but he was a remarkably stupid one. Charles I was a tragic figure, a kind of holy fool. His son, Charles II, who had been brought up in a harsher school, was certainly a brilliant politician, whatever may be thought of his statesmanship. But in a family whose trade was politics, he seems to have had a monopoly of political flair. However, it would be ungenerous to deny brilliance to the second Charles, as it would be churlish to doubt that he had charm, the most selfish and irresponsible of the more agreeable human attributes. Rupert, his cousin, a Stuart on the distaff side, son of the most charming of all the family, was himself to put charm resolutely behind him, either as a quality he could not aspire to or as one he despised. In place of charm, one must set fury; in place of brilliance – what? The trouble is that the historical image of Rupert was moulded by the events of a few months during which he was scarcely more than a boy, who had, in an hour of crisis, been raised by a distracted uncle to a position of responsibility demanding diplomacy and patience as well as gallantry. Rupert's image as it was in 1643 has hardened with time, grown bigger, been simplified so that it is scarcely more of an approximation to the man than are the scurrilous libels of the Parliament's propaganda.

The robber Prince, the diabolical Cavalier, the slaughterer, if not actually, the devourer, of children; 'The Commons of England,' Parliamentary pamphleteers of 1644 had declared, 'will remember thee! How many towns hast thou fired? How many virgins hast thou ruined? How many godly ministers hast thou killed?' By 1682, when Rupert died, those yelps of the London scribblers seemed sufficiently preposterous to 'the Commons of England' or their descendants who had recently looked to the 'Protestant Prince' as one who might save them from Popery. Yet in one respect, the image of Rupert created during the early months of the Civil War has been indelibly printed on the mind of the British while the later version has faded. He is still – and, perhaps, for all time – the wild young cavalier, who, at the head of his torrent of horsemen, would sweep away a whole wing of the opposing army. Nor is the image false, only partial. Rupert *was* a dashing leader of cavalry, cast in the same mould as Ney or Seydlitz, although there was, even in those early days, a dour edge to his panache. He had a magnetism of his own rather than the fatal charm of his family. His humour had a sable tinge. In one respect, it is true, he conformed to the Cavalier pattern. He was a leader of fashion, a man of taste who did not need social courage, since he had social prestige, to impose his taste on others. But he was also a man of principle, stiff in opinion, constant whether in the right or the wrong. Above all, as his long career in violence proved, he was an intellectual capable of applying his mind to the most diverse problems such as: improvising an insurrection in the King's name – for that is what the Civil War, in fact, was – an insurrection by the King against the Commons and settled power of England; devising a strategy which, if it had ever been put into practice, might have brought off the miracle of a royal victory in the war; managing a fleet – and what a fleet! – little better than a swarm of mutineers held together by the hope of plunder and the fear of the yardarm; founding a vast commercial empire; waging a naval war against Holland and, simultaneously, championing the seamen he led against the bureaucracy that was swindling them. In short, a man of practical ability in many spheres, one who had so many different talents that they added up to something like genius. Rupert's life was a prolonged exercise in versatility.

He began with advantages and greater disadvantages. He was a prince with the qualities of body and spirit that not all princes possess – but a prince without a principality. He was a member of a family that was not only poor but – which is different and far harder to bear – was ruined. He was a grandee of the Empire without an acre to his name, with barely a penny he could call his own, with the indignity of dependence to outweigh the dignity of his name. But he had advantages of the mind. In him the genes of Stuarts and Wittelsbachs had united to produce, under the stress of misfortune, an intellect exceptionally alive and resilient. Alongside the public side of his life, as it may be called, there was a personal side, a life of the spirit, an ingenuity which sought its outlet in art, in science, in invention. The Renaissance was over but the Enlightenment, which was dawning, was an age in which the creative process was still fluid and dispersed; in which the inspired amateur, the man of untutored curiosity, the all-rounder, could play his part. To a degree unequalled by any man of his time, of any social class, Rupert did this. He was not the stuff of which a Newton or an Einstein is made, but possibly a James Watt or an Edison.

As the years passed, he matured and changed. He was a great aristocrat who had the intelligence to learn from experience. He saw that the England of the 1660s was very different from his uncle's kingdom of twenty years earlier. By birth and by necessity a monarchist, he realised that the monarchy must change because forces had arisen to claim their share of men's allegiance. The young Rupert who, on the flushed morrow of Edgehill, wanted to march on London and seize the rebel part of the Parliament for one King, lived to petition another King to summon an elected Parliament. It was a different age, and he was a different man. Once he had seemed both ceremonious and ungracious, too grand for the English grandees – it is probable that he was simply young, shy, gauche, aware of his foreign accent, and daily more conscious that an outsider has no easy role to play in a family brawl. But the Rupert of the final phase, the lame old gentleman hobbling along the Windsor by-paths, was remembered by the Berkshire cottagers as exceptionally kindly and unassuming. He was the friend of poor cheated English sailors and of old Cavaliers brought to bankruptcy. The meteor of the Civil War had lived to become almost the grand old man of the Restoration, an era when the climate, at court at least, was not favourable to grand old men, especially those who spent so much time in the laboratory.

He gives the impression of having been an unhappy man and certainly there was much in his life to encourage melancholy – the catastrophe of the family fortunes; defeat in the war; the death of Maurice, who was closest to him: it may be that he had loved the Duchess of Richmond and that she had rejected him. That is likely enough, given the woman's beauty and the man's temperament, but it seems most probable that Rupert's melancholy sprang from no single cause; that unhappiness was originally and ineradicably rooted in his nature as it had been in his father's and as, emphatically, it was not in the character of his fascinating mother! His unhappiness was one aspect of the reflective side of his nature which, with age, grew more marked. If the first picture of Rupert is of the fiery man of action, the final portrait is that of a brooding thinker.

The story of those whom Rupert left behind is quickly told. Francesca Bard, although a Catholic, became an ornament at the court of Rupert's Protestant sister, Sophie, who loved her dearly. The Emperor paid her 20,000 crowns – the famous 30,000 rix dollars – which he owed Rupert. As was to be expected, Francesca espoused the Jacobite cause. Her son and Rupert's, Captain Dudley Bard, distinguished himself while commanding the musketeers in one of the battles against Monmouth's troops. After that campaign he went to Germany where he had some difficulty in getting possession of the estate at Rhenen which his father had left him. He took service in the Imperial army, then engaged in a war with the Turks. In 1686, aged nineteen, he was killed while leading English volunteers in an audacious attempt to scale the walls of Buda. It was a feat to be expected of his father's son. Sophie tried to arrange that the house at Rhenen was transferred to Dudley's mother after his death in action. Whether she succeeded or not is uncertain. All that can be said is that Francesca died at Karlsruhe in 1708.

Peg Hughes lived until 1719, and was buried at Lee in Kent. Her daughter, Ruperta, married Brigadier-General Emanuel Scrope Howe, a prominent Whig, a soldier and a diplomat, who became William III's envoy at Sophie's court where Francesca Bard was living at the time. Ruperta lived to a great age and, when she died, left many 'curious pieces of mechanism' made by her father.

Sophie lived to bless Rupert for insisting that she should have her son, George, taught English. For the day came when, through an improbable concatenation of political and medical events, Sophie herself, were she alive, or George, her son, became likely inheritors of the English throne. As Sophie wrote unkindly to her friend, the philosopher Liebnitz, as Queen Anne's children died one after another, 'they inherit a heavenly crown, leaving an earthly one to my children'. However, it was Anne who finally ensured that the earthly crown should not adorn Sophie's brow. Furious over what she considered Sophie's too blatant manoeuvres in England on her own or her son's behalf, she sent the Electress a tremendous rebuke by letter.* The shock was too great for Sophie. She died of a heart attack a few days after receiving it, so that six weeks later,

* Sophie had asked if George Louis, her son, should not have a writ enabling him to sit in the House of Lords as Duke of Cambridge.

when Queen Anne died, Rupert's nephew, George Brunswick of Luneberg, through his descent from the Queen of Bohemia, ascended the throne of Great Britain and reigned in Whitehall and, when he could spare the time, dwelt in Windsor Castle, which his uncle had once tried and failed to storm and of which, at last, he had been Governor. In the end, then, Rupert's mother had produced the ace of trumps that won the game.

APPENDIX

The Hole in Rupert's Periwig

Samuel Pepys was not likely to be the most impartial witness about anything Prince Rupert did, said or was. Plainly he regarded the prince as a dangerous intruder into the workings of the Navy Office, one who might, by his inconvenient complaints and investigations, bring to light various profitable little arrangements. The King might be tolerant of these time-honoured practices. But the Prince's temperament was less complaisant. So Pepys and others who wished things to go on smoothly looked on Rupert with fear and dislike. However, Pepys was unsurpassed as a reporter of what he saw and heard. He said (1667) that Rupert was suffering from 'pox' which he had caught twelve years earlier and which had now broken out on his head. Trephining would be needed. Three years later he reported that there was a hole cut in the Prince's periwig to prevent irritation of the sore by the hair of the wig.

It would not be at all unlikely that a man like Rupert, attractive to women and unattached, suffered from one of the complaints which in those days were covered by the general description, 'pox'. Is there any reason to suppose, however, that the wound on Rupert's head had anything to do with this disease? The known facts about his health are these: he was badly wounded by a shot in the head in 1647. After a dangerous sea voyage lasting four years which would have tested the strength and fortitude of any man, he returned to France and was at once very ill. It was apparently one of the diseases to which seafaring men were liable – scurvy, or one of the tropical fevers endemic in the Caribbean area from which he had just come. After a few weeks, Rupert recovered completely and was playing tennis with King Charles, in Paris, swimming in the Seine, hunting and so forth. In the autumn of 1664, Rupert was about to sail to Guinea when, suddenly, he took gravely ill: the old wound in his head had broken out again. It appears that the first attempt at cure failed and that Rupert went up to London to seek further treatment. Immediately afterwards he went to sea and, as an Admiral, fought a severe battle with the Dutch (1665). Two years later (January 1667), the head wounds opened once more and two operations (trephining?) were needed to enable him to sleep. During his convalescence, he amused himself by inventing instruments with which the surgeons could dress his wounds more easily. After 1674, Rupert lived more or less in retirement and often in bad health. It seemed that his leg troubled him at this time. He died in 1682, aged sixty-two, after four or five years of bad health. The old hurt in his leg broke out again; he had a fever and pleurisy and apparently died in great pain.

An autopsy showed 'three strange things' – a large stone in one of his kidneys with a hole in it so that 'he in his whole life was never troubled with any pain of the stone'. Another was that in the skin that covers the brain there grew a bone, and in his heart another.* About the meaning of this report, in the opinion of a pathologist consulted, Dr Rodney Finlayson of the Wellcome Museum of Medical Science, who does not pretend that anything more than a conjecture can be made, the 'bone' under the skull was probably a blood clot, an extra- or sub-dural haematoma, a legacy of the head wound of 1647, which had calcified, or ossified. The subsequent, far from aseptic, trephining may well have resulted in secondary infection of the skull and scalp. The 'bone' in the heart was very likely a calcification of the mitral valve ring. This, too, cannot be regarded as evidence of late syphilis. The trouble in the leg may have been of syphilitic origin but, as nothing is known about its nature, there is no reason to suppose anything of the sort. It was, perhaps, the result of an accident on shipboard during the war of 1667. In any case, it was not the reason why Pepys and his contemporaries spoke of Prince Rupert's 'pox'.

On the existing evidence, then – such as it is – Rupert can be given a clean bill of health, so far as syphilis is concerned. Only by opening his coffin in Westminster Abbey could a surer verdict be given.

---

* Cal (Dom.) S.P. December 2, 1682. Quotation from a Newsletter to John Squier, Newcastle.

Notes on Sources

CHAPTER I

The Luck of the Palatines

The background of the Palatine family and the explanation of the predicament in which they found themselves is set out in C. V. Wedgwood's masterly narrative, *The Thirty Years' War*, London, Cape, 1938. For the family's brief sojourn in Prague and the events that immediately preceded and followed it, two biographies should be mentioned: Carola Oman, *Elizabeth of Bohemia*, London, Hodder & Stoughton, 1938, and Mary Anne Everett Green, *Elizabeth, Electress Palatine and Queen of Bohemia*, London, Methuen, 1855. These books are useful too for various events in Rupert's later career. It need hardly be said that earlier lives of the Prince have yielded useful material; above all, Eliot Warburton, *Memoirs of Prince Rupert and the Cavaliers*, 3 vols, London, Richard Bentley, 1849. Warburton's sentimentality may be out of date, but he prints many contemporary letters that are unavailable in other sources and throw interesting lights on the personalities of the time. There is also Eva Scott, *Rupert, Prince Palatine*, London, Constable, 1899, a thoroughly worked biography. Unusual light is shed on the Palatine family's Bohemian adventure by Frances A. Yates, *The Rosicrucian Enlightenment*, London, Routledge & Kegan Paul, 1972. For a picturesque description of the Palatinate as it is there is André Simon, *Gazetteer of Wine*, and, on the historical side, the *Encyclopedia Britannica* article on *Palatinate*. An account of Prague in the seventeenth century is given in Fynes Morison, *An Itinerary* (4 vols), 1907. Throughout this story, entries in the *Calendar of State Papers, Domestic, Foreign and Venetian* provide an essential supply of information. The Palatine home at The Hague is extensively dealt with by various Dutch authorities, notably Bernard Bekmann, *The Hague and Scheveningen*, The Hague, 1956, and H. E. van Gelder, *Het Haagshe Binnenhof* The Hague, 1946.

CHAPTER II

The Prisoner of Linz

For the correspondence between the Queen of Bohemia on the one hand and the English diplomats Roe and Vane on the other, the *State Papers Domestic* are indispensable. Sir G. Bromley, *Collections of Royal Letters*, London, 1787 is likewise important. The life of these princely exiles at The Hague is recorded in the Memoirs of Princess Sophie, *Die Memoires der Herzogin Sophie, Nachmals Kurfürstin von Hannover*, ed. A. Köcher, Leipzig, 1879; C. van Sypestyn, *Het Hof van Boheme*, Amsterdam, 1886; F. E. Bailey, *Sophia of Hanover*, London, Hutchinson, 1936, and R. S. Rait, *Five Stuart Princesses*, London, Constable, 1902. The portrait of another royal lady who played a leading role in the drama of Rupert's life is drawn in Carola Oman's *Henrietta Maria*, London, Hodder & Stoughton, and C. V. Wedgwood, *The King's Peace*, London, Collins, 1955, which is indeed essential for understanding the war into which the young Rupert was plunged. The project of a marriage with Mlle de Rohan is in correspondence published in Sir H. Sidney, *Letters* (edited Collins), vol. II, 1746. For the fight at Lemgo, the Lansdowne, Bennett and Pyne manuscripts may be consulted.

CHAPTER III

A Rabble of Gentility

From this point onwards, the various histories of the Civil War provide the background against which Rupert's career can be seen and judged: G. R. Gardiner, *History of the Great Civil War* (4 vols), London, Longmans, 1894; C. V. Wedgwood, *The King's War 1641–1647*, London, Collins, 1958, which continues the masterly narrative of *The King's Peace*. Earlier, there is the classic of Edward Hyde, Lord Clarendon, *History of the Rebellion*, Oxford, 1888. A sound introduction to the purely military aspects of the struggle can be found in Michael Roberts' *The Military Revolution, 1560–1660*, Belfast, 1956. There is also Peter Young and Wilfred Emberton, *The Cavalier Army*, London, George Allen & Unwin, 1974, and C. H. Firth, *Cromwell's Army*, London, Methuen, 1902.

CHAPTERS IV TO VIII

A Bible and a Winding Sheet
A Night of Cruel Frost
London Saves Itself
This Scribbling Age
Washington's Breach

The early events of the war are best followed in a general account like A. H. Burne and P. Young, *The Great Civil War*, London, Eyre & Spottiswoode, 1959, while for the more important events from Turnham Green onwards there is Austin Woolrych, *Battles of the English Civil War*, London, Batsford, 1961.

Edgehill can be seen through the eyes of many who were there, e.g., Denzil Holles and Lord Wharton; Lord Bernard Stuart, for whose account see *English Historical Review, XXXVI*. There is also Carte, *Letters I*; there is too Burne, *British Battlefields*. Turnham Green: see *Calendar of State Papers* (Venetian) 1692–3, various pamphlets in the Thomason Collection, e.g., E. 127–8, 10,2 and 20 British Museum press marks. Warburton's *Memoirs* are valuable for Rupert's part in these events. The storming of Bristol: Warburton, vol. II, *Journal of the Siege of Bristol*; and the disagreements that followed it in the Royalist camp, Clarendon, *History*, Book VII.

CHAPTERS IX, X AND XI

Let the Old Drum be Beaten
The Rebels' Army of Both Kingdoms
'Wae's Us! We're All Undone'

The entry of the Scottish army, the prelude to Marston Moor and the battle itself: Charles Sanford Terry, *Papers Relating to the Army of the Solemn League and Covenant*, Edinburgh, Scottish Historical Society, 1917. Accounts of the battle abound: *The Diary of Sir Henry Slingsby, Bart.*, ed. Daniel Parsons, London, 1866; Leonard Watson's *A More Exact Relation* (found in the Thomason Collection in the British Museum [E.2. 14]), and the anonymous *The Glorious and Miraculous Battle at York*, a Scottish account, printed by James Lindsay, Edinburgh, 1644, and republished in *Historical Fragments Relative to Scottish Affairs*, Edinburgh, 1833. For Arthur Trevor's vivid eye-witness account of the battle, see *A Collection of Original Letters and Papers Found Among The Duke of Ormonde's Papers*, ed. Thomas Carte, 1739. Modern narratives of the battle are in Austin Woolrych, *Battles of The English Civil War*; C. H. Firth in *Transactions of the Royal Historical Society*, Second Series, XII. This is a particularly full and scholarly account of a confused struggle out of which, eventually, one decisive fact emerged, the power and discipline of the Ironsides. Biographies of the chief commanders include C. S. Terry, *The Life and Campaigns of Alexander Leslie*, London, Longmans, 1899; Antonia Fraser, *Cromwell, Our Chief of Men*, London, Weidenfeld & Nicolson, 1973; John Buchan, *Oliver Cromwell*, London, Hodder & Stoughton, 1934. A most readable account of the Marquis, later Duke, of Newcastle's life before and after Marston Moor occurs in A. S. Turberville, *A History of Welbeck Abbey and its Owners* (2 vols), London, Faber & Faber, 1938. The Duchess' *Life* of her husband is a loyal and enthusiastic document which, however, gives details of the financial sacrifice made by this family as a result of the war. There are too the character studies of the main figures in Clarendon's *History of the Rebellion*, and, of course, the various entries in the *Dictionary of National Biography*.

'Your Present Sad Opinion'
'Much Inclined to a Happy Peace'

The journal of Rupert's marches, *English Historical Review*, XIII, is useful for this and the previous few months of Rupert's war. Naseby: Cromwell's and Fairfax's letters are capital documents. In the Thomason Collection in the British Museum *A More Exact Relation* will be found (E.288. 28). Other contemporary accounts are to be found in Carte's papers in Sir Edward Walker's *Historical Discourses* (1707), Sir Henry Slingsby's *Diary* (1836), and J. Sprigge's *Anglia Rediviva* (1647). For the turmoil among the Royalist camp after the fall of Bristol, the most vivid and interesting account is to be found in C. V. Wedgwood, *The King's War*, Two, V.VIII.

CHAPTER XIV

A Beautiful Action

For the naval side of Rupert's career, which occupies much of this chapter and fills all the next, an account written for the Prince and, perhaps, at his dictation, is printed in Warburton, *Prince Rupert and the Cavaliers*, vol. III, p. 233. It begins with the surrender of Oxford and fills 150 pages, which include many contemporary letters. To this source must be added R. C. Anderson's careful, modern narrative, 'The Royalists at Sea', published in *The Mariner's Mirror*, vols 9, 14, 17 and 21 (1923–1935). For events in Portugal, see *Camden Miscellany*, and Thurloe, *State Papers*, I, pp. 132 and 136, also Violet Rowe, *Sir Henry Vane the Younger*, London, Athlone Press, 1970.

CHAPTER XV

Revenge Our Guide

Once again Warburton and R. C. Anderson are the main sources, with the Thurloe Papers and *State Papers Domestic* providing sidelights. See too Clowes' *History of the Navy*, vol. II, London, Sampson Low, 1898.

CHAPTER XVI

The Design of this Grand Pirate

For Rupert's life after his return from sea, Thurloe, passing on to his masters the reports of Commonwealth spies, is indispensable. At this point, the Clarendon State Papers afford useful insights into the various shifts and stratagems of the Stuarts in exile. S. R. Gardiner, *History of the Commonwealth and Protectorate*, vol. III, is a useful guide to the various factions within the Royalist camp as they planned hopefully their return and plotted the murder of Cromwell.

CHAPTER XVII

Family Business

For this phase of Rupert's life, the biographies of his mother by M. A. E. Green and Carola Oman require to be supplemented by R. S. Rait's *Five Stuart Princesses*, London, Constable, 1902, which deals with the lives of several of the Queen's daughters. The anonymous *Life and Amours of Charles Lewis*, London, printed for Thomas Nott, 1692, gives a somewhat biased account of the exploits of her eldest son, the Elector. The friendship of Descartes and Princess Elizabeth is a theme in Elizabeth Godfrey, *A Sister of Prince Rupert*, London, John Lane, The Bodley Head, 1905, and is more fully dealt with by Léon Petit, in *Descartes et la Princesse Elizabeth*, Paris, Editions Nizet, 1969, V. de Swarte, *Descartes, Directeur Spirituel*, 1904, and Jacques Chevalier, *Descartes*, 1924. For the Palatine family's doings in general, see also Baroness Blaze de Bury, *Memoirs of the Princess Palatine*, London, Richard Bentley, 1853. The career of Rupert's youngest sister, Princess Sophie, is narrated in Marie Kroll, *Sophie, Electress of Hanover*, London, Gollancz, 1973, and important letters of hers are printed in *Die Mutter der Konige*, edited by Robert Geerds, Munich and Leipzig, Langewiesche-Brandt, 1913. *Memoirs of Sophia, Electress of Hanover*, edited H. Forester, 1888. Léonce Raffin, *Anne de Gonzague*, Paris, 1835, gives the best modern account of the formidable lady who married Rupert's brother Edward.

CHAPTER XVIII

The King Comes Home in Peace

G. M. Trevelyan OM, *England Under the Stuarts*, London, Methuen, 1957, Whig in outlook, provides a good general picture of the political and social England of Charles II. There is also Arthur Bryant, *King Charles II*, London, 1931. The will of the Queen of Bohemia is printed in *Wills From Doctor's Commons*, The Camden Society, 83.109.

CHAPTER XIX

Such Judgments and Calamities

For the amorous letters addressed to Rupert see G. Bromley, *A Collection of Royal Letters*, 1787. The naval war with the Dutch may be followed in Arthur

Bryant, *Samuel Pepys, the Man in the Making,* 1947, and *Samuel Pepys, the Saviour of the Navy,* Collins, 1949; Clowes, *History of the Navy,* vol. II, 1942, and Samuel Pepys' Diary. *The Calendar of State Papers Domestic,* vol. XV, 1673. The same source, 1666, for Choqueux's fees for treating Rupert. K. H. Haley, *The First Earl of Shaftesbury,* OUP, 1968, tells of Rupert's business and political association with Shaftesbury and throws light on Rupert's activities at the time of the Popish Plot.

CHAPTER XX
Inventions and Discoveries

For Prince Rupert's commercial interests, see Beckles Wilson, *The Great Company*; E. E. Rich, etc., *The History of the Hudson's Bay Company,* Hudson's Bay Record Society, vol. 21, 1958; W. R. Scott, *Constitution and Finance of English, Scottish and Irish Joint Stock Companies*; H. E. Egerton, *Short History of British Colonial Policy,* 1932. For Rupert's scientific work, Daniel Defoe, *An Essay upon Projects,* 1697; Alice Lounsberry, *Sir William Phipps*; Sir Harold Hartley, ed., *The Royal Society,* 1960; Thomas Birch, *The History of the Royal Society* (4 vols), 1717, and Gail Ewald Scala, *Index to Birch,* reprinted from Notes and Records of the Royal Society, 1974. There is also a valuable article by Kenneth Dewhurst, 'Prince Rupert As a Scientist', in *The British Journal for the History of Science,* December 1963. In this Rupert's medical preparations, chemical processes and mechanical inventions are set out. John Evelyn, *Sculptura,* London, 1662, describes Rupert's part in developing this mezzotint. See also John Evelyn's *Diary,* ed. F. S. de Beer (6 vols), London, 1955. For the politics of the time John Kenyon, *The Popish Plot,* London, Heinemann, 1972, may be read. Information about Choqueux's part in these affairs will be found in *The Narrative and Case of Simson Tonge, Gent. Printed for the Satisfaction of all True Protestants,* London, Langley Curtis, 1681, also Roger L'Estrange, *The Shammer Shammed,* London, Joanne Brone, 1681.

CHAPTER XXI
A Night at the Theatre

For details of the career of Margaret Hughes see the *Dictionary of National Biography* and also Notes and Queries, 2nd Series, III. More fully in William van Lennep and others, *The London Stage,* Southern Illinois University Press, 1967. Rupert's stay at Tunbridge Wells and his meeting with Mistress Hughes – a satirical account in Anthony Hamilton, *Memoirs of Comte de Gramont,* 1930.

Rupert's will is reproduced in *Wills from Doctor's Commons,* Camden Society, p. 142.

Index

236